Who are the Jews? A complicated people with a complicated story — discover how they tell it in their own words, in some of the greatest, saddest, funniest books of the century.

Babel Guides are a new series on contemporary world fiction available in English. The *Reviews* introduce a hundred and fifty of the best, most representative books, with a quotation as a taster. The *Database* gives useful details on fiction by Jewish authors written in thirteen languages and now available in English.

'a brilliant idea, well executed'

— *The Good Book Guide*

'accessible and entertaining'

— *Traveller's Literary Companion*

The Babel Guide to *Jewish* Fiction

by Ray Keenoy & Saskia Brown

with

Mark Axelrod, Marion Baraitser, Brian Cheyette,
Fiorenza Conte, Marina Coriolano-Lykourezos,
Clara Corona, Richard Crownshaw, Patrick Curry,
Barry Davis, Alex Gordon, Tony Hammond,
Theo Hermans, Tamara Levine, Derwent May,
Mike Mitchell, Giovanni Pontiero, Giose
Rimanelli, Gareth Stanton, Louise Sylvester &
David Treece

Illustrations by Jackie Wrout

in association with the European Jewish Publications Society

Babel Guide to Jewish Fiction

©Boulevard Books 1998.

First published 1998 by Boulevard Books

8 Aldbourne Road, London W12 OLN, UK

Tel/Fax 0181 743 5278

email: raybabel@dircon.co.uk

website: www.users.dircon.co.uk/~raybabel/

The European Jewish Publication Society is a registered charity which gives grants
to assist in the publication and distribution of books relevant to Jewish literature,
history, religion, philosophy, politics and culture. EJPS c/o The Joseph Levy
Charitable Foundation, 37-43 Sackville Street, London W1X 2DL

Special thanks to;
Clara Corona, Tamara Levine, Jason Wilson, Tony Hammond and Alex Gordon
at Spiro, Patrick Curry, Gareth Stanton and Barry Davis.

Produced with editorial advice and assistance of staff at the Spiro Institute
for the Study of Jewish History and Culture, London. Final responsibility
for content rests with Boulevard Books.

ISBN 1 899460 25 X

Boulevard Books are distributed in the UK & Europe by Kuperard/Bravo London
01714240554 fax 01714240556

and in the USA & Canada by Paul & Co. Publishers Consortium Inc. c/o
PCS Data Processing Inc, 360 West 31 St, NY, NY 10001
212-564-3730 ext. 295 Fax 212-967-0928.

Cover Art: Jackie Wrout
Typeset & Design: Studio Europa
Printed and bound by the Guernsey Press, Guernsey, C.I.

Index of authors reviewed

AGNON, Shmuel Yosef
APPELFELD, Aharon
ASCH, Sholem
AXELROD, Mark
BABEL, Isaac
BASSANI, Giorgio
BECKER, Jurek
BELLOW, Saul
BRENNER, Joseph Chaim
BROOKNER, Anita
CAHAN, Abraham
CASTEL-BLOOM, Orly
COHEN, Leonard
FRIED, Erich
FRIEDMAN, Carl
GARY, Romain
GINZBURG, Natalia
GOODMAN, Allegra
GRAB, Hermann
GRADE, Chaim
GROSSMAN, David
GRUNBERG, Arnon
HAREVEN, Shulamith
HELLER, Joseph
JACOBSON, Dan
JACOBSON, Howard
JOFFO, Joseph
KAFKA, Franz
KANIUK, Yoram
KIŠ, Danilo
LASKER-SCHÜLER, Else
LEVI, Primo
LIEBRECHT, Savyon
LIND, Jacov
LINETSKI, Isaac J
LISPECTOR, Clarice
LITVINOFF, Emanuel
MALAMUD, Bernard
MANDELSTAM, Osip
MEMMI, Albert
MICHAEL, Sami

MICHAELS, Anne
MINCO, Marga
OLSEN, Tillie
OPATOSHU, Joseph
OZ, Amos
OZICK, Cynthia
PEREC, Georges
PERETZ, Isaac Loeb
PERUTZ, Leo
PRAGER, Emily
PRESSBURGER, Giorgio & Nicola
PROUST, Marcel
RABON, Israel
RICHLER, Mordecai
ROSTEN, Leo
ROTH, Henry
ROTH, Joseph
ROTH, Philip
RUBENS, Bernice
SCHULZ, Bruno
SCLIAR, Moacyr
SHABTAI, Yaacov
SHAHAR, David
SHALEV, Meir
SINGER, Isaac Bashevis
SINGER, Israel Joshua
STEINER, George
TAMMUZ, Benjamin
WEST, Nathanael
YEHOSHUA, Abraham B
YIZHAR, S.
ZANGWILL, Israel

Anthologies

Wisse, R (ed.)
A Shtetl and other Yiddish novellas
Howe, I & Greenberg, E (ed.s)
A Treasury of Yiddish Stories
Howe, I & Greenberg, E (ed.s)
Ashes out of Hope. Fiction by Soviet-Yiddish Writers

Kalechofsky, R &R (eds.)
Echad, an anthology of Latin American Jewish writings
Stavans, I (ed.)
Tropical Synagogues
Forman, Frieda et al (ed.s)
Found Treasures: Stories by Yiddish Women Authors
Blocker, Joel (ed.)
Israeli Stories
Spicehandler, Ezra (ed.)
Modern Hebrew Stories
Lappin, Elena (ed.)
Jewish Voices, German Words
Perova, Natasha & Tait, Arch (ed.s)
Jews and Strangers. Glas New Russian Writing 6
Domb, Risa (ed.)
New Women's Writing from Israel
Abramson, Glenda (ed.)
The Oxford Book of Hebrew Short Stories
Ben-Shaul, Moshe et al (ed.s)
PEN Israel 1997: A Collection of Recent Writing in Israel
Litvinoff, E (ed.)
The Penguin Book of Jewish Short Stories
Rosenfeld, Max (ed.)
Pushcarts And Dreamers
Solotaroff, Ted & Rapoport, Nessa (ed.s)
The Schocken Book of Contemporary Jewish Fiction (formerly 'Writing our way home'),
Neugroschel, Joachim (ed. & tr.)
The Shtetl: A creative anthology of Jewish Life in Eastern Europe

Lyndon, Sonja & Paskin, Sylvia (ed.s)
The Slow Mirror and other stories. New Fiction by Jewish writers
Cheyette, Brian (ed.)
Contemporary Jewish Writing in Britain and Ireland

The Reviews

The reviews of selected fiction that follow are by writers of Jewish descent writing with a consciousness of their Jewish identity, in books or stories available in English. The editors and contributors have chosen major and lesser-known works to give an overview of Jewish writing around the world in the twentieth century. For words marked with an asterisk* see glossary on page 249.

Publication details on books reviewed can be found in the *database* section.

The transcriptions of Yiddish and Hebrew names and titles here vary because they are based on how they appear in the individual translated books and have not been standardized by the *Babel Guide*.

Osip Mandelstam

Isaac Bashevis Singer

Bernard Malamud

Twenty-One Stories [Hebrew]

Agnon, who won the Nobel Prize for Literature in 1966 was the first writer in Modern Hebrew prose to give the language real international standing. He was though, radically unlike other great, Nobel-winning writers of the century like Thomas Mann or Albert Camus. Some of his preoccupations, such as the struggle to live a religiously-observant existence in a modern world, seem archaic but this somehow fits well with the whole notion of Modern Hebrew; the revival of a literature and a language from the past for a revived Jewish nation.

In this 'modern archaism' there is a similarity with Isaac Bashevis Singer, more a less a contemporary and also born in Poland. Perhaps the fact of the Holocaust — which finally destroyed a traditional Jewish civilisation already under attack from many directions; scepticism, emigration, Communism and Polish nationalism — it could be this made the contrast between traditional and modern ways of life so stark that both tried to re-create Jewish history and experience, often particularly cherishing archaism and tradition. In any case, reading Agnon is distinctly an odd experience. An experience perhaps better to undergo with the short works that are collected in *Twenty-One Stories*, in *Two Tales: Betrothed and Edo and Enam* or *The Book that was Lost*.

Some of the most outstanding, and perhaps representative, of the *Twenty-One Stories* are the short, uncanny *To the Doctor*, which is as disturbing as a nightmare or *The Document*, where its protagonist is caught up in a Kafkaesque bureaucracy; 'So one day passed and so a second... The clerks sat on — their faces bent over their papers and their pens writing automatically, incessantly. The clock ticked gloomily away. Its hand moved slowly, and a dead fly was stuck to it and moved along with it.' A simple, vivid story but constructed out of effortless transitions from one mood, one thing to another. Agnon is the writer of abrupt changes, he makes them seem natural — which is alarming to the reader unwittingly caught on his narrative thread.

Perhaps these sudden shifts are appropriate for a man whose own life shifted several times, dramatically enough between countries and states; Austria-Hungary, Poland, Palestine, Germany and Israel. Agnon's 'shifting' reaches a peak here in *From Lodging to Lodging*, the story of a man who is seeking a cure for a physical illness but is also suffering from profound spiritual wounds. A story too of separation — as often in Agnon — the man's wife and children are far away. Ultimately though, and to the reader's surprise, *From Lodging to Lodging* is a powerful and convincing story about human compassion that manages to emerge from a seemingly flat re-telling of banal events. One of his short masterpieces.

Also a masterpiece, but with a streak of humour too, is *Friendship*. In *Friendship* life is slowed down for us by this master of narrative time and space. Slowed down, as in a film by Andrei Tarkovsky or Robert Bresson, we realise how much fiction (or film) usually depends on narrative excitement — but that if we stop and contemplate we might see as much or much more.

Love is an Agnon theme too, charmingly in the often-anthologised *First Kiss* and, more sombrely, in *The Doctor's Divorce*, a highly original story, the theme is love but also 'the worm in the rose' of a great love; jealousy. It's Agnon in his gloomy rejection-of-the-world mood; the world can only be a snare and a delusion because of the self-tormenting perversity of the human heart.

Finally, *At the Outset of the Day* is one of the very best in the *Twenty-One Stories* collection, combining many major Agnon themes elegantly, elegaically, heart-breakingly. Read it and be moved, amazed, grateful. R K

'After the enemy destroyed my home I took my little daughter in my arms and fled with her to the city. Gripped with terror, I fled in frenzied haste a night and a day until I arrived at the courtyard of the Great Synagogue one hour before nightfall on the eve of the Day of Atonement. The hills and mountains that had accompanied us departed, and I and the child entered into the courtyard. From out of the depths rose the Great Synagogue, on its left the old House of Study and directly opposite that, one doorway facing the other, the new House of Study.

This was the House of Prayer and these the Houses of Torah that I had kept in my mind's eye all my life. If I chanced to forget them during the day, they would stir themselves and come to me at night in my dreams, even as during my waking hours. Now that the enemy had destroyed my home I and my little daughter sought refuge in these places; it seemed that my child recognised them, so often had she heard about them.

An aura of peace and rest suffused the courtyard. The Children of Israel had already finished the afternoon prayer and, having gone home, were sitting down to the last meal before the fast to prepare themselves for the morrow, that they might have strength and health enough to return in repentance.' (p252 *At the Outset of the Day*)

Two Tales: Betrothed, and Edo and Enam [Shevu'at emunim; Edo ve-Enam] [Hebrew]

This book comprises two novellas that expose the reader to Agnon's stately prose at greater length than his short stories but less overwhelmingly than in a novel like his *Shira*.

The first novella, *Betrothed*, is set in Turkish Palestine in the early days of Zionist settlement before the World War One, a period when Agnon himself lived there for a time. He shows us a world that seems to be a very different place from contemporary Israel; 'Life was unexacting, very little happened'.

Jewish though any book written in Hebrew must be, borrowing so much resonance from the language of the Bible, Agnon here also seems deeply classical. There is a trance-like, elegiac quality to the unreeling of events, that creates a contemplative vision rather than a narrative noise.

In this early Zionist world we hear about the dreams of pioneer life; 'He saw himself joining a settlement and becoming a farmer, sowing seed with one hand and holding his Talmud in the other'. Here we can smell and taste a quiet pre-war world — but it is not a 'traditional' one, for one thing rather self-assured women feature in *Betrothed*, some have emigrated alone and are particularly radical and independent while others are the more respectable daughters of emigrating fathers. *Betrothed*, as the title suggests, is the story of a love but with a very unexpected ending.

Edo and Enam is set in a later and now British- rather than Turkish-run Palestine, in around 1947 — except that this is a highly mysterious text, like science fiction at times and does not seem set in a real time or place. It moves by subtle narrative transactions, it is a work of genius, unlike anything else. For example, another story irrupts inside the story of *Edo and Enam*; about a Lost Tribe in the mountains, who have retained a Biblical Jewish life-style.

If sometimes bewildering, *Edo and Enam* is also often very beautiful; Agnon could effortlessly discover beauty in his language and deservedly counts as one of the founders of its modern literature. R K

'Jaffa is the darling of the waters: the waves of the Great Sea kiss her shores, a blue sky is her daily cover, she brims with every kind of people, Jews and Ishmaelites and Christians...' (p3 from *Betrothed*)

'But winds of change began to blow through the yeshiva walls; among them, a purifying wind that brought new promise of national revival. The students of the yeshiva began to speak of God's prophecies, of the return to Zion and the sprouting of the horn of salvation for the house of Israel in Israel's holy land. Some of them were later to belie their own words; others had the privilege of fulfilling in their lives what they sought after in their hearts. And when Yehiel heard that in the Land of Israel there were Jews who lived upon the soil, he resolved to go there and fulfil the Torah through work. He saw himself joining a settlement and becoming a farmer, sowing seed with one hand and holding his Talmud in the other; or following the plough with his copy of the Jerusalem Talmud resting upon it, thus at once fulfilling the Torah of the Land of Israel and the working of its soil.' p34-5 from *Betrothed*

'Perfect as the moon was Gemulah; her eyes were sparks of light; her face was like the morning star; her voice was sweet as the shades of evening. When she lifted up her voice in song, it was as if all the gates of melody were opened. she knew, besides, how to bake *kavanim* and how to roast meat on hot coals. Though Gemulah was only twelve years old when Gamzu first chanced upon her home, her wisdom shone out like that of a mature woman, for her father had passed on to her the secret knowledge laid up by his ancestors.' (p200 from *Edo and Enam*)

ALEICHEM
Sholem
The Tevye Stories and others [Tevye der milkhika] [Yiddish]

Sholem Aleichem was the most famous and popular of the Yiddish writers and both the musical *Fiddler on the Roof* and Barbara Streisand's film *Yentl* were based on Aleichem stories. When critics call the tone of Yiddish literature rather sentimental, taking a romantic and idealised view of Shtetl* life and personalities, it is often this writer that they have in mind. Nevertheless, amongst his huge production of work there is plenty of excellent reading and he's indispensable for an understanding of the turn-of-the-century Russian-Jewish world — with the proviso that many Jews did *not* live in the 'typical' small rural communities where he usually sets his work.

There are various collections of Aleichem's short stories and these are a better place to meet him than his often over-ambitious novels such as *Marienbad* where he takes himself a little too seriously. Overall, the short stories feed us the texture of Shtetl life, its comings and goings, the network of relatives, the poverty and the everyday difficulties. In the popular 'Tevye' stories — which can be found in most Sholem Aleichem collections — we get to know the 'Little Man' Tevye the Dairyman who perennially struggles to make a living, marry off his daughters and look after the horse that pulls his dairy wagon around the villages and dachas (country villas) of his corner of Russia. Tevye is an earthy character who loves his grub —'You should taste her noodle pudding. Then you would know what heaven and earth can be.' — but also has pretensions to be an educated Jew and constantly drops garbled or inappropriate quotations from sacred texts into his speech.

Another of the 'typical characters', one-dimensional yet telling, that populate Tevye-land is the distant relative, the *Luftmensch*★ who is a great talker, a *spieler*★ who sells Tevye a useless 'investment' in the cautionary tale *The Bubble Bursts*. What this story also tells us is that in those times people lived on air ('luft') and hope as much as herring and blintzes★ and borscht★.

Sentimental as he can often be, something Sholem Aleichem was quite unsentimental about was the caste or class division amongst East European Jews — the Shtetl wasn't all 'one big happy family', and, in the story *Modern Children*, the harshness of social distinctions is made quite clear when a mere 'stitcher' applies to marry one of the dairyman's daughters; '"A tailor" gasps Golde. [Tevye's wife] "Where does a tailor come into our family? In our family we have had teachers, cantors, Shamosim★, undertaker's assistants, and other kinds of poor people. But a tailor — never!"'. Similarly the story *The Enchanted Tailor* shows conflicts between poor Jews and the better-off individuals who held the official posts in the Jewish community This is a less-than-rosy view of social relationships in the Shtetl and is well-sprinkled with the pithy and often heavily ironic folk-sayings that Aleichem loved to reproduce, like this one; 'Silver and gold make even pigs clean'. The reaction of many young Jews to the widespread social and ethnic inequality and political stagnation of Czarist Russia is suggested when a suitor for another of Tevye's daughters — Hodel, in the story of the same name — turns out to be a young revolutionary who ends up getting deported to Siberia.

The story entitled *A Wedding without Musicians* is about a pogrom★ that is miraculously forestalled

There's plenty more about the tricky ethnic situation of the Jews in Russia — who were subjected to all kinds of legal and economic restrictions — in other stories here such as *The Lottery Ticket*, the bitter story of an impoverished young Jew who has to renounce his religion to enter university while *The Miracle of Hashono Rabo* is a leg-pull at the expense of an ignorant Russian Orthodox priest who displays great arrogance towards his Jewish neighbours.

Sholem Aleichem's stories are unmissable for their populist artistry and their flavour of the Russian Jewish world, so track down a collection of them — don't be satisfied with the Hollywood version! R K

'The main thing is that what you bring must be good — the cream must be thick, the butter golden. And where will you find cream and butter that's better than mine?

So we make a living... May the two of us be blessed by the Lord as often as I am stopped on the road by important people from Yehupetz — even Russians — who beg me to bring them what I can spare. "We have heard, Tevel, that you are an upright man, even if you are a Jewish dog..." Now, how often does a person get a compliment like that? Do our own people ever praise a man? No! All they do is envy him.' (p141 *Tevye Wins a Fortune*)

AMICHAI
Yehuda

Not of This Time, Not of This Place [Lo me'Akshav, lo mi'kan] [Hebrew]

This work is exquisitely composed, rich and profoundly layered, symphonic, with motifs being played out and developed gently but resolutely. Amichai was born in Würzburg, Germany, in 1924, and moved to Israel with his parents in 1936. In this novel the main protagonist, Joel, is an archeologist who wants to reconcile himself with and re-evaluate many of his past experiences. He feels the need to return to Germany, to 'Weinburg', his birthplace, to better understand the people, the past conflicts — the haunted world that inhabits his thoughts twenty-three years after first leaving. Amichai presents this physical and metaphysical journey, its themes and sub-themes in a modern symbolist style in harmony with the poetry work he is most known for.

We are introduced to the concept of duality, of the need to pursue perhaps two strands of thought and exploration in the early pages of the novel, on 'one of those summer evenings when people talk to each other about their plans'. Joel's friend Mina, revealed to be a schizoid personality, encourages him to both return to Southern Germany and to stay on in Jerusalem to address the doubts in his marriage to Ruth. During this 'overture' we meet several of Joel's circle of friends, each one in transition, at a moment of uncertainty and change; Einat, who is deciding to fall in love, Yosi with his violin, who also wishes to travel, and Patricia, with her seductive, strangely familiar face. Once this stage is completed, the novel-as-symphony starts up, and the rich interplay of voices and melodies begins.

The narration switches to the first person, and Joel is the 'I' who decides to travel back to his German birthplace. He becomes overwhelmed by memories of his dearest childhood friend, Little Ruth, crippled in an accident in childhood, and then dying at the hands of the Nazis. He is first reminded of her in his conscious memory (she has never left his subconscious one) once her father, Dr Mannheim, reappears in a hospital in Jerusalem, elderly and frail. With insight and delicate probing Amichai presents this retracing of the stages of his childhood. Joel talks of the need to examine the faces of the older generation of Germans — a common experience of Holocaust survivors — to decide their roles in his personal fate, to try and determine some path of revenge.

The Joel who stays in Jerusalem is presented in the third person: he needs to pursue various relationships in his contemporary world, including the question of whether the main attraction of his wife Ruth was her name, as the re-embodiment of his childhood love. He develops a passionate, physical alliance with Patricia, woman doctor, Christian, American. Clearly he is exploring the aspects of 'otherness', hoping perhaps to be healed by a different reality, one where his Jewishness and his Israeli personality are rehabilitated in a different way.

With both scenarios or major motifs established Amichai commences the brilliant contrapuntal section of the novel. Joel intersects with a motley crew of people in Weinburg, who have their resonance in the characters he is interacting with in Jerusalem. He spends many hours with his original nanny, Henrietta, at a home for the elderly in Weinburg; through her he can scan all those incidents of his childhood that trouble him, the existential questions and the factual truths. This is echoed in Jerusalem by his conversations with Dr Mannheim. As both the personas of Joel peruse these ancient faces, he senses that all of his life is contained and reflected in a few significant faces.

In all his encounters and explorations in Weinburg, Joel needs to redefine his identity, literally rename himself, to gain access to inhospitable places. These vignettes are the most amusing of the novel. For all the seriousness of the subject, Amichai presents it with a lively pace and honest and witty self-reflection. His inanimate objects are revealed with heart and soul, e.g. the 'tree which loved chocolate' from his childhood, or the changing faces of society, reflected by the bizarre conference he intrudes upon near the end of his stay in Weinburg, which changes its name and purpose at every turn.

The book's two scenarios are finally brought together both philosophically and thematically as Joel reflects on the rewriting of biography in the light of the past.

Within the whole range of his personality, Joel has needed to admit to the major significance of his past on his current life. Amichai, regarded as the 'poet laureate' of Israel, has created a novel exploring intimate and profound material that reverberates with lyrical grandeur. T L

'The tailor across from the cafe opened his shutter. An unfinished suit is always on display in his window. No finished garment catches the eye the way a suit does that still shows the white basting stitches and has but one sleeve. It is possible that Joel, too, was like that, unfinished. But only Patricia, the American, who looked in through the café window, realized that Joel's life was incomplete, despite the fact that in age and status in society he seemed completed long ago. She went in, and when he turned around he noticed her gray skirt and sleeveless blouse loosely tied at the neck with a golden thread. She came toward him like a ship in full sail, and her face was like the painted faces of women that adorned the prows of ships in years gone by. And in fact she began by saying, "This skirt is made of sailcloth." She anchored and sat down beside him and smiled and lifted a questioning finger: "Where are all the others? The gang? The people? The friends?" And he gave her some sort of answer, and she smiled slyly and knowingly.' p53–4

APPELFELD
Aharon

The Age of Wonders [Tor ha-pela'ot] [Hebrew]

The single central experience in the childhood years of Aharon Appelfeld was the Holocaust and all his memories and experiences are seen in juxtaposition to that reality, never directly described but always alluded to.

Born in Czernowitz, Bukovina (Romania) in 1932, he was sent as a boy of eight to a concentration camp. After managing to escape he spent the next three years in hiding in the Circassian forests. He arrived in Israel after the war, and has become one of the major authors writing on this period. Appelfeld has taken a particular perspective: he describes the build-up to the moment when all became nightmare, expressing the sense of confusion and disbelief, the shifting of all standards and norms of expectation. This can be seen very movingly in his earlier work, *Badenheim 1939*, where a holiday resort favored by the Jews becomes in effect their prison. Appelfeld has also described the years after the war when survivors with broken personalities found great difficulty adapting to a normal existence and regular family relationships, in *The Immortal Bartfuss*.

In *Age of Wonders* though he explores the late childhood years of his character Bruno. Events are presented in terms of milestones: the holidays spent with his mother and father in familiar places, his growing awareness that some things are changing irreparably; the family members that flow in and out of the narrative. We meet, for example, Uncle Salo and his many mistresses and young Aunt Theresa, sensitive and troubled.

By far the most striking sensations for the young boy are the various train rides he takes. The opening scenario where he and his mother are stopped on their overnight voyage, because all Jewish passengers are required to register at some obscure roadblock, sets the tone of eerie fatalism. The book is intersected with other such journeys predicting the gradual disintegration the family. The descriptions are highly evocative, as the colours, the shadows, the times of day, the seasons, all reflect the inner states of mind of his parents and himself. We are aware too of the unforgettable universal image of the Holocaust, of Jews on cattle trains being herded off to death.

A major theme in *Age of Wonders* is the role of his father as an author; the vicissitudes of his fortunes, both in reputation and in earning capacity, seem to echo the destiny of the Jews in Austria at the time. Originally well regarded, his standing is questioned when a series of articles begin appearing in journals and newspapers. These decry his 'Jewish' writing, 'the unhealthy beauty of the parasite'. The accusations are even more hurtful when it becomes clear that their author is himself Jewish. Father's own anti-Jewish feelings and his denial of any particular Jewish qualities in his writings throw into sinister relief the fate that awaited him.

The second part of the book *Many Years Later When Everything was Over*, explores the return of Bruno to his hometown after twenty years. The narrative is presented now in the third person, compared to the first person immediacy of the first part. We find out the name of the protagonist and his native town of Stalheim near Vienna for the first time, as a certain objective tone is introduced. Bruno returns by train, and the wealth of associations flood back to the reader, linking all the other train journeys taken in the earlier part of the book.

The narrator explores his past environment, and begins by examining the places he used to see and visit. There seems to be a need to find whether the buildings and surrounding nature bear witness to the tragedy. Certain routines return to his mind: holidays with his elderly Grandmother, or Aunt Theresa; taking coffee with his mother after those excruciating Latin lessons; being ragged by his fellow schoolmates after class; and the hours and days he spent with his maid Louise. Certain figures reappear, as if in a dream. Here is Louise, overblown and ungainly, recalling the attentions of all Bruno's uncles. There is Lonka, the waitress at the coffee shop, with no sign of remembrance in her eyes. Bruno meets with others at the bar and in the street, all seem to be living in a disoriented world as misfits. Those Jews who have returned are all only half-Jewish; their lives are incomplete and filled with existential anxiety.

Days turn into weeks, his encounter with the unknowing and elusive character Brum, also a personality from his past, troubles him. Once this is reconciled, in another dream-like sequence that typifies much of the writing of this second half, Bruno can return to his new home, Jerusalem.

As a young man attempting to come to terms with the weight of his experiences, Aharon Appelfeld met with and was encouraged by S.Y. Agnon [reviewed in this Babel Guide]. Agnon encouraged him to persevere with his writing and write from the heart about that which he knew. This book bears witness to the value of that advice. T L

'Bruno entered the Old Bouquet of Flowers next to the crossroads without thinking. Brum's resounding voice had held him for a moment, trapped with no way out, and he had gone into the café seeking refuge. Here was the silence found only in old wooden buildings. For some reason he took off his hat, and the aroma of coffee fortified with chicory flooded his nostrils.

Every Tuesday in the early hours of the afternoon he used to come here with his mother. It would be after the interminable Latin lesson when his head was clenched like a fist. These unforgotten little outings were usually uneventful, but they left behind a train of sweetness that would seep into his sleep together with the smell of chicory. On Tuesday afternoons the customers were mainly pensioners, each sunk in his own proud loneliness; but the place had a charm all its own due to the proprietress, Lonka — Lonka and her Slavic accent so full of vitality amid the dry formality of the Austrian petite bourgeoisie.

"Does the boy drink coffee yet?" Lonka would ask. "Coffee with lots of milk," Mother would say softly. And Lonka would take his head in both her hands and say, "A wonderfully Jewish face. The kind of face I love." "Why expose the child's disgrace in public?" Mother would whisper with a wink. "Madame," Lonka would say, "Jews are the finest people in the world. I grew up among Jewish students, you know." And Mother would respond, joining in the spirit of the thing, "In that case, Lonka, I must bow to your superior knowledge." And Lonka would say, "My lust for Jews, Madame, knows no bounds."

He opened his eyes and was glad to see that nothing had changed. The big front window, full of blue flowers, looked modest and natural, as it always had. The aromatic steam of the coffee hung almost imperceptibly in the air. In this café, as in all old-fashioned cafes, some of the corners were brightly lit and some were dim and shadowy. By the front window adorned with its blue garden flowers he would sit with his mother for hours, listening to music.

While he stood there wondering, an old woman appeared and raised her voice as if she were deaf. "What can we do for the gentleman?" It was Lonka. All that was left of her mane of brown hair was a wispy down of gray. Her ears were exposed; the heavy words sticking in her throat seemed about to break out of her mouth.

"Coffee with chicory, please," said Bruno.' p154–5

APPELFELD
Aharon

Badenheim 1939 [Badenheim, 'ir nofesh] [Hebrew]

Appelfeld's early life was as terrifyingly eventful and shocking as his novels are terrifyingly calm and understated; born in Romania, he had lived through the murder of his mother and his own deportation to a labour camp before he turned eight. He then escaped into surrounding forests where he survived for 3 years before the wanderings (including time in the Red Army) which eventually took him to Palestine in 1946. The marks of this past are most obvious in the settings of his novels, although living all his adult life in Israel, Appelfeld's settings are frequently the end-of-an-era resorts, spas and crumbling hotels of Austria on the eve of the Holocaust, populated by genuinely unsuspecting, strong-willed and sometimes complacent individuals who are about to be lead to terrible, anonymous deaths — Jewish Central Europe as it was never to be again.

Badenheim 1939 is perhaps his most accomplished portrait of this world as we witness an Austrian spa town — Badenheim — preparing for the summer season and annual music festival with its full range of averagely well-to-do Jewish guests, from Dr Pappenheim the Festival director to the two respectable prostitutes Sally and Gertie. This summer will be different though; what was to be a buoyant normal summer season, filled with people from the cities with the usual mix of neuroses, longings, pettiness and generosity will begin to seize up, as the Sanitation Department carries out inspections, wanting to know 'all kinds of peculiar details'. Beginning with the inspections then there are registrations (of Jews), restrictions on movement and worse... While the book opens, tellingly enough, on the chronically ill Trude through whose eyes the world takes on the pallor and translucency of life waning, it is the Sanitation Department's invisible growth in the book which is the real and unrecognised disease taking hold on the root of all these lives, and through which everyday reality will be steadily, irreversibly and fatally transformed.

Appelfeld conveys this gradual transformation through a limpid prose so restrained yet so eloquent that it bears what is *not* said like a distant rolling mist, an optical illusion which one has to double-check. What is crystal clear, though, is that these Jews have no room for disbelief or scepticism. When the pressure is on, they shield themselves not exactly with lies, but with two well-worn strategies: *trust* that the authorities know best, have procedures, committees, appeals and reason on their side; and *blame* — Austrian anti-Semitism here is devolved down to the Jewish population itself, feeding on the friction between the established Austrian Jews and 'those clowns' the *Ostjuden*, recent arrivals from Poland or Russia , poor pious 'riffraff' as the woman nicknamed 'the Duchess' witheringly puts it, and all of them 'little shopkeepers', who are implicitly blamed for antagonising the non-Jewish population.

In response to these tensions and the enforced proximity as Jews flood into the designated area of Badenheim, some individuals revert movingly to links with animals: Karl is ever watchful over the aquarium, quick to weed out the killer fish which threatens to gobble up all the rest, and the headwaiter patiently and painfully attends to his starving dogs, which by the end will mutely long for death.

It is finally only the rabbi, a late arrival to the crowded hotel in Badenheim, who is openly sceptical about what is going on around him. Confined to a wheelchair, speaking an incomprehensible mix of Jewish languages (Yiddish and Hebrew) and ignored by all, he 'placed no faith in these delusions' and his final emotion is one of anger.

Perhaps we too should feel anger, but the lasting impression of this gripping book is of terrifying smoothness. The transition from normality to abnormality is aided by the seeming impartiality of bureaucracy and also by active deceit: the Poland the Jews are to be transported to is advertised as some kind of holiday camp, or 'Pitchipoï' (the child's word in Yiddish for a faraway idyllic village). But the transition is also smoothed over by obstinate refusals to see (Dr Pappenheim's resounding remark as he approaches the deportation train: 'If the coaches are so dirty it must mean that we have not far to go').

The Badenheim Jews have all forged their own paths — they are secular, think of themselves firstly as Austrians, their parents have converted or they have married out, in other words, they have left a certain Jewish identity behind, and think that now they can go their own way. Particularly shocking, then, especially in an age which worships the notion of choice and which sees identity or identifications — spiritual, musical, cultural, ethnic — as attributes one can happily shop around for, is the unflinching gaze of Appelfeld on the fact that one can also be an identity one does *not* choose. Appelfeld seems to say that as soon as certain powers (political, economic etc.) start doling out identities — later, the obligatory yellow star — it is perilous to ignore who sets the terms and for what ends. S B

'The nights were now high and transparent. The hotel throbbed to the sounds of music. Even the laziest of musicians practised. No one could say anymore: "Why don't you rehearse?" Never before had Badenheim heard such a concentration of sounds.

"Isn't that a feast for the ear!" exclaimed Dr. Pappenheim.

"They're driving me crazy", grumbled Mitzi.

"You wouldn't like us to appear in Poland unrehearsed, would you? What would people say?"

The summer had not smiled on Mitzi. No suitor, no friend. This one busy practising, that one in love, that one adding up his savings. Even the dull, heavy musicians had suddenly taken it into their heads to rehearse. Fussholdt was completely absorbed in his proof-reading. Mitzi wept. Her petty vanity, cultivated with so much femininity lay in ruins around her — and without this little vanity what did she have in the world? Fussholdt again, Fussholdt and his eternal proofs. And that was all there would ever be. So what difference did it make to her if they were here or in Poland?' p88

APPELFELD
Aharon

The Healer [Be-'et uve-'onah ahat] [Hebrew]

In *The Healer* Appelfeld takes us on a voyage to the Carpathian mountains on the eve of the Second World War.

A family is taking a journey from the urban splendour of Vienna into the wilds in search for a cure which medical science is unable to offer. Their brilliant daughter, Helga, a talented musician, has lapsed into a mental torpor from which even Viennese psychoanalysis can provide no respite.

In desperation her mother, Henrietta, persuades her businessman husband, Felix, that there might be salvation to be found amongst the healers of her ancestral mountains. The very figure of the assimilated Jew, as Appelfeld puts it, Felix is reluctant, but after repeated entreaties and in the face of the failure of medical science he agrees to the venture and the family set out on the arduous trip. On arrival at their destination and disgusted by the reminders of his own past, the poverty and absence of modern amenities such as electricity, Felix watches as his wife slots into a routine of caring for Helga and visiting the healer who instructs them both in the importance of returning to a religious life. Felix sees only imposture and superstition in this regime and clings ardently to his secularism and his memories of life in Vienna.

Cut off in the mountains by the weather, however, aspects of Felix's personality are systematically undermined. His son Karl has been a failure at school and had been a source of shame to the father. Outside the urban environment, however, Felix begins to see qualities in his son which hitherto he had ignored. Karl's gargantuan appetite for food and servant girls comes to be a secret source of pride, but he is stung by the son's accusations that it is Felix who is responsible for Helga's illness, for turning her into a 'Jewish weakling'.

During their time of exile he comes to realise that his wife too has been transformed in her efforts to affect a cure for Helga.

In his increasing detachment from the familial dramas that unfold he begins to detect his own emotional neglect of the children as they grew up. His own strivings for recognition in a secular world have somehow led him here. His own selfish desire for his daughter to become a famous musician have brought about her illness.

Observing those around him, the merchants and peasants of the region, he occasionally glimpses moments of shared heritage in their mutual imprisonment in the mountains, but he still lusts for Vienna and at the first opportunity he takes Karl with him back to the big city and its cinemas and theatres. In so doing he breaks up the family. A temporary gesture, he suggests, but the story gives every indication that in clinging to his secular identity he has lost his wife and daughter forever to their faith, and himself stumbled back into a world of darkness where even healers will offer no succour. In this sense the journey of Felix's family becomes itself an allegory for the gathering darkness. The spare prose renders a complex worldview and a haunted foreboding crackles through the book's pages. G S

'After a prolonged silence, he spoke about foreign parts again, about the expanse of foreignness surrounding us on every side and destroying everything good. "We constantly retreat before that cruel invader, though we no longer have anywhere left to flee." The old man spoke in a whisper, but Henrietta caught every word. The subject was clear to her as though that language had been hers from time immemorial. He spoke of the urgent need to withdraw into our bright, warm homes. The outside is a lie. A lie. He closed his eyes.' p141

APPELFELD
Aharon

The Retreat [Hebrew]

The Retreat of the work's title could be any number of large mountain resorts in the Austrian Alps, except for two distinctive features: it is peopled exclusively by Jews and — this is the highly original and chilling premise of the book — it has been set up *for* Jews *by* a Jew (the brooding Balaban) in order to eradicate the 'hereditary defects' which Balaban and most of the guests assent to having: the Retreat is there to build good Aryans.

This work of Appelfeld looks at some of the themes of the earlier *Badenheim 1939* (also reviewed here), such as Jewish self-alienation and forms of anti-Semitism, but looks at them from a different angle, and picks up on different facets of late 1930s Austria. For example, *The Retreat* can be read as an oblique commentary on the racist theory of 'Entartung' (degeneracy), a concept which the Nazis harnessed to justify their separating off or 'concentrating' the Jews; in this respect, it is significant that the novel is set in 1938, the year after the large Munich exhibition of 'Entartetete Kunst', where works by Modernist artists from all over Europe were publicly displayed and ridiculed as 'degenerate art'. The desire to eradicate 'hereditary defects' can be seen, in this light, as a direct response to Nazi theories.

While in *Badenheim 1939* we see the 'divide and rule' logic which sets Austrian Jew against Polish or Russian Jew, one of the focal points of *The Retreat* is how the racial vilification of the Jews is internalised as Jewish self-hatred, a self-hatred so familiar to all and sundry that the non-Jewish coachman can present as a compliment to the vain actress Lotte Schloss the words: 'But you do not look like a Jewess, my lady'. We forget for a moment that Lotte, like so many other of the 'guests', ends up at the Retreat because she was fired from her job — precisely for *being* Jewish.

The model which the guests of the Retreat are encouraged to emulate is that of the 'simple peasant' whose powerful body and stunted mind incarnate a collective fantasy of wholeness and heartiness. And it is a fantasy which is so powerful that it goes unchallenged by most of the guests. So Lotte nurses her desire for 'tall blond Austrians', while we find out in a way which seems almost casual, such is Appelfeld's technique of understatement, that Lotte's daughter Julia is regularly beaten by her farmer husband, just such a 'tall blond Austrian'.

So the guests of the Retreat benignly set about building themselves up into 'simple peasants' through a regime of heavy foods, sports and 'non-Jewish' leisure activities (billiards rather than poker for example). Nevertheless disorder reigns, and the guests are subject to 'disgracefully Jewish arrangements', as the haughty Jewess Isadora states, that is to say the guests are forever involved in argument and dissent, and quickly reverting, incorrigibly, to their own chaotic ways. Even the founder Balaban's efforts to reform himself prove fruitless: in his last days, struck down by illness, he loses his acquired perfect German accent and babbles inconsolably about his ancestors in his mother tongue of Yiddish.

So the days pass by and Appelfeld sketches with precision

how each character cultivates their own faint dreams over empty days: Lotte prepares the poems of the German lyric poet Rilke for some imagined future performance, the ever-chattering Betty longingly pursues the janitor Robert, Lauffer and Lang argue over their visions of life, the former altogether unimpressed by nature, muscle and tankards of beer, the latter still hoping for transformation (and 'salvation') through strenuous exercise. For the Retreat is a place where 'everything is different, including the climate', where time seems frozen in an aimless present, marked only the rhythm of breakfast, lunch and dinner (over which presides a formidable matron who slams the serving hatch on the dot, intent as she is on teaching Jews punctuality). It is an ugly fairytale whose spell is hardly broken.

Yet it is broken. For although never stated in so many words, such is the spareness of Appelfeld's style, the reader knows that just outside of this hushed, unreal realm on a mountain-top policies of segregation and persecution are preparing the way for extermination, not of character traits or habits, but of lives. In fact this menacing outside world makes itself felt as supplies run out, suicides take place, and the suave Herbert — formerly a leading journalist — returns from the plain at the foot of the mountain where he has been beaten up.

In this short, flowing novel, Appelfeld achieves a compelling portrayal of the terrifyingly good-natured faith of these assimilated Jews: they believe that somehow life will go on and things will get better. The fatal blindness is most poignantly summed up by Lotte who, still resisting the incontrovertible evidence, stares down at the grave of the first suicide victim at the Retreat and murmurs: 'there must be some mistake'. S B

"'I told him', said Mrs Kron in her old maternal voice, "but he wouldn't listen to me. He refused to give up his evening run. What sane person goes running in winter, in the frost?" Rauch, his morning running mate, stood wrapped up in his winter coat, silent and erect, looking for some reason like the possessor of vast properties. To tell the truth, it was Betty who was now the centre of attention. She ranted and raved, screaming at the top of her voice. "What am I doing here? Why did I let myself be talked into staying here?" Her outburst was a mixture of words, complaints and ancient fears. Herbert's pleas were in vain. She was insistent: "What am I doing here?".

"Becoming a human being", said Rauch, raising his voice.

"I'm a woman".

"You're a jellyfish, not a woman".

"Did you hear what he called me?" Betty interrupted her screaming.

This exchange, for some reason, relieved the tension.

Order, needless to say, was not maintained. The search party descended the hill, holding on to each other and shouting at the tops of their voices: "Lang, Lang, where are you? Give us a sign of life". And a certain satisfaction was felt. Some of them were reminded of scouting camps in the winter season, and some of the First World War.' p96-7

ASCH
Sholem

The Nazarene [Der man fun Nazres] [Yiddish]

Mottke the Thief [Motke ganev]

Three Cities [Moskve, Peterburg, Varshe]

Asch burst on to the literary scene in 1907 with his play *God of Vengeance*, a lesbian love story set in a brothel, with a sharp attack on the hypocrisy of religious piety, a play which today would probably provoke riots amongst the ultra-Orthodox Jews of Brooklyn's Crown Heights or Jerusalem's Mea Shearim. It was immediately translated into German, Russian, Polish, Hebrew, English, Italian, Czech and Norwegian, and performed in most of them. In 1923 the play was banned in New York as obscene. Asch sought controversy, indeed he wished to be that very modern thing, the celebrity, about whom everybody would talk and who kept up public interest by constant surprise. Criticism spurred him on. When, for example his novel about Jesus — *The Nazarene* — provoked hysterical hostility amongst Jews on its publication in 1939 (significantly in the English translation alone) he went on to write not one, but *two* sequels. Asch was bitterly attacked for what has now become a literary and academic commonplace — the depiction of Jesus as a Jew.

Asch's own upbringing was to provide the two staple motifs for his work. The youngest of ten children, his own brothers were fervently religious in an enclosed Jewish world, whilst his stepbrothers and his father moved in the outer world of the market place and the Polish peasantry. When his parents suspected that he was no longer religious he had to flee from the first to the second. This conflict became dramatised in the clash between earthly desire and heavenly purity, which so often figured in his work.

Though he strove for realism in his writing, and went to

great pains to research the background of his subject, he could not stop himself writing in a romantic manner. Hence his writing veered between romantic nostalgia and gritty realism. The former predominated in *The Shtetl* (1904) where he distilled memories of his childhood, producing a portrait of small town Jewish life, that was unusually positive for that time. The negative view predominated however in *Mottke the Thief (1916)* where he was unstinting in his depiction of the brutality of the Warsaw Jewish criminal underworld. Still, he could not resist the happy ending. The villain is finally saved from damnation by the love of a pure woman. This kind of thing was probably what made him so eminently popular, carrying the reader along with him, even if the reader didn't always stop to think too much. Sometimes his novels are reminiscent of Hollywood screenplays of the 1930s and 1940s.

Although Asch probably thought of himself in the literary tradition of Tolstoy or Thomas Mann, his style was closer to that of James Mitchener or Leon Uris with a touch of Boris Pasternak... Asch was very definitely however the first Yiddish writer to write a 'great European novel'. *Ancestry* (1909) was his first attempt and the culmination was *Three Cities*, the trilogy of *Petersburg, Warsaw* and *Moscow*, published between 1929 and 1931. Here, he looked at the Jewish *nouveaux riches* striving desperately for recognition in the anti-Semitic world of Tsarist Russia. He depicted poverty and unrest, despair and hope, with the people ground down by a corrupt and oppressive officialdom. Finally, he looked at the outcome of war and revolution, analysing the social forces unleashed in 1917 and the clash between personal integrity and party discipline in the Bolshevik regime. There are few works which give such a vivid portrait of the social history of the period and of the intellectual ferment, but whether it is effective as literature is another matter. It has been said that the unity of the novels is artificial, that the character who links the parts, Gregory Mirkin is weakly drawn, that the dramatic changes he undergoes in order to figure prominently in all three are not convincing. This, indeed, was an accusation frequently made against Asch, that his novels were too contrived, that they stretched the reader's credibility, that monstrous figures all too easily and unexpectedly become saints. Mirkin starts off as the son of a rich industrialist. He flees from an arranged marriage, only to discover that his former fiancee has married his father. In anger, he retreats into the working classes of Jewish Warsaw and emerges as a leader of the proletariat. After the revolution, he falls foul of the Party in Moscow, escaping to the reborn Poland, with no power or resources, but with his soul intact.

If any Yiddish writer could be said to have made a great noise in the wider world, such was the case of Sholem Asch, that is until the later success of Isaac Bashevis Singer from the 1960s onwards. In that sense, Asch achieved what he wanted in his own lifetime. 'I am not a Jewish artist, I am a universal artist' he declared and his non-Jewish readership was immeasurably larger than his Jewish one. Yet it was his fate to be much read in his lifetime, but neglected afterwards. Not such an unhappy one though, since he was at least able to benefit personally from his book royalties. B D

'The autumn nights in Poland are pitch-black. Sky and earth are wrapped in a close embrace within which broods the mystery of creation.

With the first glimmer of dawn the sky lifts from the earth and, receding upwards, leaves a fresh, untrodden layer of white frost on the fields and meadows. The earth lies silent. no animal is yet astir. Nobody as yet owns this earth, new-born under the ascending sky: like a foundling it lies outstretched with a bloom of dew upon it...

From beyond the fields comes a metallic clinking like the trickle of single water-drops from some invisible gutter; out of the gray half-light, the first milk-cans resound far and wide in the pure, clear emptiness and rouses the sleeping world.

When these have gone past, the gray half-light gives up other wagons; over the stone bridge appear high loads of cabbages and potatoes, carts packed with egg-boxes, with fowl-crates, with jars of plums, baskets of pears, casks of cranberries; all brought by Jews and peasants from the small towns and villages into the great city of Warsaw. The wet dew of the night-fields is still thick upon the wagons. From the lofty bales of hay, from hollows in the straw, there peer fresh, round-cheeked country girls, peasant women with weather-beaten red faces under bright head-shawls, shivering Jews muffled to the ears, dripping peasants in steaming sheepskins.

Weary, with hanging heads, drops of sweat frozen on their flanks, the horses set their hoofs on the hard stones of the bridge.' (p277 *Warsaw* in the trilogy *Three Cities*)

Cardboard Castles [English USA]

Cardboard Castles, chronicles the adventures of Duncan Katz, a Jewish Brazilian-American from chilly Minnesota but the plot is merely a conveyance for the language he uses and for the digressions that possess him. Through various diversions, the novelist/protagonist goes from Minnesota to Los Angeles to Paris and back by incorporating simulated images and non-literary objects for literary use and meets many other characters, fictional or otherwise, all randomly arranged in the device of 'digressions', borrowed from Laurence Sterne.

The motive for Axelrod's narrative ducking and diving is to talk about evanescence and appearance, the problematic relativity of truth and how we perceive it.

Axelrod is a literary collage-maker after Joyce but with the demented linearity of Céline; here we get concrete poetry, stage dialogue, exilic narrative, controlled stream of consciousness and exotic vocabulary served up in a diverse combination of lexical and typographic flavours.

Because of its construction it would be difficult to give an account of what the novel is about overall but meaning clings to the digressions, whether Katz/Axelrod is tackling nostalgia, world hunger, basketball, the Holocaust or the reciting of Kaddish [*the Jewish prayer for the dead*].

Cardboard Castles is an S.O.S. message from the far edge of Jewish America, from a California world held ransom by consumerism and Hollywood cringe, it is a *Herzog* on acid. Hold tight and enjoy the ride. G R & R K

[part of this review originally appeared in *World Literature Today* 71:3 Summer 1997]

'Those were the no-star sections of Marseilles where old men lay curled up in the corners of vacant doorways, hallways, passways, ways away from the ways of others; stubbled, stumbled, and stabbed from the cold or disgrace, in tattered clothes and blankets with no pull or pile or thickness to their thinness, they lay uncovered. No teeth or only a few or teeth with blackened gums and chancres on their lips which spoke in sustained mumbles or no hands or hands with no fingers or hands with fingers besmudged in shit and garbage or hands with soiled fingers and nails extended towards cleaner hands and fingers. Lips beseeching food, hands beseeching lips to answer.'

**Collected Stories [includes Red Cavalry [Konarmiya],
Tales of Odessa [Odesskie rasskazy] [Russian]**

(Trilling, L., Ed.)

You Must Know Everything Stories 1915-1937

(Ed. Babel, N.)

Isaac Babel 1920 Diary

(Avins, Carol J. Ed.)

Isaac Babel The Forgotten Prose

(Stroud, N. Ed.)

We have to read Babel because he's a breathtakingly good writer and because his work is about a fascinating and rather terrible moment in the story of the Jewish worlds of Poland and Russia. His own curious life-story is that he felt himself picked out to be a writer and deliberately placed himself in a dangerous 'real life' situation to discover his material.

Babel, the spectacle-wearing little Jewish intellectual, went off to serve in the ranks of Marshall Budyonny's piratical (and famously anti-Semitic) Cossack division of 'Red Cavalry' in the Russo-Polish war of 1920-21. The result was a wonderfully written book, *Red Cavalry*, made up of series of vignettes of war, cruelty and pillage in a new and humane vein of war-reportage which made him an overnight success. Further collections such as *Tales from Odessa* and single stories published in magazines focused on Jewish communities in Russia and Poland either just before or just after the October Revolution of 1917.

Babel's take on Eastern Jewry is radically different from the Yiddish writers of the 1910s and 1920s; there is never a strip of sentimentality or heroism in his picture of the Jews. He seems to view things as an outsider, as 'Mr. Soviet Writer' or 'Mr. Red Cavalryman'. His 'outsiderdom' is more than a pose though, because he realises, as he stands in a Polish Synagogue where even the light-bulbs have been methodically pillaged by marauding soldiers, or sees an old Jewish man have his throat cut by his Cossack comrades for 'spying', that the traditional Jewish society, ground between the mills of Civil War, Communism, Modernisation and Slav anti-Semitism has no future. Indeed, one of the shocks of reading Babel is to realise how awful things were in the Russo-Polish borderlands even before the German mass murderers arrived.

Astonishingly though Babel perceives moments of great beauty in his sad campaigns across the Eastern lands; in a looted Polish manor he finds 'the satin of feminine letters rotting in the blue silk of waistcoats' and a despoiled church reveals the mysterious (to a Russian and a Jew) and fascinating religion Catholicism which he understands as 'a fragrant poison to intoxicate virgins'.

An extraordinary individual in an extraordinary situation, as Babel, the young man from a comfortable Yiddish-and-Russian speaking home in sunny Odessa, becomes a witness-participant in the campaigns of this *pogromnik** army. Even more extraordinary is that recently Babel's private version of events during the military campaign (*Isaac Babel's 1920-21 Diary*) has come to light. Here are the not-for-publication thoughts of a Red Soldier, to put alongside the published 'story' version of events in *Red Cavalry*. The rather post-modern flavoured conclusion we reach is that in the *Diary* — which of course like any diary is itself a literary construction — we can read another layer of what was going on and how it could be described, which is, in the case of such a great writer (and witness) as Babel, fascinating.

In his not-for-publication (in Bolshevik Russia) version Babel constantly questions the whole nature of this war and this army; 'We are the vanguard, but of what? The population await their saviours, the Jews look for liberation — and in ride the Kuban Cossacks' or 'Boratum, beautiful evening, my heart is full, rich householders, pert girls, fried eggs, fatback [bacon], our soldiers catching flies, the Russo-Ukrainian soul. I'm not sure I'm really interested.' Or, poignantly, in a village with a large Jewish population 'Demidovka, night, Cossacks, all just as it was when the Temple was destroyed.' And finally 'the filth, the apathy, the hopelessness of Russian life are unbearable.'

Like all of Babel it's very striking stuff. However, in the *1920 Diary,* there is there is yet another Babel version; Babel served in the Red Cavalry as a journalist and sent despatches to his newspaper about the campaign, some of which are reproduced as an appendix to the *1920 Diary*. Here is the heroic propaganda version of the campaign, that emphasises, for example, the Polish Army's atrocities against Jews but 'forgets' the looting and murdering of the Red Cavalry Babel himself witnessed. So we have three versions of the same reality written by the same author at the same time, — heady stuff and probably quite unique.

In *Red Cavalry* and elsewhere part of the rich Babel mix is a kind of critique of Jewishness and, in contrast, a romantic admiration (well-tempered with disgust) of what Lionel Trilling in introducing the *Collected Stories* calls Cossack 'boldness, passionateness, simplicity and directness — and grace'. Babel's complicated view of his Jewishness perhaps arises because he was on the fault line of the modern Jewish world when Yiddish was deserted in favour of Russian or another majority language. This movement implies a necessary absorption, an intimate coming-to-terms-with an other, previously 'outer' culture.

Apart from the stark but exciting war stories there is also a funny Babel as he talks of low-life in Odessa and Moscow, applying an ironic humour to a society in dissolution, corrupt, matter-of-fact, incredibly Russian (and Jewish) and universal. Don't miss Babel! R K

'There, only two paces away, stretched our front line. I could see the chimneys of Zamoste, stealthy lights in the defiles of its ghetto, the watchtower with its broken lantern. The raw dawn flowed over us like waves of chloroform. Green rockets soared above the Polish camp. They shuddered in the air, scattered like rose-leaves beneath the moon, and went out.

And in the stillness I could hear the far-off breath of groaning. The smoke of secret murder strayed around us.

"Someone is being killed," I said. "Who is it?"

"The Poles are crazed with fear," the peasant answered. "The Poles are killing the Jews." (p169-170 *Collected Stories*)

'Toward evening the bank-manager came home. After dinner he placed a wicker chair right on the edge of the bluff overlooking the moving plain of the sea, tucked up his legs in their white trousers, lit a cigar, and started reading the *Manchester Guardian*. The guests, ladies from Odessa, started a poker game on the veranda. On the corner of the table a slender tea urn with ivory handles hissed and bubbled.

Card addicts and sweet-tooths, untidy female fops with secret vices, scented lingerie and enormous thighs, the women snapped their black fans and staked gold coins. Through the fence of wild vine the sun reached at them, its fiery disc enormous. Bronze gleams lent weight to the women's black hair. Drops of the sunset sparkled in diamonds — diamonds disposed in every possible place: in the profundities of splayed bosoms, in painted ears, on puffy bluish she-animal fingers.' (p296 *Collected Stories*)

The Garden Of The Finzi-Continis [Il giardino dei Finzi-Contini] [Italian]

This beautiful, melancholy story is set in the fascist era of the 1920s and 30s. The garden lies behind a villa in the prosperous Northern Italian city of Ferrara and is the centre of the happy world of Alberto and Micòl, children of a wealthy Jewish family. Walled away from the ominous rumbles of an Italy slipping more and more under the influence of Nazi Germany, their world eventually shrinks to just this garden — a metaphor for the extirpation of their own lives and that of their community. As their horizons draw in, Alberto slowly sickens and dies of a mysterious wasting disease while the spirited and beautiful Micòl gradually relinquishes both her brilliant career — all professions were closed to Italy's Jewish citizens after 1938 — and, sensing that she has no future, renounces any fruitful love.

Bassani's book is a tender, delicate requiem for a drowned world of beauty and intelligence, a diverse and cosmopolitan way of being Italian that Italy robbed itself of, leaving it a country that shares, if to a lesser degree, the curious postwar 'moral vacuum' of Germany; a nation on parole, frightened of its own misdeeds and yet also frightened to own up to them.

What makes this requiem effective is the way it transcends these particular events and celebrates the mysteries of beauty, intelligence, friendship and kindness, which are thrown into relief by a melancholy destiny. R K

'When I went back... at the beginning of May I found spring bursting out every-where, the sprawling fields between Alessandria and Piacenza already yellow, the country lanes of Emilia full of girls out on bicycles, already bare-armed and bare-legged, the great trees along the walls of Ferrara already in leaf.' p183

The Heron [L'airone] [Italian]

The protagonist of this psychological novel personifies the post-liberation (1945) generation in Italy and the frustration of the ideals experienced in those years. Bassani follows a day in the life of Edgardo Limentani — his last day. It's a long, drawn-out day in which memories of his past that have been soothed by time and emotions which he has long pursued but never captured come floating to the surface as he hunts in the River Po delta near Ferrara, an unending landscape of plains and water. From the hide where he awaits his prey, Limentani, a lawyer, suddenly sees a heron flying unhurriedly across the sky. One cruel shot brings the creature plunging to the ground and he plans to turn its solemn, graceful beauty into an object stuffed with straw. The wounded heron's attempts to stay alive are futile, and become in Limentani's eyes a symbol of human suffering, of man's vain efforts to acquire values that he has been stripped of from the start and that only death can give back in the frozen beauty of embalming.

The idea of suicide dawns on him a little later on while he is standing by a shop window with a colourful display of stuffed birds and in that moment it appears to him as the only liberating and —redeeming act he can undertake.

Edgardo Limentani seems to be 'yesterday's man', moving through a landscape forever changing and slipping away, a watery, misty flat land, where a trick of the light renders everything insubstantial. Perhaps he's not even yesterday's man — that seems to be the ex-fascist Bellagarta who has moved away from politics into becoming a hotelier catering to the *nouveaux riches*. Limentani is like the heron, a large impractical bird; inedible and not really worth stuffing either. A terribly haunting figure somehow, he evokes other denizens of 'the drowned world' of the European Jews. In *The Heron* there is something of the same tone as in the work of the East European Jewish/Israeli writer S.Y.Agnon who in puzzling, deeply allusive stories conjured up what cannot be conjured — immense loss, loss on the scale of genocide. F C & R K

'He walked in haste, now at the end of the Via della Resistenza, — determined not to glance toward the great lighters and the barges lined up, as they had been that morning, along the bank of the river port. But once he had sensed at his side the presence of these mouse-coloured immobile forms, so immobile that you would think they were resting, rather than on water, on the mucky bed of the river, he couldn't resist the temptation to stop and look at them.

He had seen boats lined up in that way countless times, especially as a boy, in the canal ports of Cesenatico, Cervia, Porto Corsini: in the days of the blissful endless holidays that were the custom then, before the first war and immediately after it. But from these — low, broad, and surmounted, not by vast, gay sails of bright colours, but by pitiful skeletal rigging in which, light and transparent as gauze, lazy shreds of fog lingered — from these there was no extracting any sense of joy, of life, of freedom.' p146

Jacob the Liar [Jakob der Lügner] [German Poland & East Germany]

Becker was a Jewish Pole who settled in East Germany and became a leading author there. *Jakob the Liar* is set in one of the ghettos created by the Nazis in occupied Poland by stuffing thousands of Jews into a barricaded part of a city with very little food and under various harsh regulations. Eventually nearly all the surviving inhabitants would be transported to extermination camps.

Extraordinarily enough in this setting Becker creates a story with a good deal of humour and warmth. The ghetto denizens are, after all, ordinary people only recently torn from everyday lives and in their conversations emerge poignant details of their pre-deluge lives; their little shops selling potato pancakes, haircuts or tobacco; the tricky loose ends of love-affairs and marriages, all evoked by a particular kind of sardonic Yiddish wit and warmth. In fact, although writing in German, Becker draws on a Yiddish oral storytelling tradition.

One of the conditions of ghetto life was that any contact with the world outside was forbidden, including the possession of any radios. Jakob, the former proprietor of a potato pancake (*latke*) and ice-cream shop, claims one day to have a radio and this story of the imaginary radio rapidly develops under its own strange logic bringing in the hopes for survival of various very different individuals including a eight-year-old child that Jakob looks after, one of the stray children of exterminated parents who often died of starvation in the Ghettos. The relationship of these two is at the emotional centre of this tremendous and humane book. This tenderly described odd couple and the light shed by their human warmth only goes to illuminate the monstrous crime of the Holocaust, leaving open all those questions still unanswered as to how should the nation that perpetrated it be thought of today.

R K

'Come on, lean back and close your eyes, let's not spoil the pleasure by talking, let's take a few puffs and dream of old times, which will soon be back again. Come on, let's think of Chaim Balabusne with his thick steel-rimmed spectacles and the tiny shop where we always bought our cigarettes, or rather the tobacco to roll our own. His shop was closer to yours than mine was, it was between our two shops, yet we never became real friends with him, but that was his fault. Because he wasn't interested in pancakes and ice-cream, or in a haircut or a shave. Many people said he let his red hair grow so long out of religious piety, but I know better, it was out of stinginess, nothing else. Ah well, never mind, mustn't speak ill of the dead, Balabusne always had a good selection, cigars, pipes, cigarette cases with little flowers, gold-tipped cigarettes for the rich, always tried to persuade us to take a more expensive brand but we stuck with 'Excelsior'. And the stand with the little gas flame and the cigar cutter on the counter, the brass stand he was always polishing when one went into his shop, it's that brass stand one always remembers in thinking back to the old days, though we only bought tobacco from him once a week at most and never used the stand.' p91-2

BELLOW
Saul

Herzog [English USA]

Herzog, published to great acclaim in 1964, probably still holds the title of Greatest American Jewish Novel of All Time. Its real greatness, although Yiddish-speaking Herzog (and Bellow) are classic American Jewish types, is that it is much more than a Jewish book or a book about the Jewish experience in America. That it is, but it is also manages to be a manual of the ideas and philosophical crises of the century — Dr Moses Herzog is an academic and writer covering the History of Ideas and Literature and, in the guise of telling us about his aborted master work on these matters, Bellow slips in a fascinating series of references to the intellectual debates of our times. Further and most poignantly *Herzog* is about a time of crisis, a decisive watershed in a human being's life.

Herzog, forty-ish, chaotic but loveable, is too clever for his own good, with the naivete very clever people sometimes have ('somewhere in every intellectual is a dumb prick'); a special kind of immaturity and lack of practical wisdom. We meet Moses Herzog after he has tripped over badly, very badly, in love. He married a woman who, it turns out, has a personal agenda out of hell and she eventually fillets poor old Moses and has him for breakfast — with the help of a few of Herzog's own 'good friends', men seduced by this winsome, cunning and quite mad *New-Yorkaise* wife Madelaine.

It's the tale of a good (but unconsciously very arrogant) man brought down by his own stupidity, an inspired descent into a man's own ignored truths; 'considering his entire life, he realised that he had mismanaged everything'.

Herzog in defeat and licking his wounds gives Bellow the opportunity to dissect the middle-class intellectual American Jewish male of the early 1960s. Gloomy and broody but successful with women, surrounded with friends and admirers and children who love him, Herzog still carries around lots of that good old Jewish *schmerz* [pain]. Consciously in his intellectual work but unconsciously in the way he leads his life he is driven by the 'meaning problem' — the one problem America can't buy its way out of; 'that people can be free now but the freedom doesn't have any context', as Bellow/Herzog puts it.

Perhaps that problem is particularly clear for Jews who, escaping persecution and penury in the Old World, in a generation or two found themselves with everything material but with a sense of spiritual emptiness in a country with little in the way of history or certainty.

All this is wrapped in Bellow's writing which is never slipshod and often sparkling, as in this couplet on a Borough of New York; 'Queens far off to the night, a thick document of brick, veiled in the atmospheric dust'.

Herzog is, finally, something of a morality tale, Moses Herzog has everything his forefathers went to America for but ends up pointlessly crucifying himself on the altar of love. Maybe he's just bored and, as Bellow knowingly shows us, the most sublime taste of love comes when it is conducted on the edge of danger. Wife Madelaine is permanent danger, her beauty and fire at their height when most deranged; she is the most seductive thing possible to a bored, self-destructive male.

One could go on and on, but let's say that, to the wise, reading *Herzog* is worth five years of Psychoanalysis and a Masters in the History of Ideas, such is Bellow's grasp of the inner perverse workings of the soul. Save the money and the time; buy the book.

R K

'He repressed the impulse to dial Sono Oguki's number from a sidewalk booth and got on the subway instead, which carried him to Penn Station. In his long brown coat, tight in the shoulders and misshapen by the books stuffed into his pockets, he walked the underground tunnel of shops — flowers, cutlery, whisky, doughnuts and grilled sausages, the waxy chill of the orangeade. Laboriously he climbed into the light-filled vault of the station, the great windows dustily dividing the autumn sun — the stoop-shouldered sun of the garment district. The mirror of the gum machine revealed to Herzog how pale he was, un-healthy — wisps from his coat and wool scarf, his hat and brows, twisting and flaming outward in the overfull light and exposing the sphere of his face, the face of a man who was keeping up a front. Herzog smiled at this earlier avatar of his life, at Herzog the victim, Herzog the would-be lover, Herzog the man on whom the world depended for certain intellectual work, to change history, to influence the development of civilisation. Several boxes of stale paper under his bed in Philadelphia were going to produce this very significant result.

So, by the expanding iron gate with its crimson plaque, lettered on gold, Herzog holding his unpunched ticket marched down to the train. His shoelaces were dragging. Ghosts of an old physical pride were still about him. On the lower level the cars, smoky red, were waiting. Was he coming or going? At times he didn't know.' p104-5

BELLOW
Saul

Mr Sammler's Planet [English USA]

Distinguished by Bellow's characteristic fusion of high seriousness and acute comic observation, *Mr Sammler's Planet*, like his earlier *Herzog*, is richer in character and ideas than in dramatic incident. At its centre is Arthur Sammler, a Holocaust survivor living in New York, and by his own description 'an Anglophile intellectual Polish Jew and person of culture — relatively useless'. The novel spans two days, focusing upon Sammler's thoughts and experiences as his nephew, Dr Elya Gruner, dies in hospital. Gruner, a kindly gynaecologist who brought Sammler and his daughter Shula to America after the war, is one of a cast of variously eccentric, unhappy and damaged characters whom Sammler confronts during the course of the novel.

Amongst these are Shula, condemned by her traumatic wartime childhood to profound instability and child-like irresponsibility; Gruner's dysfunctional children, Angela and Wallace; and Dr Govinda Lal, an Indian scientist whom Sammler encounters when Shula steals the single copy of his manuscript, *The Future of the Moon*.

Each of these characters embodies in different ways the crisis of post-Enlightenment Western civilisation that haunts Sammler throughout the novel. As a young journalist in inter-war London, Sammler had cultivated a friendship with H.G.Wells, through which he became enamoured of Wells' utopian vision of the perfectibility of humankind through scientific advance. Sammler's subsequent experience of history, however, was to give him a shatteringly different picture of the fate of humanity in the modern

40

world. Both the horror of Nazi-occupied Europe and the 'madness' of America in the late 1960s serve to eradicate his faith in human progress.

Sammler had to crawl to survival from beneath a mass grave of Jewish corpses, including that of his own wife; and he has himself felt the visceral urge to kill when a surrendering Nazi begs him vainly to spare his life. Sammler's loss of one eye at the time of his narrow escape from extermination comes to symbolize the way in which his subsequent trauma irreversibly transforms his perception of the world.

Contemporary America, far from serving as a shelter from this trauma, only confirms the triumph of 'dark romanticism' over Enlightenment humanism. The culture of 'limitless demand' is everywhere visible, most poignantly when Sammler, addressing a student audience at Columbia, is lambasted as an 'effete old shit'. Governed by artifice, greed and the cult of the individual, America is the sick heart of the West; consequently, the Indian scientist Dr. Lal fails to persuade Sammler that the Wellsian dream of societal perfection can be attained on the moon — for there is no escaping the crisis of the modern age.

If Bellow's portrait of late 1960s America as a place of social, cultural and spiritual decay sounds overwhelmingly conservative, it's worth pointing to his extraordinary ability to leaven even Sammler's most apocalyptic ruminations with brilliantly funny dialogue and incidents (for example, Wallace's obsessive belief that his dying father has received money from the Mafia and secreted it in false water-pipes leads him to interfere with the house plumbing and cause a full-scale flood). Bellow's gift for comedy rescues the book from mere high-mindedness, revealing the intense warmth and humanity underlying its horrified vision.

J C

'New York makes one think about the collapse of civilization, about Sodom and Gomorrah, the end of the world. The end wouldn't come as a surprise here. Many people already bank on it. And I don't know whether humankind is really all that much worse. In one day, Caesar massacred the Tencteri, four hundred and thirty thousand souls. Even Rome was appalled. I am not sure that this is the worst of all times. But it is in the air that things are falling apart, and I am affected by it. I always hated people who declared it was the end. What did they know about the end? From personal experience, from the grave if I may say so, I knew something about it. But I was flat, dead wrong. Anybody may feel the truth.' p244-245

Out of the Depths [Min Ha-Metsar] [Hebrew]

Joseph Brenner represents that moment in the history of Hebrew literature when the center of creativity moved from Eastern Europe to Palestine. He personified the well-educated young Jew of the time, schooled in traditional learning in Hebrew, learning modern European languages through his own efforts and knowing in any case his mother tongue, Yiddish.

Dissatisfied with the narrow confines of life in their hometown or village, frustrated with traditional ways, young idealists like Brenner left to seek fulfillment elsewhere. Writers influenced by Zionism and the plan to revive Hebrew as an everyday modern language would eventually head East to Palestine. Writers influenced by the Bund* and who preferred Yiddish as the national language of the Jews tended to head West to Warsaw, America etc.

As *Out of the Depths* tells us, Brenner himself initially left his hometown of Novi Malini (Bulgaria) to try his chances in London.

Arriving in the Jewish East End, where he edited an early Modern Hebrew periodical, *Hameorer*, Brenner struggled with the way of life, the values being adopted by his compatriots and the English language.

Out of the Depths presents the lives of new immigrants to London around the workings of the Jewish newspaper, named ironically '*The Daily Crabb*'. Mr Crabb himself is shown as a power-hungry exploiter of his workers and fellow countrymen. Here Brenner is able to expound his growing disdain for capitalism and self-indulgent materialism. Consistent though with his unromantic view of reality, Brenner is as demanding of his other characters: the sycophantic foreman, Jacobson, who struggles to implement the boss' harsh terms of employment; or the ever co-operative Mr. Katlansky, 'Mr Editor', as Crabb calls him sarcastically.

Brenner explores the ideological changes of the turn of the century, particularly in the lives of the women characters like Hayyah-Rahel, an emancipated woman with left-wing values. The young girl Eve Taler on the other hand, innocent and hopeful, is abused by a society where moral values are in decline, and everyone is out for himself.

The most interesting characters are the narrator and his

mysterious friend, Avraham Menuhin. Conversation is mainly eavesdropped at the general meeting place 'Maisey's Kitchen' where matters and personalities of the day are discussed, issues regarding the new typesetting machine and the possible 'brigands' who may eventually train to work with it. As the printing house passes through the phases of modernization, we witness the early efforts of Jewish union movements, (Brenner went on to found the *Histradut* labour federation in Israel) seen here in opposition to the British trade unions.

Brenner, along with S.Y.Agnon, the most important of the second generation of Modern Hebrew writers, was a stylistic innovator. For immediacy and authenticity, he uses his favoured diaristic format: — sharp impressions and half-conversations remembered soon after the event. Within this diary format though, characters are sometimes presented via dialogue and sometimes via stream of consciousness, where the narrator reflects on the significance of each episode. Considering the date it was written, 1908-9, it is groundbreaking stuff.

Although *Out of the Depths* reflects Brenner's work in the pre-Palestine period, it introduces the reader to his unrelenting realism in both style and content. *Out of the Depths* prefigures his importance as author, mentor of other literary personalities and active socialist in Palestine after 1908. His achievement as a founder of Modern Hebrew prose is all the more poignant when we realize he died in an Arab uprising near Jaffa in 1921, aged only forty. David Paterson has presented a masterful and accessible translation. T L

'Tomorrow's paper. The Sunday edition is headed "Monday," the Monday edition "Tuesday" and so on until the Friday edition which is headed "Sunday." The paper has four pages. The front and back contain big advertisements, those yellow tasteful advertisements. Inside: news from the English press, both this year's and last year's, put together by Spinner, the newsman, a Jew who spends the rest of his working day teaching the holy tongue according to the English method. Although a jolly man by temperament, he dreams of writing a searing tragedy drawn from the life of emigrants, revolutionaries and members of the self-defense units, and presenting it in the local Yiddish theatre — "which will reduce the audience to a state of hysteria." Katlansky himself, the editor, the "advisor" (at his master's behest he would spend an hour every evening in the office proffering advice to abandoned wives, widows unable to remarry, impoverished Jewish emigrants, suppliants of whatever kind) writes almost every day, at Crab's direct instigation, a column entitled "Seen and Heard" devoted to parliamentary sessions, to matters of state in general, to public institutions in need of support, to local scandals, to the question of ritual baths for Jewish women and to cantors who have gone off the rails. The rest is filled with snippets taken from the "Freynd" *[another Yiddish newspaper — ed.]* and other overseas papers, with romances and penny dreadfuls which are put in the paper lock, stock and barrel without acknowledgement. For the distributors and vendors there is an additional "poster" — an eye-catching announcement summarizing the main feature: "Eighty year old Jew weds fifteen year old girl; English woman strangles her three children and then kills herself; terrible new pogrom in a Jewish community ... a hundred killed and three hundred wounded ... Tomorrow's edition will contain a detailed picture of the slain".

And I stand on a street-corner in Whitechapel, crying over and over again:

Buy the paper, Jews... buy... the daily... the daily... one ha'penny, one ha'penny ... tomorrow's Crab, tomorrow's Crab...

On my left — the copies; under my arm — the poster with the pogroms, both real and imagined...

I make my living out of pogroms.' p 30–31

BROOKNER
Anita

A Family Romance [English Britain]

Anita Brookner was born in London in 1928. In interviews she has often talked about her Jewish parents, and her introduction to English culture through reading Dickens. In her novels Jewishness has tended to be represented obliquely through the themes of the alienation that comes from being an emigrant, or from having foreign parents (see for example *Providence* and *Latecomers*).

A Family Romance tells the story of the narrator's life-long involvement with Marie-Jeanne Schiff, known as Dolly, who is her aunt by marriage. We are told that Dolly was born in Paris in 1922. Only her father is Jewish but Dolly is presented as a Jewish type in a number of ways. She is married to the narrator's uncle Hugo, and is a kind of mirror-image of her mother-in-law Toni Ferber, daughter of a Viennese ophalmologist and around whom the Freudian associations of the title, *A Family Romance,* cluster.

Brookner represents her idea of Jewishness mainly through Toni and her family. Jewishness is referred to directly, and is also presented as a quality of otherness and excessiveness as opposed to the calm norms of Englishness. Toni's husband leaves her after twenty-five years of marriage and the narrator comments that

'Marriage to Toni had bred in him a mild strain of anti-Semitism, but the more he disapproved of her the more perversely attractive he found her to be.'

The novel's narrator is Jane, Toni's granddaughter. She and her parents constitute a quiet and peaceful English family: 'I grew up English and unafraid' notes Jane, as though fear is a concomitant of not being properly English. The depiction of Dolly underlines the truth of this, and presents the qualities of 'un-Englishness'. Both Dolly and Toni pass from girlhoods of ravishing beauty and unbearable eagerness to the various frustrations of middle age.

A Family Romance is written with great delicacy, in fine cadences, but ultimately these cannot mask the transformation that occurs. Dolly, always either going out or entertaining, finally meets her downfall through a sexual liaison with a vulgar and slightly younger businessman. Jane, who has inherited almost entire the fortunes of her grandmother and her parents, also inherits Dolly's financial troubles, and at this point buys her a flat in which she becomes indistinguishable from the English ladies who live in the block, a transformation symbolized by her new style of dress. Having always worn exquisite hand-made garments, we learn that she now dresses 'discreetly' in department-store dresses. We also learn that Jane comes to love Dolly, a love almost painful in its depiction, as the opening lines of the novel suggest that it will be, but a love too which is almost painful in its implications.

To become loveable to the invisibly Jewish Englishwoman Jane, Dolly has had to shed the qualities which marked her out, throughout her life, as excessive, ardent, difficult, foreign, *Jewish*.

L S

'I have mentioned the primal scene, that imaginary sexual encounter which children reconstruct for their parents and which some believe that they have actually witnessed. This primal scene I unhesitatingly ascribe to Dolly and Hugo. Her angry smiles, her sidelong glances at her husband, her brightening of expression as the day drew towards evening, all put one in mind of a sexual life lived not too far out of sight. At the time of our first meeting Dolly was in her middle forties: was it the anguish of ageing that had brought these matters to the surface? Yet I do not believe that she thought of her substantial attractions as waning, rather the opposite. Her impatience, as I now see, had to do with frustration, as if the amiable Hugo had failed to come up to the mark. In this respect, as in so many others, she might have been the natural daughter of my grandmother Toni. Toni too had been embroiled in a primal scene, although of a more authentically Viennese stamp. Toni too had had expectations of men and had been disappointed. Both Toni and Dolly had the same restless imperious turn of the head, the same beautiful predatory hands. I see those hands now, stretched out to take the cards, be-ringed, vainly admired. Their initial ardour, which was succeeded by the most virulent antagonism, also indicates a closeness of relationship which was always denied to my mother. For this reason my mother became involved as a witness to their drama, from which she always considered herself to be slightly removed. In this, as in most other matters, she felt apologetic. I upheld her, of course, as I always did, even when such feelings were still a mystery to me. But then, for as long as I can remember, our particular closeness had no need of explanations.' p45-6

CAHAN
Abraham

The Rise of David Levinsky [English USA]

The work of Abraham Cahan, especially his novel *The Rise of David Levinsky*, is a significant point of departure in understanding the fabric of the Jewish-American immigrant experience, its evolution, and the assimilation of a people in a new homeland. Both its literary and socio-historical content establish it as a seminal influence in American letters. Abraham Cahan was Russian-born and immigrated to the United States in 1882 at the age of twenty-two.

Born near Vilna (today in Lithuania), Cahan's grandfather was a rabbi and his father a schoolteacher. Possibly because of those influences, Cahan was an imaginative and inquisitive student who was more apt to question the existing order of things than to capitulate to it. Upon leaving the Vilna Teachers' Institute in 1881 as a teacher, Cahan applied those critical faculties and got involved in the radical politics of the day. By the time he reached America he was giving lectures on Marxist philosophy to Jewish workers. He went on to establish himself as a Yiddish journalist, which eventually led to a career in creative writing.

By 1886 Cahan was contributing short journalistic pieces to a Jewish-Russian weekly called *Russky Yevrey* with pieces devoted to what would eventually become a Cahanian motif, immigrant life in America.

In 1897 Cahan founded the New York *Jewish Daily Forward*, a Yiddish newspaper which he edited from 1903 until his death in 1951, and which offered him a unique opportunity to deal with the varieties of Jewish experience on New York's burgeoning East Side. His editorial experience there enabled him to mediate between various social and ethnic levels: the Yiddish, the Russian and the American, so to speak. Cahan's familiarity with these various cultures made Cahan's contribution to North American literature and social history significant, since as a Russian-Jewish-American writer privy to this cultural richness, Cahan, more than any other writer before him. laid the foundations for one of the major themes in Jewish-American writing of the twentieth century: the problems inherent in cultural readjustment or 'acculturation'.

As can be witnessed in later Jewish writing in North America, Cahan influenced Saul Bellow, Alfred Kazin, Bernard Malamud, Phillip Roth, I.B. Singer, and Mordecai Richler who are all, in some way, indebted to Cahan for an approach to the difficult dualities of Jewish Europe and Jewish America.

Cahan established himself as a serious novelist in his three novels in English: *Yekl A Tale of the New York Ghetto* (1896) *The White Terror and the Red* (1905): and his masterpiece *The Rise of David Levinsky* (1917). This work is especially influential in his marvellous adaptation of American Jewish experience in the dialect of his immigrant characters. Cahan invigorates his characters by making them speak in a raw, idiomatic fashion which exposes the vulgarizing effect that America has had on them. Cahan's use of Judeo-American dialect predates the work of Henry Roth or Bernard Malamud.

Cahan's work reflects the change in Jewish perceptions of the world, specifically through the loss of language. In Cahan's fiction we see the slow but definite assimilation of his characters into American society, as expressed in their use of language. This is most poignant in Cahan's last and best known novel, *The Rise of David Levinsky*. Here the language of his characters expresses most fully their complete or nearly-complete assimilation into American society and, concomitantly, their gradual loss of their most important source of identity: their native language.

What Cahan presented in a way not presented before was a unique narrative treatment of a slowly evolving social, ethnic, and linguistic process which transformed the European Jew, with all his cultural, ritualistic, and mystical sensibilities, into an American Jew almost devoid of any tradition.

The novel begins with a successful middle-aged David Levinsky flashing back on his apparent rise to fortune. In the first four sections of the book, Levinsky recounts growing up in and finally leaving Antomir, his Russian village home. Eventually he gets the money needed to emigrate to America. The remaining nine sections deal with David's gradual disassociation from his heritage and assimilation into a new culture, for once David is in America he undergoes the slow process of acculturation. He shaves his beard, loses his chastity, learns English, begins his business career in the garment industry, falls in and out of love and finally becomes a successful businessman. Yet with all his apparent success he is not fulfilled. The lack of fulfilment and the loss of homeland and language have been a large price to pay for success in America.

Cahan's masterpiece prophesies that without a willingness to reinstate the past prosperity of Jewish-American roots, American Jews are doomed to an existence of increasing dispirited spiritual poverty while living within the luxury of American materialist 'darkness'. In short, Jewish-Americans are doomed to live, like David Levinsky, within the success of his failure. M R A

'Sometimes when I think of my past in a superficial, casual way, the metamorphosis I have gone through strikes me as nothing short of a miracle. I was born and reared in the lowest depths of poverty and I arrived in America in 1885 with four cents in my pocket. I am now worth more than two million dollars and recognized as one of the two or three leading men in the cloak-and-suit trade in the United States. And yet when I take a look at my inner identity it impresses me as being precisely the same as it was thirty or forty years ago. My present station, power, the amount of happiness at my command, and the rest of it, seem to be devoid of significance.'

CASTEL-BLOOM
Orly

Dolly City [Dolly City] [Hebrew]

Orly Castel-Bloom is one of a lively generation of younger Israeli women writers. Born in Tel Aviv in 1960 to French-speaking Jewish Egyptian parents, this is her first major work published in English, translated on the initiative of a small British publisher (Loki Books) dedicated to international women's writing.

Dolly City is a controversial novel, executed using the flat and violent language of the cartoon or the world of punk, not expecting to understand or interpret the world, but looking on, to quote David Gurevitch (in *Modern Hebrew Literature 15/1995*) with 'anxiety and wonder' at the inhuman, indefinable and inexpressible', at a world, which like Alice in Wonderland's, exists in a no-man's land outside time and space.

Yet, even though *Dolly City* aims at times to offend, forcing us to react to the contemporary issues of child abuse, to the horror of city life (Tel Aviv is shown as an alienating 'cancerous city'), the style remains light and witty and laughter is mixed with the horror.

Eventually the reader realises that the book's main characters, Doctor Dolly and her son 'Son' are a joint metaphor for Israel itself, and the novel is also a satirical parable on the 'Yiddishe-mamma' complex. On this point the Israeli critic Ariana Melamed wrote; 'I do not know of any other attempt in literature so persistent and determined to expose the terrifying epic of motherhood to its core, with no compromises, restraint or clichés'.

The story concerns a half-crazy woman doctor, Doctor Dolly, who has a laboratory in Tel Aviv where she slices up various animals for investigation. Into this charming scenario she brings an abandoned, shivering infant boy she happens on by the roadside. As 'Son' grows, she treats him, in her deluded self-involved state, as one of her experiments. She even carves the map of Israel into his back, the borders enlarging as he grows. Miraculously, with the help of a saintly aunt and an earthy grandmother, the boy manages to survive into adulthood despite everything done to him by his mother. He even manages to save her from a suicide attempt by fishing her out of the sea. He joins the navy, then the army, tries to highjack an aeroplane to escape, fails, and we last see him disappearing into the desert, chased by police.

With this futuristic fantasy-satire Orly Castel-Bloom is suggesting that perhaps Israel can be cured of the obsessive need to control (and kill for) its borders. 'Madness is a predator', she writes in the novel, 'It eats the soul. It takes over the soul as fast as our army occupied all of Judea, Samaria, and the Gaza District in '67.' The writer is strongly critical of Israeli 'Arabo-phobia', of the ultra-Orthodox and the bureaucracy of Israeli politics.

Adrift in a hostile city, Mother Dolly (Israel) doctors her son with a love that destroys, until she learns the meaning of compassion. M B

'One night I woke up at three o'clock in the morning with an intense desire to operate. Once upon a time, when the urge took me, I would find myself in my laboratory, opening and closing animals, but now that research was shelved and the lab was taboo, there was nothing for me to do, and, in any case, there was nothing left for me to operate on since dissecting dead bodies bored me stiff.

At the bottom of my heart, I knew I must not, must not go into the baby's room. He was sleeping soundly. I advanced on him wearing my green surgeon's uniform, undressed him and laid him on his belly on the cold metal table. He shivered with cold. I counted his vertebrae. It seemed to me that there was one missing. I counted them again and again, and after I was one hundred per cent, two hundred per cent — and so in arithmetical progression up to a million per cent — sure, I started feeding all kinds of data on my child into the computer, until it began to groan like a woman in labour.

The baby was still lying on his stomach. I put him to sleep, even though I still didn't know where I was going to cut. I tried desperately to suppress this drive of mine to mess with the child, I tried to fob it off with a simple enema, but to no avail.

I took a knife and began cutting here and there. I drew a map of the Land of Israel — as I remembered it from the biblical period — on his back, and marked in all those Philistine towns like Gath and Ashkelon, and with the blade of the knife I etched the Sea of Galilee and the Jordan River which empties out into the Dead Sea that goes on evaporating for ever.

Drops of blood began welling up in the river beds cutting across the country. The sight of the map of the Land of Israel amateurishly sketched on my son's back gave me a *frisson* of delight. At long last I felt that I was cutting into the living flesh. My baby screamed in pain but I stood firm. When I had finished marking all the points my neglected education succeeded in pulling out of the creaking drawers of my mind, I went back to being what I am — a doctor — and I disinfected and dressed the cuts, and sewed them up where necessary.

I contemplated the carved-up back: it was the map of the Land of Israel; nobody could mistake it.' p43-4

COHEN
Leonard

Beautiful Losers [English Canda]

Leonard Cohen, along with his (Jewish) contemporaries Bob Dylan and Lou Reed counts amongst the greatest singer-songwriters of North America. A lot of their best work is as Jewish as it comes: an identification with the outsider, the downtrodden, the *losers* that probably has its roots in the exclusion, persecution and marginalisation of Jews in many moments and places of the Diaspora.

Leonard Cohen established his reputation as a poet and novelist before he became internationally known for his songs. So this is a case of a good writer excelling in different media rather than a gifted musician turning out an unreadable novel, as Bob Dylan did with *Tarantula* (which apparently he was never keen to publish).

Beautiful Losers is a real book by a real writer — if at times a little stuck in the sands of hippie time, circa 1966 — and with a youthful and passionate sense of life. In Montreal, the ethnically divided and politically unstable heart of Quebec, a sensitive young scholar is researching, in a strange, obsessive way, into a tragic but colourful Native American tribe, the Iroquois, and in particular a seventeenth century Catholic convert, the young Catherine Tekawitha, 'fragrant as a birch sapling'.

Like an English-speaking Jew in French-Catholic Montreal, Catherine was someone living at the margins of a powerful, larger world, in her case the advancing colonial presence in North America, in his case the renascent Quebeçois nation, at that time testing its political muscle through mass Nationalist movements and a terrorist ginger group the *Front de Libération du Québec*. Catherine, after much penitential self-chastisement — prancing naked in the snow at minus forty degrees and wearing spiked iron accessories — dies at the age of twenty-four and, as the Jesuit missionaries who have sponsored her career as a Catholic report, in death her face miraculously turns white as she entirely casts off her heathen heritage.

In fact, between his Quebeçois friends, his seventeenth century heroine and Cohen's own profound attraction to both religiosity and sexuality the novel explores the real wonders of Canadian history; raw, romantic and wounded. Like his singing.
R K

'If all the breeze it took to ruffle a tea rose suddenly became flesh, it would be like her belly button.' p42

FRIED
Erich

Children and Fools [*pieces from* Kinder und Narren, Fast Alles Mögliche, Das Unmaß aller Dinge, Mitunter sogar Lachen] [German Austria & Britain]

Children and Fools is an extraordinary collection of thirty-four short prose pieces by a Jewish Austrian poet who was exiled from Vienna as a teenager. Fried settled in England and some of the best pieces in the book are sad/amusing vignettes of Austrian exile life set in North London.

This is a poet's book, with a poet's sudden unexpected swooping down onto bright fragments of truth; sometimes found in minor but illuminating objects or moments; the day (*The Green Suite*) when the green sofa, the Viennese grandmother's lifetime pride and joy, is finally ignominiously lugged up into the attic (prefiguring her own end) or the little handful of damp 'sand' picked up at Auschwitz (in *My Doll at Auschwitz*) that, casually pocketed, turns out, back at the hotel, to be composed of human bone fragments; the sole remains of thousands of exterminated people.

There is no avoiding the shadow of Nazism that passed over Fried's life — his father was beaten to death by a Gestapo officer who, he notes, later pursued a successful career in West Germany, and the Grandmother touchingly described in *The Green Suite* was 'transported' at the age of 76, blind and frail, to be executed by the good citizens of Greater Germany. The charming, humorous tales of pre-1938 Vienna are mixed with pieces about the succeeding barbarism and bittersweet stories of exile — of love and friendship but also desperate attempts to get relatives out of Nazi Austria.

There are also some satirical pieces about the post-war world concerning different kinds of terror. *Tortoise Turning* is an ironic fantasy about contemporary power brokers such as the oil companies, destroying the planet while distracting us with adverts featuring the odd wild animal they are 'protecting' and *The Real* which points out that the final perfection of the extermination technique Hitler started piecemeal is now available through the deployment of nuclear weapons.

It is however the most autobiographical pieces, mainly at the end of the book, including *My Heroic Age*, *The Unworthy Families*, *Three Library Users*, *Läzchen* and *Fini* that demand to be read and which provide an impeccably artistic and sympathetic account of times and people close enough to touch and far away enough to forget. R K

'One day a few of those who were not taken to the gas chambers right away are said to have called out at the end, "Watch out, we don't burn well! More will be left of us than you bargained for! Our smoke will suffocate you!"

These were their last words before they were burned. Their predictions have not, however, come true. They burned well, very well even, care had been taken of that. Although petrol was already in short supply then, it had not been spared, and had been poured or sprayed on most shortly beforehand. "Emergency baptism" it was called by the others, who drove them into the fire, the last part with long poles, in order not to come too close to the flames themselves.

Not one of the drivers and commanders of the drivers were suffocated by the smoke of those burning. From experience they knew very well how far back they had to stand and also that they had to take account of the wind. And since these burnings, which they used to call "Minor Resettlement Without Special Facilities", were basically an insignificant, little noticed episode which was not to be compared to the simultaneous so-called "Major Resettlement Action" with the Zyklon-B crystals manufactured by Degesch, the German Pest Control Company [Deutsche Gesellschaft für Schädlingsbekämpfung], they also did not attract much attention, and some of the burners who later returned to their homeland, still live today as respected elderly gentlemen in their postwar professions, or as pensioners, loved by their grandchildren. The last words of the burned were therefore mistaken at best.' p59-60

FRIEDMAN
Carl

Nightfather [Tralievader] [Dutch]

This is as much a story about the children of those who survived the extermination camps as about the survivors themselves. The 'nightfather' of the title is seen through the eyes of his daughter, a girl of about ten. She and her two brothers were born after the war (we are in the early 1960s) and they have grown up with a father traumatised by his concentration camp experiences.

Although they realise their father is different from other fathers in their neighbourhood, to them this is just the way he is, and they accept it. He 'has camp', and it gives him nightmares, it makes his reactions unpredictable, it means he has to spend periods in the sanatorium. His wife gives him her unconditional, loving support. As the children grow up, the elder boy has moments of rebelliousness, venting his frustration at a father who never stops relating everything around him to the concentration camp.

Despite the father's grim condition the book paints a remarkably upbeat picture. The girl's innocence and her matter-of-factness create an unsentimental perspective and leave much of the pain unspoken. Friedman's uncluttered style adds considerably to the freshness and humour of the forty short, vignette-like chapters. Its immediacy renders the book's progression unemphatic. But progression there is: the father's stories not only cover a chronological sequence but contain an element of suspense which is not resolved until the end, when it becomes clear that in the final months of the war, as the factory where he worked was bombed, he killed a German guard. The concluding chapter has the father relating his homecoming to his Bette, the children's mother and the father's sweetheart. She too remembers everything. As the book ends we realise that *Nightfather* is as much about her love as it is about his survival and readjustment. And since *Nightfather* has its basis in autobiography, it is also Carl Friedman's homage to her parents. Theo H

'He never mentions it by name. It might have been Trebibor or Mafkawitz, Soblinka or Birkenhausen. He talks about, "the camp", as if there had been just one.

"After the war," he says, "I saw a film about the camp. With a prisoner frying an egg for breakfast." He slaps his forehead with the palm of his hand. "An egg!" he says shrilly. "In the camp!"

So camp is somewhere where no one fries eggs.

Camp is not so much a place as a condition. "I've had camp," he says. That makes him different from us. We've had chicken pox and German measles. And after Simon fell out of a tree, he got a concussion and had to stay in bed for weeks.

But we've never had camp.

Most of the time he drops the past participle for convenience, Then he says "I have camp," as if the situation hadn't changed. And it's true, it hasn't. He still has camp, especially in his face. Not so much in his nose or his ears, although they're big enough, but in his eyes.' p1-2

GARY
Romain [pseudonym: Emile Ajar]
Momo [La vie devant soi] [French France]

So who is 'Momo'? Momo is the ten-year-old boy who tells this delightfully sharp and funny story about himself and is looked after by the enormous Madame Rosa in the Parisian quarter of Belleville, an area populated by North African Arabs, Jews, Black Africans and some Vietnamese, some of whom are involved in trades of the sort one doesn't talk about in front of the children.

Except that Momo has seen and heard it all before, takes it all absolutely for granted, knows that he, like the other children in Madame Rosa's care, are the offspring of women who 'peddle their ass'; knows that when a Nigerian pimp is killed in a settling of accounts no-one bats an eyelid because 'that was between blacks and they had no identity, because they're not French like the American blacks and the police only bother about people who exist'. He also knows that Madame Rosa lugs her 210 asthmatic pounds of flesh down six flights into the cellar (and then back up) at secret times in the night, to visit her 'Jewish hideaway' (originally from Poland, Madame Rosa had 'served' with the French Foreign Legion in Morocco and Algeria, then returned to Paris from where she was deported in the 'Vélodrome d'Hiver' round-up of July 1942 — a massive swoop by French police on Jewish quarters — returning to Paris a survivor of Auschwitz); and, finally, Momo knows that on really bad days, when life is intolerable, Madame Rosa takes from under her bed a picture of Hitler and immediately feels better because — such is Momo's watchful conclusion — that is 'one less thing to worry about'.

What Momo *doesn't* know is that one has to have a mother. The overwhelming discovery that he should have one and doesn't is the starting point for Gary's beautiful and insightful story of coping, caring and loving, for which, under the pseudonym of Emile Ajar, Gary — the Russian-born son of a Jewish mother, who moved from Moscow to Vilna (Lithuania) to Warsaw before settling finally in France — earned the most prestigious French literary prize, the Goncourt Prize, in 1975.

With the seriousness of the child who has a whole life behind him, Momo narrates how he first responded to the awareness that others, but not he, had mothers by 'shitting all over the apartment'; but, as he maturely concludes, 'that was no life'. Subsequently he steals openly from the local market stalls, on the lookout for a clout abound the ears, since he knows that 'that's what a mother does when she notices her kid'. This naivety is never twee, and the book manages to preserve the crispness of this child's often bizarre interpretations of the world without sinking into quaintness. Indeed, far from quaint, Momo's experiences show the groping, troubled and burdened world of the child, as well as a growing awareness of the way the world works — racism, police, doctors, euthanasia, trauma, transvestites...

But what makes this book a really important and unusual read is the presentation of the bond between Momo and Madame

Rosa. Gary maintains an exquisite focus on the oblique, contradictory and inherently clumsy ways which people find to give love and to get it: Momo's way of showing his anxiety that Madame Rosa will die is to stay out late and hope he'll get caught shoplifting 'to show how I felt' or to try his hand at becoming a pimp (aged ten), since he sees his role as, naturally, either pimp or cop, since both are devoted to protecting women (and it can't be cop because Madame Rosa is scared stiff of cops 'because of the home where she was exterminated in Germany').

Gary is also exceptional and daring in his treatment of old age, genuinely compassionate as well — Momo doesn't understand why someone should be forced to go on living 'just because they are suffering'. The novel is striking in its presentation of this ten-year-old's matter-of-fact but always solicitous care for Madame Rosa's body — when, as he conscientiously informs the reader, Madame Rosa is 'disintegrating' — chewing her meat for her, cleaning her up, while amazed only at how alone she can feel 'given how much of her there is'.

This is a delightfully told story (we are warned, for example, that a freshly introduced character will die by the end of the book: 'I'm telling you this right now so as not to upset you later on'), linguistically vivid and with a sharp sense of humour, but also deeply moving: the messy, inarticulate ways through which love and needs are expressed, the adult, almost melancholic sense of responsibility which this child carries, and the obtrusive physicality of life, treated with all the tenderness and respect it deserves. S B

'So Le Mahoute — the name doesn't mean a thing, that's why it stuck to him — shot Madame Rosa full of heroin. First Madame Rosa was stricken with amazement, then she went into a state of satisfaction that was horrible to look at. Think it over, sixty-five and Jewish — that was all she needed. I ran for Dr. Katz, because with heroin there's a danger of what they call overdoze, and you end up in an artificial paradise. Dr. Katz didn't come, because he was too old and forbidden to climb the six flights except in case of death. But he phoned a young doctor he knew, who turned up an hour later. Madame Rosa was drooling in her armchair. The doctor looked at me as if he'd never seen a ten-year-old kid.

"What is this place? Some sort of nursery?"

I felt sorry for him standing there so indignant. He just couldn't believe it. Le Mahoute was on the floor, bawling because he'd shot his happiness into Madame Rosa's ass.

"How could such a thing happen? Who supplied this old lady with

56

heroin?"

    I looked at him with my hands in my pockets. I smiled at him but I didn't say anything. What was the use? He was so young, maybe thirty, and still had so much to learn.' p58

GINZBURG
Natalia

Voices In The Evening [Le voci della sera] [Italian]

Family Sayings [Lessico Famigliare]

The Little Virtues [Le piccole virtù]

Natalia Ginzburg was born to a liberal Jewish family in Palermo, Sicily and spent her whole life in some of the finest intellectual and literary circles in Italy. One of her friendships was with the celebrated Cesare Pavese, [see *Babel Guide to Italian Fiction*] a writer whose work still burns brightly today.

    Voices In The Evening covers Ginzburg's favourite terrain, family life, awkwardly realistic family life and she is working at the height of her style, a powerful and seducing *matter-of-factness*. How matter-of-factness can be so seductive, so surprising and real is her great achievement as a writer.

    Ginzburg, whose first husband died at the hands of the Fascists, seems to feel the beauty of everyday living particularly sharply and alongside the kind humour of her half-bitchy, half-affectionate family conversations there is a melancholy realism.

    Family Sayings, one of Natalia Ginzburg's most celebrated works is a family memoir that became a best-seller in 1963. Among other things it reflects her kind of Italian Jewish identity, a sense of the division between the restricted small world of Jews and the wider world of Italian letters, politics and society. *Family Sayings,* as its title suggests, draws its material from that most Jewish (and Italian) of institutions, the family and a kind of intense, domestic intimacy unknown amongst cooler Northern cultures.

    In her book Ginzburg shares with us the soundtrack of the family; its words, sayings, dicta, its repetitive and emotive special language. We are allowed to eavesdrop on the inner workings of a family of anti-Fascist Italian intellectuals of the 1930s; it is an extraordinary experience.

    Apart from meeting all the great intellectual figures of political and literary life in Turin between 1925 and 1950 we also hear about the various marriages, the brother who joins the underground resistance to Mussolini's dictatorship, about Natalia Ginzburg's father, a Professor of Anatomy kicked out of the university by the Fascists and her own journey into 'restricted exile', a form of arrest meant to isolate intellectuals and political activists, that she undertook with her husband Leone Ginzburg.

Her later book *The Little Virtues,* is set in calmer times but this too is an extraordinary work, by an author who has really succeeded in sharing her wry, humane and spirited take on life with the reader. From this collection of eleven short pieces, particularly of note are *My Vocation*, in which Ginzburg speaks of her life as a writer in terms that will cheer anyone who has genuinely dedicated themselves to a profession or art; the two hilarious, charming sketches of England, *England: Eulogy and Lament* and *La Maison Volpé* and *Portrait of a Friend*, her panegyric to Cesare Pavese.

Although outside the mainstream of her work, the novella of family affairs, *The Little Virtues* is perhaps Ginzburg's greatest (and most contemporary) achievement. R K & C C

"'Because after she had lost her voice," said my mother, "she went practically mad through grief and was treated in a clinic. Once a week a dentist visited the place to see the patients' teeth, and thus he fell in love with her. She had a very beautiful mouth."

"You have told this story to me millions of times," said my father. "Why do you want to bother Tommasino with it, with persons he has never seen and never will see?"

"It serves to make a bit of conversation," said my mother. "Do you want us to sit here all evening gazing into each other's eyes? One tells stories and talks, someone says one thing, and someone else another.'" (p136 *Voices In The Evening*)

'I have always wondered why there is such a feeling of desolation in English cafés. Perhaps it comes from their desolate social relationships. Every place where the English gather to chat to one another exudes melancholy. Indeed, nothing in the world is sadder than an English conversation, in which everyone is careful to keep to superficialities and never touch on anything essential. In order not to offend your neighbour, not to violate his privacy — which is sacred — an English conversation revolves around subjects that are extremely boring for everyone concerned, but in which there is no danger.' (p25 *England: Eulogy and Lament* in *The Little Virtues*)

The Family Markowitz [English USA]

At the age of twenty-one Allegra Goodman published a precociously mature short story collection under the title *Total Immersion*. Included in it (alongside *Variant Text*, an outstandingly funny and penetrating study of an agnostic but strictly observant Orthodox Jew set in Oxford) we find a story called *Oral History*, which introduces us to Rose Markowitz. It is in these two stories that we best discover Goodman's qualities of wit and observation and her ability to draw out of the everyday stuff of life a sense of the weightiness of personal relations, as well as a comic, at times satirical, detachment from the foibles and pretentions that encumber people's lives. *Oral History* reappears in Goodman's *The Family Markowitz* as a chapter integral to her study of three generations of a contemporary American Jewish family, strung out from the West Coast to the East, and reaching to Israel and England.

Rose Markowitz, twice-widowed, orphan refugee and mother of Henry and Ed is the hub of the family Markowitz. The novel moves chapter by chapter into the lives of each of the family members in turn, so that we penetrate the diverse worlds of Henry, the Anglophile art-lover and aesthete, who leaves California to settle in England; Ed, the academic, specialising in terrorism and the Middle East; Sarah his wife, home-maker and writer; Miriam, their medical student daughter who has turned to religion, and most intriguing of all, Rose herself, whose capacity to bridge the generations, to be connected to her old Viennese past, but not to allow herself to be entrapped by her history and whose vitality acts in itself as an affirmation of life, make her the hub of the book.

This novel, as its title might indicate, takes its place ostensibly within the genre of Jewish 'family epics' (We can think of I.B.Singer's *The Family Moskat* or Bernice Rubens' *Brothers*, among others of lesser fame) but Goodman's *Family Markowitz* is not a historical novel. It is a novel in the present tense and continually alert to the conditions of the present. The chapter *Oral History* emphasises this, as Rose bewilders and frustrates the oral historian engaged in taking down her story by refusing to allow her memories to be contorted into stereotypical sociological formulae and by playing fast and loose with the 'truth' to satisfy her researcher's requirements: 'Well, we'll make something up, dear. The university will never know'. Goodman understands the elusive nature of our experience, always in danger of being diminished by the analytical mind. Her own writing respects and conveys the fluidity of feelings and events, so that for the reader nothing is dull.

In her first book *Total Immersion*, she explored the rather exotic hybrid of Jewish-Hawaiian culture and mores, while here she reveals the interest and urgency of less apparently colourful lives. Moreover the book provides a persuasive rebuttal to the idea that Jewishness in America cannot survive acculturation. It is in Rose's, and her family's, embrace of the world she inhabits, as related by her author, that we sense the survival of the Jewishness in such families as these. T H

"Hello, it's Rose. Tell me her name again."

"Susan McPhearson."

"I know that; I mean the spelling."

Sarah spells it for her.

"That's not a Jewish name," Rose says."

"It's not a Jewish person, Ma," Ed calls out. He can hear Rose's voice over the receiver.

"You tell Ed," Rose says to Sarah on the phone, "that there are a lot of women and gentlemen in this world pretending they are what they are not."

"I don't think anyone is pretending," Sarah ventures.

"Fine", Rose says. "Remember, I told you about the Winston couple on the Alaska cruise. At the Chopin concert I met the couple, last name Winston. I looked, at this old gentleman. Winston? Never. A Weinstein... He understood Yiddish perfectly."

Ed grabs the receiver from Sarah. "Susan McPhearson doesn't know Yiddish, Ma."

"Neither do you," Rose points out. "Let me tell you"

"She's not pretending", Ed says.

"I wasn't just thinking of her", Rose says. "There's also Henry."...

"What do you think she meant by that?" Ed asks Sarah after he hangs up the phone. "That Henry is pretending?"

Sarah looks up at the ceiling. They are lying together on the bed. "That he's pretending he's English, I guess."

"Oh, he's been doing that for years," Ed says. "I really think she's wondering what he's doing taking up with a woman after all this time.'"

GRAB
Hermann

The Town Park [Der Stadtpark] [German Czechoslovakia]

Hermann Grab, like Franz Kafka, was a 'Prague Jew', part of a German-speaking group of great cultural importance. As a Jew Grab was forced to leave Prague and emigrated to the United States were seven of the eleven pieces in this book are set.

In one of the American stories *Wedding in Brooklyn* he captures the unsettled awkward world of those whose settled, established lives in Prague, Vienna or Berlin were thrown on the table like so many dice. They were then doomed to try to eke out a living, starting from scratch in their forties or fifties, in a foreign country. And these of course were the lucky ones! Just one of the many crimes on the chargesheet of the Germans under Hitler was the virtual crippling of European intellectual life as a result of their domination of Central and Eastern Europe.

In the title piece, a novella, we discover quite what a loss Hermann Grab's exile was to literature in German. His writerly gift is immediately apparent as the young boy passes through early morning city streets: 'Renato would notice how one or other of the shop windows would already be illuminated at that hour, thereby transplanting an interior into the midst of the cold streets'. There is a powerful visual imagination here that recalls the master, Proust, especially as this is a story of childhood and youth constructed from memories of school (where reigned the quirky Dr. Wanka) and Mama ('Visiting Mama in her bedroom, Renato would look at the elongated glass drops which were always just on the point of falling from the chandelier'). With the other stories in the section 'Early Tales' there is a wonderful evocation of the atmosphere of Austria-Hungary (of which Prague was a part) in its last years before 1918.

Whether reminiscence unfolded out of the unforced logic of childhood or the intelligent naïveté of adolescent thwarted love — 'I probably am fond of her, he declared and immediately reflected how strangely it was arranged that one was fond of people who seemed quite indifferent to one.' — Grab is strange, original and striking.

He can also be tender and humorous as in *The Lawyer's Office* which, set in Prague between 1920 and 1938, evokes in the petty existence of minor office staff a vivid human world, just like our own with its office politics, lonely people and claustrophobia; but different in that by the end of the story Jewish or Communist employees are starting to disappear into thin air...

The Nazis tried to write Grab and his fellows out of history so congratulations to the small transatlantic publishing house (Verso) that has restored this excellent writer to the English-speaking world and the present day. R K

'Her betrothed sometimes remained away over a Sunday. Then Fräulein Lange would ask whether Fräulein Kleinert would like to spend the afternoon with her. They would go to a picture theatre, to a promenade concert or to the big pastry shop. Here they would sit at one of the little gilt tables with their princely ornamentation and, when they had consumed the plump doughnuts with coffee-flavoured or chocolate icing and scraped up every last remnant of whipped cream from their plates, they would watch the families slowly endeavouring to forge a way between the close-packed tables, they would see the Sunday bustle of the waitresses, the impassive faces of the customers who had found a place and the cigarette smoke which hung in the teatime air. Fräulein Lange always spoke only about her betrothed and his dazzling prospects and, if he were not travelling, Fräulein Kleinert would say she was quite content on a Sunday afternoon to alter a dress, brush her carpet or rear-range her cupboards. In her room in the high-lying suburb, which afforded her fresh air and also a view over a small children's playground, she would hear the occasional radio and sometimes piano-playing too, since, like her, a few families in the building would be spending the afternoon at home.' p149 (from *The Lawyer's Office*)

GRADE
Chaim

The Well [Der Brunem] [Yiddish USA]

Chaim Grade re-creates in a wonderful and poetic way the world of the religious Jews of Vilna, a great Jewish centre in Lithuania. If overall it seems a slightly sentimental picture of Jewish Vilna what is not so sentimental are some of the characters which people it. The misanthropic and embittered 'Lazar the Scribe' who copies out sacred scrolls for religious use but whose heart is consumed by antipathy for his fellow-men. Then there is the sad old bereaved couple whose children starved to death during the lean times of 1914-1918; the highly religious husband, although he suffers just as much as his wife, feels it was 'God's Will' while his wife sees it more as God's injustice to the poor...

The book, apart from the colourful characters, is loaded with fascinating and highly palatable ethnographic detail; the marvellous folk-remedies of 'Grandmother Sarah' who claims great power against the Evil Eye; 'I conjure up every evil eye, every wide eye, long eye and narrow eye, every sunken eye and every goggle eye'; the highly-charged disputations at the great Rabbinical assembly of Lithuania which reveal the troubles of learned Rabbis in the modern world. In fact a large theme of the book is the conflict between highly religious — fundamentalist if you will — Jews and modernizing ones who believe in, for example, medical doctors rather than the healing power of Talmud and righteousness. There are conflicts too over the organisation of a Zionist film show and whether it was right for a synagogue choir to sing the *Hatikvah* * on the Sabbath at a secular occasion as well as other endless arguments about observance and the Sabbath which prefigure deep conflicts today in Israel.

The Well explores 'from the inside' — as Grade himself came from a pious background — the continuing division between highly religious and rationalist Jewish points of view, a theme present in many Yiddish writers. The Jews of Eastern Europe lived in an ideological pressure-cooker of forces with the pressure of both the surrounding Christianity and the state machinery of Russia and Poland operating alongside that of the secular strands of Enlightenment and Socialist ideas. If one adds to this the cultural factors of language, the switch from Yiddish to Russian, Polish or German as languages and cultures accessible to Jews then the response by what are now known as the 'Ultra-Orthodox' of refusing to accept anything that wasn't 'traditional' in ways of thought makes more sense. Grade is especially interesting on the world of the religious Jews because, although as a Yiddish writer he is ultimately a secularist — the super-pious have no time for novels —one can also read in him an enormous sympathy too.

An accessible and colourful Yiddish classic with many amusing passages, well worth tracking down. R K

(one of Grandmother Sarah's magic charm remedies)

"'When a man is deathly sick you should stand him under a tree, drill a hole in the tree above his head, cut off a lock of his hair and put it into the hole, then say: 'Three devils standing on a mountain peak. One says: Sick. The second says: Not sick. The third says: Healthy. Take a lock of his hair, devils, but let him go.'" p130

The Book of Intimate Grammar [Sefer Ha-Dikduk Ha-Primi] [Hebrew]

This is a book about changing perspectives. It opens with its young protagonist, Aron Kleinfeld surveying his world from the balcony of the flat opposite his home, watching his parents taking their evening stroll and meeting their neighbours. Everything seems in control: he has his closest friends with him, Gideon and Zacky, and as usual they are embarked on a project of espionage and counter-espionage, with Aron as decision-maker supreme.

David Grossman builds this novel in a poignant and unconventional way: his hero grows and develops, but not in the classic *Bildungsroman* genre where a young man's growing maturity and knowledge of the world lead him to accept and flourish in his environment. Exploring and trying to understand the realities around him Aron withdraws into his own 'intimate grammar' which he creates for himself in that place 'under his heart' where words that have been cleansed, purified and made dependable can be stored.

We meet Aron's family: his sister Yocheved, a talented ballet dancer; his parents, archetypal caring Jewish parents, offering their children attention, affection, advice and food, to the point of smothering them; and Grandma Lilly, ailing, and apparently near to death. As the story progresses we experience through Aron's eyes the claustrophobia building up around him and his frantic need to delineate a space and a vocabulary all his own, where he can exist in peace and safety, away from all the unpredictable forces of parenting, love, life-and-death and friendships.

Grossman writes here with great sensitivity and empathy about the early adolescent, as in other of his works. He reflects with moving intensity on the resources a young and highly sensitive youth will draw on to counteract the misery growing in his heart.

Literary comparisons can be made between *The Book of Intimate Grammar* and Henry Roth's *Call it Sleep* [*reviewed in this Guide*]: both protagonists are young Jewish boys, living in an unpredictable and sometimes alien environment, David Shearl in 1920s New York, and Aron in a distinctly unromantic Jerusalem, presented without beauty or spiritual nuance. Both ponder the issues of language surrounding them, and both learn the same bar mitzvah portion, a reading from the Prophet Isaiah, that impacts on their sensitive minds with great significance.

The bar mitzvah itself is gloriously and sensitively described, with Aron confounding all his parents' hopes. The Rabbi in the synagogue seems fierce and disappointed, whilst at the party that follows in their home, Aron wants to hide from the fairly grotesque array of family and friends, telling coarse jokes and promoting their own children at his expense. Aron again feels betrayed by those surrounding him.

Grossman, born in 1954 and one of the most significant writers living in Israel today, has written a masterful novel about the pain of adolescence. The reader becomes involved not only as observer, but as perhaps the only witness who can salvage the overwrought young protagonist from a world where everything and everyone seem to be colluding against him. T L

'Last year in English class they learned the present continuous. Aron was thrilled: I em go-eeng, I em sleep-eeng. You don't have that eeng tense in Hebrew. Gideon didn't understand why he was so excited. Well, Gideon was like that, dead set against anything non-Israeli, non-Zionist, especially anything English, because the British loused up our country under the mandate, and if we had one drop of pride we wouldn't be learning their stupid language. Aron wanted to point out that the Hebrew language has just as many exceptions to the rule, but he held his tongue and reveled in "I em jum-peeng…" Jumping far. Far out in space, halfway to infinity, and soon he was utterly absorbed and utterly alone; jum-peeng; it was like being in a glass bubble, and someone watching from the outside might think Aron ees only jum-peeng, but inside the bubble, there was so much happening, every second lasted an hour, and the secrets of time were revealed to him and the others who experienced time the way he did, under a magnifying glass, and inside you feel private, intimate, and the people watching you, pressing their faces against the bubble, wonder what's going on; they stand on the outside looking in, puzzled and sweaty and filthy, and again he asks himself what it will be like when his bar mitzvah comes around in a year and a half, will he start growing those stiff black hairs all over, his might be blond, though; what happens, does some mysterious force squeeze the hairs out through the epidermis, and does it hurt, and he vows that even when he's big and hairy someday, with coarse skin like papa and other men have, he will always remember the boy he used to be, and engrave him deep in his memory, because otherwise certain things might vanish in the course of growing up, it's hard to say what, there's a quality that makes all adults seem similar, not in looks so much, or even in personality, it's this thing they have in common that makes them belong, that makes them law-abiding citizens, and when Aron grows up to be like them, he will still whisper, at least once a day, I em go-eeng; I em play-eeng; I em Aron-eeng; and that way he will always remember the individual Aron beneath the generalities.' p36-7

GROSSMAN
David

See under: Love ['Ayen 'erekh: ahavah] [Hebrew]

'There are no simple stories anymore' says the children's writer Anshel Wasserman to the German extermination camp commander when ordered to tell him 'a simple story'. And one need have no nostalgia for simple stories, if this astonishing, bold and imaginative work is anything to go by.

We start with Momik, a child growing up in Israel to parents and grandparents who have strange habits and mutter darkly about 'Over There' and 'the Nazi Beast'. Momik, like any child, wants to know and to understand, so he sets about drawing his own conclusions on the basis of the scant information he can gather.

Grossman skilfully captures the blend of logic and fantasy which the child's world consists of, at once the utter seriousness of dealing with grownups, noting down their words and actions like the best of detectives, and at the same time elaborating his own fantastical interpretations of them. Sometimes the research is frustrating: the whole family resolutely refuses to translate the words in German which Momik's father screams out in his sleep, or to disclose where the buried treasure is which is locked with a combination whose numbers are marked on his parents' and relatives' arms. His research draws a blank, but Momik finds a seemingly promising source in Grandpa Anshel whose gibberish, Momik is sure, conceals a comprehensible thread which may even be the key to the whole enigma, and anyway 'only Momik knows how to handle him'.

The 'Nazi Beast', Momik surmises, has frozen everything with its icy breath 'like the Snow Queen', such that 'Over There everyone is covered in a very thin layer of glass that keeps them motionless, and you can't touch them, and they're sort of alive and sort of not...'. This is the potently anxious world of the child, but treated with a warm irony, such as the deadly serious attempts by Momik to tame the 'Nazi Beast' by secretly cooping up in the cellar a range of animals from toads to ravens, hoping for their transformation...

The child's fantastical constructions set the tone for the book as a whole; a kaleidoscope of four superimposed and also interlocking tales, breathtaking in their range, surprisingly light given the difficulty of the themes and always retaining a fine line of coherence. The second section shows us an adult Momik, an aspiring writer living in Tel Aviv, now married and with a child. This adult Momik has a fascination for the writings of Bruno Schulz, a Polish Jew shot down in the street of his home town by an S.S.-man. In one of Momik's versions of Schulz's death, the latter does not die, but plunges into the sea, the very same sea which laps the shores of Tel Aviv, a connection which sparks some extraordinary poetic writing: massed ranks of twisting and shining bodies (of which one is Bruno, surviving as a salmon...), gory fish massacres headed by sharp-toothed leaders, vast treks across reefs and currents, frenzies of fins and gills and bulbous eyes... .

If the sea fantasy is one way of talking about fighting back and survival, the third section is another, where Grandpa Anshel tells a story nightly to the camp commander. In this bold variation on the *Arabian Nights* theme, Anshel nurtures the only power he has; that his stories are all his own. Each word is poised on a knife edge as he plays on that last remnant of human need within Obersturmbannführer Neigel: the need for stories, for their seductive worlds, for their realms of possibility... Grossman never lets you forget the unbearable jarring of contexts — at its most powerful when in Anshel's story a baby is born (but will he live?), while outside, again: trains, cudgels, dogs, smoke.

In contrast to this tensely claustrophobic world, the last section of the book, entitled *The Complete Encyclopaedia of Kazik's Life* appears to abandon storytelling in the name of a pseudo-scientific classification of 'basic mechanisms animating all members of the human race'. At the same time, however, new narratives breed under cover of these encyclopaedic ambitions: we can 'see under' the names of characters in Anshel's stories, for example, and so we read stories within stories (within an encyclopaedia...). This section therefore also manages to subvert the cold classificatory logic and totalising pretensions which an encyclopaedia represents, infiltrating it with personal stories and with the general inchoate mess of the human (see under: 'eczema', 'cigarette', 'trap', 'feelings', even 'love'...).

If there is one thread worked and reworked through this

extraordinarily inventive book, it is perhaps a question: how commemorate, in writing for example, someone or something who is dead? Or perhaps: how go on (to live, to write) in the face of deaths which no-one is left to commemorate and in the face of events which shake our capacity to comprehend them? David Grossman's supple and mature writing looks both backwards and forwards, it turns back to the Holocaust while affirming a possible future, it works over old forms (children's story, sea-ballad, encyclopaedia...), and breaks them open to bring out of them completely new worlds. This is a profound, beautifully written and utterly readable work. S B

'Sometimes they come into his room at night and stand next to his bed. They just want to take one last look at him before they start with the nightmares. That's when Momik strains every muscle to look as if he's asleep, to look like a healthy, happy boy, just as cheerful as he can be, always smiling, even in his sleep, ai-li-luli-luli, we have the most hilarious dreams around here, and some-times he has a really Einsteiny idea, like when he pretends to be talking in his sleep and says, Kick it to me, Joe, we're going to win this game, Danny, and things like that to make them happy, and once on a really horrible day when Grandfather wanted to go outside after supper and they had to lock him up in his room and he started hollering and Mama cried, well, that horrible day Momik pretended to be asleep and he sang them the national anthem and got so carried away he wet his bed, and all to make them understand they didn't have to get so upset, they didn't have to waste their fears on him or anything, they ought to be saving their strength for the really important things, like supper and their dreams and all the silences...' p51

GROSSMAN
David

The Zigzag Kid [Yesh yeladim zigzag] [Hebrew]

David Grossman's favoured narrator is the young boy on the threshold of adolescence facing the world and its larger realities for the first time. He has presented us with a 'family' of such protagonists in his earlier novels — Momik in *See under: Love*, Aharon in *The Book of Intimate Grammar*, even David, in his children's story, *Duel*. Here we have Nonny (nickname of Amnon) on a voyage of discovery. The search is for his own identity, plunging him into a racing, helter-skelter trip from train, to motor-chase, to confrontation with his own family background. It's a detective story set in motion by Nonny's father, a prominent Israeli detective, and his companion and secretary, Gabi, warm, emotional, *sympathique*. The result is the unravelling for the young boy of the mysterious elements of his past, who his mother was, and who he himself will choose to be. The story takes place in the days immediately before Nonny's Barmitzvah, a pivotal moment of transition in the life of every Jewish child. Written with a wink at the genre of detective novel, Grossman nevertheless moves beyond the frivolous to real questions.

Written as it was for the author's own teenage children, it is imbued with mischief and a wonderful sense of fun, with a much lighter hand than most of David Grossman's fiction. He himself was surprised at its tremendous reception by the adult reading public. Magical realism at its most captivating, it encompasses both the narrow spaces of self-exploration in the confines of a train compartment, in an exotic Bugatti car, folded up in bed, in a strangely familiar room, or tied up in the vaults of the bank; and the expanse of a soaring imagination, racing through visions of action and discovery, such as the real meaning behind Lola's purple scarf and Felix's talismanic coin. David Grossman's great sensitivity towards the inner voice of the child means that Nonny's thoughts, his range of intense and conflicting emotions all strike a vivid chord in our own hearts. He filters the impressions of all the other characters through Nonny's teenage vision and intuition. In trying to answer the question 'Who am I?', the leitmotif of the story, we perceive all the other voices talking in his head. The stringent, unsentimental voice of his father conducts a dialogue with the impudent, engaging Gabi, whilst the bewildering Felix, archetypal con-man, constantly calls for a reappraisal of everyday expectations.

Nonny must continually, during this Adventure, reassess his world, his preconceived beliefs of life within the law, steadfastly represented by his father, and life outside of the law, boldly represented by Felix, with his dark, magnetic power.

The book's success and charm lie in this combination of poignant introspection, questioning the very existential issues of life, and the witty, detailed, spirited relationships of a young Israeli with those who inhabit his world.

At the end of the book Nonny suceeds in drawing together all the strands of his heritage and in the final showdown between all the forces at play; we travel with the young protagonist, through disguises and red-alerts, luxuriating in this fantasy. His musings reverberate through the story; 'While it is true that knowledge has power, mystery has its own special sweetness'. T L

'It was strange that I had never asked such a simple question before. I knew who I was, everybody knew, I was me, Nonny, the Jerusalem district mascot, with a father and a Gabi, and a best friend named Micah, and future plans to work with Dad, but just then, for some reason, I had a feeling maybe there were a lot of other answers, maybe things weren't so cut-and-dried, and my heart sank, weighing me down till I almost didn't care anymore about this adventure, and wondered glumly, What's the matter with me, who am I?...

Just then I caught sight of someone gazing at me through the glass partition with a strange look in his eye, as though he didn't really see me. I stopped; that is, I was stopped in my tracks by the expression on his face. I knew, I just knew I reminded him of someone, because he kept looking at me with a dreamy, faraway smile. I stood directly in front of him, keeping perfectly still. He seemed to want me to stand there and pose so he could concentrate on his memory.

Then his eyes focused sharply. They penetrated the bewildering reflections in the train windows and stared directly at me, yes, me, with quizzical affection, as his long leg jiggled over his knee, and he fished something out of his pocket, a round piece of glass hanging from a fine gold chain. He put the glass to his eye, wedged between his cheek and his eyebrow. I had seen something like this in a movie once: a monocle, that's what it's called. The kind English gentlemen wear.

Hey, I'm being watched through a monocle! I realised happily, raising my head high and thinking noble thoughts to improve my reflection, because it isn't every day an Israeli kid makes an appearance in a monocle.' p 38

GRUNBERG
Arnon

Blue Mondays [Blauwe maandagen] [Dutch]

This is one of the most hilarious books to have come out of Holland in recent decades. A first novel, written for a dare by a twenty-two year old, it is not simply a carefree comedy but, if anything, a tragicomedy.

The story traces the exploits and misadventures of one Arnon Grunberg as he struggles through adolescence and early adulthood in late 1980s and early 90s Amsterdam. School offers little of interest to him. He feels no compunction to attend and sells his schoolbooks so as to be able to spend time with his great first love, Rosie. On an otherwise disastrous weekend trip to Antwerp he has his first, still rather innocent sexual experiences with her. When Arnon is eventually kicked out of school altogether and Rosie has moved on to other boyfriends, his parents urge him to make decisions about a job, a career, the future. Arnon has no idea, and no ideals either. The parents hardly serve as role models in any case. The mother, highly strung, keeps going on about the death camps, screams and smashes the crockery when she is at her wits' end, which she is very often. The father drinks heavily and, following a stroke, becomes incapacitated. The family scenes with Arnon propping up an incontinent father who is being rude to the visiting nurse while the mother is jabbering away in the background are horrendous and slapstick at the same time. The father eventually dies, choking on his own food.

The novel's second part picks up the story two years after Arnon's leaving school. He is now nineteen and has had a couple of dead-end jobs. But he spends his energy, and most of his money, on visiting prostitutes. The addresses he selects at random, and he rarely returns to the same brothel. Exactly what drives him remains unclear — one of the book's deeper mysteries. It may be his way of escaping from an oppressive family atmosphere, or it may be the memory of Rosie which haunts him. Although there is never any emotional involvement with the prostitutes, they are described with gentle, almost tender care. The sex scenes on the contrary are deadpan and incongruous; the humour has a wry, absurd touch. At the end Arnon decides — he finally makes a decision! — on a decidedly off-beat career: he becomes a male prostitute, working for an escort agency called Blue Moon, whence the book's title. Theo H

'I didn't want anything at all. I just wanted to go on sitting on that sofa and talking about this and that until the hour was up, but I was too scared to say so.

"Let's get undressed then."

"Right, let's do that."

She took her clothes off very quickly, but I was pretty quick too. I was surprised to find that I didn't feel embarrassed in the slightest, which I generally do if I get undressed in front of other people. We stood there at the foot of the bed and for a little while there was silence, and eventually I asked, 'Do you have any pets?'

"We'll go and wash now," she said.

I looked at her wrinkled belly and at her breasts, which drooped like wilting flowers, and I followed her to the washbasin. She washed herself with the blue washcloth, first her pussy, then her ass. That didn't seem all that promising. I was about to pick up the other washcloth to wash myself but she said, "No, let me do it."

I put the cloth down again. "That's nice," I said, "I haven't been washed since I was seven."

"But you've been under the shower since then, I hope."

"Of course. What I meant was that I've washed *myself* since then."

She washed me very thoroughly, just the way my mother used to.

"Now a quick wash of your hands too," she said, seizing my left hand and squirting liquid soap into in, while the music went on twanging away.

"Go lie down," she said.' p135-136

HAREVEN
Shulamith

The Miracle Hater [Sone ha-nisim] [Hebrew]

This intriguing short novel is a fictional reconstruction of the story of the Exodus of the Jews from Egypt. In contrast to the histrionics which this genre of Biblical reanimation tends to produce, this is a compact and spare account of wandering and wondering. For here there are no heroes: Moses emerges in the midst of rumours which say that he has killed an Egyptian and is fleeing retribution, that he has both a Hebrew and an Egyptian heart, and that he is talking about return to the Ancestral Land. The Hebrews gathered in their oasis camps tolerate this madness because they all knew his mother, just an ordinary woman like any other... To make matters cloudier still, Moses reverts to speaking his native Egyptian, much to the puzzlement of the masses who are now vacantly gathering around him: imagine the confusion, a leader and a saviour talking to one in a language *one does not understand.*

If Moses is an unlikely leader, the Hebrews are an unlikely people: they spend generation after generation aimlessly in the desert, such that; 'like doorless and windowless houses, they had no other memories'. We are not in the grip of a mesmerising force felt by all, and the triumphant fulfilment of a desire or a will, but at best an inexplicable doggedness. Even Moses striking the rock with his staff and bringing forth water for his parched flock is viewed from the perspective of two mothers whose babies have just died of thirst anyway, and who are not impressed.

The Hebrews' tenacity is partly due to ignorance and lack of imagination (at many points the Hebrews could have set their course out of the desert) but also due to an ill-defined sense that they are doing the right thing, submitting to the commandments (all we hear about the giving of the Law at Mount Sinai is that Moses goes missing for a few days); why not, after all... As they approach the Ancestral Land, they feel themselves to be in the presence of 'someone smiling and forbearing who expected something... without... knowing what it was'.

The novella gently demystifies the role of leadership, putting forward a model of 'leader of a people' which does not correspond to the troubling figure of ultimate authority we have come to be suspicious of. With respect to that model, Moses fails on most accounts; he's awful at public relations, at once impatient and distant, 'grim and remote'; bad on communication (long unexplained absences); bad on prioritising (in camp he spends all his time listening to his followers' thoughts and complaints until Joshua sets up guard outside the tent to fend people off); he has no charisma and no clear aims and objectives.

If hero there is, it is a minor character called Eshkar. Eshkar was born in secret, like all the children of the enslaved Hebrews, who were forbidden to have children, and he keeps his distance from the camp; he doesn't live in the family tent but strays far away to graze his sheep while always somehow coming across the wanderers in the desert again at pivotal points. He wants nothing to do with God, yet even he is gripped by a restless new energy as the banks of the Jordan loom into sight... .

Quietly haunting, unpretentious and interestingly unheroic, this is a lyrical book with a fine narrative momentum, as well as being a fascinating reworking of an important story. S B

'A smell of roast meat, of blood, of spilled beverage, and of date honey hung in the swiftly darkening air. The trampled, muddy clay paths of the camp glittered in the sunset, and later in the flickering light of the torches, with a gross, dark, bloody sheen. It was almost as if the quick of life itself, now shamelessly exposed for all to see, were being readied for transfer to some other place: the utensils of women thrown about out-of-doors, the now useless guts of sheep, the chamber pots and slop bowls, broken shards, the bare frame of a spinning wheel that never would spin again.

With the first stars, the bonfires leaped higher.' p18'

HELLER
Joseph

Good As Gold [English USA]

'Gold had been asked many times to write about the Jewish experience in America'. So writes Joseph Heller, the author and originator of a phrase in the English language 'Catch 22', at the start of this, one of his funnest comic novels.

Bruce Gold, professor of English literature, novelist and essayist finds himself at odds with his family. His wife does not notice he is no longer living with her, his octogenarian father thinks he is an idiot and his own children no longer recognise him. While his family ignore him, the government in Washington is courting him. Garnering attention for his flair with soundbites for newspaper interviews — 'I don't know', 'It boggles the mind' — his old friend Ralph Newsome assures him that he is about to get an important job in the administration without ever actually revealing what it is.

Newsome's ability to say something and nothing in the same sentence: 'You'll figure it out on your own once it's been explained to you' leads Gold to success and promotion without ever knowing his true position. In the end Gold trails through a series of hilarious disasters; wrangles with publishers, an obsession with Henry Kissinger and an engagement to the daughter of an establishment anti-Semite.

In the end, *Good as Gold* is about avoiding writing the book on the Jewish-American experience. Firstly because that type of book has already been written and secondly because the Jewish-American experience is in the end no different from any other sort of American experience. Bruce Gold suffers from the same doubts as any other American; failing marriage, worries about health, fear of war, ineffectual government, the future of the nation and concerns over his career. He is the American middle-class everyman.

The book ends up making a larger statement about the Jew in America — particularly given its protagonist's discomfort with his ethnic background. Heller, in putting his character into the heart of the government machine, suggests that the Jew, traditionally presented in literature as the outsider, can no longer claim that position. Accepted by universities and the civil service, Jews have become part of the American mainstream. In a wonderfully subtle literary sleight of hand, Heller, rather like his character Ralph Newsome, manages to make a grand statement about the Jew in America without actually stating anything. A G

"'This President doesn't want yes-men. What we want are independent men of integrity who will agree with all our decisions after we make them. You'll be entirely on your own.'

"I think I might fit in." Gold decided.

"Good. Don't say anything about it yet. We'll want to build this up into a big public announcement, although we'll have to be completely secret." Gold listened for some sign of jocularity in Ralph's voice. He listened in vain. "If the appointment we give you is unpopular," Ralph went on in the same informative way, "we'll start getting criticism about it even before we announce it. If the appointment is popular, we'll run right into tremendous opposition from the other party and from our own left and right... and centre. That's why it's good you're a Jew."

That word, Jew, fell with a crash upon Gold's senses. "Why Ralph?" He managed to say. "Why is it good to have someone who is ....who is Jewish?"

"That will make it easier at both ends, Bruce," Ralph explained with no change of tone. "Jews are popular now and people don't like to object to them. And a Jew is always good to get rid of whenever the right wing wants us to."

JACOBSON
Dan

The God-Fearer [English Britain & South Africa]

The informing idea of this short novel is a simple historical reversal, whose implications are, however, far from simple. Set in a period and a place suggestive of the late middle ages in Central Europe, but which in a subtly disorientating way belong to a fictional parallel history and political geography, *The Godfearer* follows the story of the elderly Kobus, a bookbinder. He is suffering blackouts and partial paralysis and is nearing his end. Through his own eyes the reader witnesses the strange, hallucinatory appearances of two small children, a brother and a sister. They wear the distinctive clothes of the 'Christer', a persecuted people, it slowly emerges, who have retained their obstinate belief in Jesus Christ ever since the Roman Empire adopted Judaism, and in its aftermath, that religion became the dominant cultural force in Europe. Through a series of long-buried memories which the mysterious appearances of the children exhume in Kobus' confused mind, we relive a poignant story of personal betrayal and public persecution, whose implications as a description of the historical persecution of the Jews of Europe are at one level unambiguous.

At the level of the personal history of Kobus, however, a more far-reaching understanding of the function and the ravages of prejudice and scapegoating emerges, along with a sense of the helplessness of the individual in a world whose cultural politics are obdurately resistant to the conscience and actions of individuals. This story is engaging with strong narrative suspense, but ultimately it is probably most memorable for the challenge it poses to easily assumed liberal and humanistic responses to anti-Semitism and, possibly, by extension, to most other destructive prejudice-based ideologies and social controls. By assuming that a historical reversal would find Judaism as susceptible to the scapegoating of other 'God-fearers' — as lacking as Christianity has in fact proved to be in mechanisms that might control disastrous excesses — Dan Jacobson has created a bold and, I would argue, profoundly Jewish response to one of European history's most intractable and destructive dilemmas. T H

'One old Christer woman died during the riot; several people were injured; a dozen homes set on fire. None of those responsible were arrested. The following day, mild young Kobus along with many others went on a kind of patrol through the Mishkennet; not, as far as he was concerned, to intimidate the Christer still further, but simply out of curiosity, to see what the quarter looked like after such an event... Later that day Sannie and three other Christer girls were taken into custody. "For their own protection", it was said, initially. Several more days passed; then Sannie alone was put on trial. She was charged with practising witchcraft, with trying to seduce Malachi from his faith, with inflicting cruel harm on him. The widow spoke up strongly against her. So did the widow's children, who had played with Sannie and been cared for by her. Other people, none of them of much standing in the community, soon came forward with tales of what they had seen and heard. Someone had seen Sannie and other Christer girls drawing squares in the dust, throwing stones into these squares, and then taking turns to jump on one leg from square to square: clearly the actions of people engaged in sorcerous rituals of some kind. Another witness had heard Sannie and other girls singing Christer songs at inappropriate times. Sannie had been seen surreptitiously making the sign of the cross with her two forefingers as she passed the House of Prayer...'

JACOBSON
Dan

Inklings [English Britain & South Africa

A Dance in the Sun

These are stories by a very effective writer of growing up Jewish in South Africa in the 1940s and 50s, with the focus on the uncomfortable relationships between White and Black South Africans. One story, *A Day in the Country,* also takes a look at a different uneasiness, the one between the Afrikaner minority and the Jewish one. If nothing else these books will make you realise that South Africa has long been a fascinating, if often nightmarish, laboratory of complex inter-group relations.

The most famous, often anthologised story of Jacobson is the nuanced *The Zulu and the Zeide*, which continually walks the edge between various racial cultural and even generational sensibilities in its story of the unlikely bond that develops between an old and quasi-senile Jew, the *Zeide* ('grandfather' in Yiddish) and the young African he chooses as a companion and helper.

The Little Pet probes deeper into the mentality of the Jewish community itself by throwing an intense and uncomfortable light on the relationship of a young boy to his over-anxious parents, who live out what seems like the classic nervousness of a group still insecure about its acceptance in a new society. A slightly older boy is shown rather unsuccessfully learning Hebrew in an ironic nod at the Jewish religious heritage in *Through the Wilderness*.

Unsurprisingly given his obvious awareness of social and racial tension in his South African stories, Jacobson left the country and emigrated to Britain, and the story *Fresh Fields* contains a convincing portrait of the 1950s and early 60s in 'post-war, comfort-clutching, cigarette-grabbing, shabby, soiled Britain' and combines it with an interesting and unusual South African theme. *Led Astray,* set in London in the same period is wonderfully bleak and atmospheric; 'The house as a whole was a run-down ramshackle place, with peeling stucco frames around its windows, all its brickwork much in need of re-pointing, and a sodden little garden at the back where a few clothes-lines were strung...'

Jacobson is someone who manages to let some strong African light in on people who are normally reticent, and on corners of life that are usually hidden, as is clear in these highly readable short stories. R K

'All the attempts that had been made in my childhood to teach me Hebrew had ended in failure. I had been determined that they should. For all the usual, obvious reasons. I had associated the Hebrew language with being alien, set apart; exposed; implicated in what I was convinced at an early age was a con-tinuing, unendurable history of suffering and impotence; involved with a reli-gion in whose rituals I could find no grace, no power, no meaning, and that had no connection I could discern with the dusty, modern mining town in South Africa in which I was growing up. I can still remember how intensely I hated the very pictures in the books from which we had been taught Hebrew. They were old books, who knew how old, and the pictures in them were ugly, small, cramped, full of thick black lines. The boys who appeared in the pictures were physically puny, dressed in skullcaps, long jackets, and grotesque knickerbockers; they had earlocks hanging from their temples; they were imprisoned in rooms that looked both over-furnished and poverty-stricken... I cannot describe the claustrophobia, the anguish of embarrassment and distaste they aroused in me....Yet — or hence — here I was, a Zionist now, learning Hebrew once again. And what was more, learning it from the same Mr. Saltzmann who had tried so hard to teach it to me in my childhood. Three times a week we sat at the big table in the dining-room, surrounded by sideboards with mahogany roses worked all over them, mirrors in heavy frames, a clock in a glass and mahogany case five feet tall, complete with pendulum, which unfortunately did not work. When we looked up from our books we stared into a marble fireplace, and a mantel that incorporated a melancholy lithograph of three sheepdogs in a hut somewhere in Scotland. One could tell that the hut was in Scotland because the largest of the dogs was standing guard over a plaid and a tam o'shanter, presumably the property of the shepherd, who was nowhere to be seen. His absence lent a touch of drama to the picture which it otherwise sadly lacked.' (p160-1 from *Through the Wilderness*)

JACOBSON
Howard

Coming From Behind [English Britain]

'Because he was Jewish and short and knew all the answers they loved him in return'. Meet Sefton Goldberg, lecturer, lover, comic hero; the recipient of this unexpected adoration. If Bernard Malamud identified the literary product of 'urbanised Jew in a *goyishe* pastorale', then Howard Jacobson expanded the franchise and gave it a particularly British flavour. *Coming From Behind* is a campus novel from the Malcolm Bradbury/David Lodge school of British academic manners which follows the picaresque adventures of its Jewish protagonist with all of the attendant self-absorption, gossip, egomania, envy and intrigue.

The novel is more character than plot-driven and the story itself is secondary to the purpose of the novel, an examination of the interactions of its Jewish character with a typically English inner-city college and the people who work in it. The book, set in 'Wrottesley Polytechnic', includes a variety of amusing descriptions of Sefton Goldberg's pronounced aversion to the bleak gentile environs, before establishing the plot around the removal of the Twentieth Century Studies Department to the Wrottesley Ramblers football ground and Sefton Goldberg's attempts to be awarded the Disraeli Fellowship at Cambridge and thereby leave Wrottesley for good.

The action is constantly interrupted by reminiscences of family life (in particular his father's conjuring tricks), academic and boyhood rivalries, professional misconduct and a variety of peccadilloes, misplaced affections and petty vanities. Along the way we meet a cast of characters which includes Cora Peck, a radical feminist pornographer with a Ph.D. in masturbation, the bookishly reverential Jacqueline, whom Sefton relieves of all innocence, and Sir Evelyn Woolfardisworthy, Master of Holy Christ College, Cambridge whose vowels make Laurence Olivier sound like an East End publican.

This is a book for those familiar with the idiosyncrasies of the Jewish family, the portrayal of the Jewish man as intellectual satyr and the supposed hostilities of a non-Jewish environment — the literary type most recognisable in Philip Roth. While Jacobson's hero constantly flirts with self-destruction, he is always granted a degree of humour which secures redemption over self-imposed furies. A G

'The light trickle of perspiration down Sefton Goldberg's back had now swollen into a river. Already he couldn't distinguish his shirt from his skin. In another five minutes the cheque book in his breast pocket and the little wad of paper money in his trousers would be sodden. He hoped that he wasn't going to be expected to pay for anything before he had the chance to dry out. Sherry and dinner, presumably were free, and a game of brag or poker didn't look imminent. But what if a collection plate were to be passed round at some point in the evening? Didn't Christians always have some nave or chancel (whatever they were) in need of repair? What then would be the effect on Woolfardisworthy (who had in all likelihood been kept away from Jews by a strict family and solicitous friends) of seeing Sefton Goldberg produce a couple of steaming one-ers from somewhere in the region of his groin? That would confirm an ancient Christian rumour or two, would it not?'

JOFFO
Joseph

A Bag of Marbles [Un sac de billes] [French France]

This true story opens on two young brothers playing marbles, tussling with their friends in the playground, chasing along the streets home, saying goodbye for the day and heading back to their parents' hairdressing shop somewhere in the Clignancourt area of Paris, an area where many Jews from Eastern Europe settled in the first decades of the twentieth century. But we are in the early 1940s. Marbles, playgrounds, friends even will soon be a thing of the past.

As Nazi raids and deportations in Paris intensify, the two brothers Maurice and Jojo the narrator (only ten years old and an undisguised Joseph Joffo) are sent away by their parents to unoccupied France (the armistice between France and Germany in 1940 created a Northern 'zone' which was occupied by Germany and a Southern zone, known as 'Vichy France' which remained unoccupied). The boys survive on their wits and the kindness of strangers as they dodge guards on overcrowded trains, masquerade as the flock of a Catholic priest, run errands for farmers in return for food and shelter and manage to nose out the right people to take them across the border. Eventually they cross into unoccupied France only to encounter the less militantly anti-Semitic but by not entirely benign Italian military occupation of Nice...

The story of the highly eventful lives of these brothers is told in a sprightly and optimistic tone, even at times when everything points to disaster — their parents are in the infamous deportation camp of Drancy, they themselves are captured by the Gestapo (who succeed the Italians) in Nice and are ordered to prove that they are not Jews by showing baptismal certificates... The tale sparkles with the young boys' inventiveness and resourcefulness in the face of huge odds, and they retain throughout a kind of innocence and integrity which makes this a charming read. No wonder it was an immediate best-seller, much translated, and read by old and young alike. S B

'The first slap rang out like a pistol shot. I had just arrived and I saw Mancelier's head strike the wall. When I saw those old lips, from which I had heard so much drivel, begin to tremble, I squeezed past the onlookers and went up to Mouron.

"Let him go. He's kept me hidden here a long time, and it could have cost him his neck to hide a Jew".

A silence fell over the room that amazed me as much as anyone. But Mouron proceeded doggedly. "All right, you're a Jew, but did that old fool know it?"

I turned to Mancelier who was wild-eyed with horror. I knew what he was thinking; I could still hear his endless "Those Jewish bastards", "Jewish scum", "A good clean sweep is what we need", "When we've wiped out half of them, perhaps the other half will stop and think". ...

"Of course he knew!"...

When he climbed into the back of the lorry he was trembling all over, but I was the only one who really knew why. To owe his neck to a Jew after applauding Henriot every evening for four years was not the sort of thing he found it easy to stomach.' p198

The Trial [Der Prozeß] [German Czechoslovakia]

Franz Kafka, a member of the German-speaking Jewish community of early twentieth century Prague, was, like Marcel Proust, a highly assimilated Jewish genius who revolutionised the art and essence of the novel. His working career was largely taken up as 'the token Jew' working for an insurance company; his whole perspective is of a man living the everday but profound anxiety of the accepted/not accepted Jewish citizen of a Christian state. No doubt this perspective helped create the particular anxious, analytical and sardonic sensibility with finds no better description than 'Kafkanian'.

A key work, *The Trial* is an uncanny book, written in the early 1920s before the totalitarian bureaucracies, Communism and Fascism, that reduced everyone to frustrated impotence were fully in place, and yet capturing exactly the powerlessness of the citizen of an uncivil society.

In *The Trial* We are given an imaginative reconstruction of a textbook case; a man is kidnapped by the state but has no redress or argument to make because his kidnappers act under orders of a higher, impersonal authority — 'we are humble subordinates'. The victim is the profoundly respectable, respectful man *K.* Happy with his routine life as Chief Bank Clerk and his regular visits to his mistress, he only wants to smooth out the waves created by his arrest. Predictable enough, but far less predictable, and with a delicious element of truth, is the scene where he acts out with a female accomplice an eroticised version of his arrest and appearance before the elusive but powerful 'commission' that is investigating him. In the course of this private action replay we realise that the 'application of the law' sexually excites them both; we are then forced to realise that the obedient citizens of the state may be, *au fond*, in some kind of masochistic thrall to it. Kafka is poking about into the deepest, darkest most secret links between man and man (and no doubt woman and woman) in a hierarchical system of power... He is the literary sociologist and psychoanalyst of our modern corporatist society.

As well as this *The Trial* is a metaphor for how we experience life; the self-doubt and the appeal to outside opinion for reassurance. All this is told with Kafka's unique and hard to replicate style of apparent naturalism interlarded with bizarre details — a fat old washerwoman is endlessly pursued by an infatuated young student — why? No explanation, no rationale, just the juggernaut of a reality somehow made more real by details that don't appear realistic at all.

Kafka himself had studied law and worked in a bureaucracy and flashes of sardonic wit based on close acquaintance with the real procedures of authority light up the book — the court 'is impervious to proof... but it is quite a different matter with one's efforts behind the scenes'. The tribunal that arraigned K. is always associated with rooms full of stifling never-changed air; a hallmark to this day of the machineries of justice and bureaucracy, with their sealed windows and their sealed-off mental and physical environments impervious to commonsense and humanity.

After K.'s multiple and hopeless battles with the wily and nebulous operations of the law the book finally reaches an abrupt and terrible ending, which chillingly prefigures the operations of the Stalinist and Nazi law courts whose 'judges' and officials have never, in Russia or Germany or Austria, been punished for their cruel assaults on ordinary citizens... R K

'The great privilege, then, of absolving from guilt our Judges do not possess, but they do have the right to take the burden of the charge off your shoulders. That is to say, when you are acquitted in this fashion the charge is lifted from your shoulders for the time being, but it continues to hover above you and can, as soon as an order comes from on high, be laid upon you again. As my connection with the Court is such a close one, I can also tell you how in the regulations of the Law-Court offices the distinction between definite and ostensible acquittal is made manifest. In definite acquittal the documents relating to the case are said to be completely annulled, they simply vanish from sight, not only the charge but also the records of the case and even the acquittal are destroyed, everything is destroyed. That's not the case with ostensible acquittal. The documents remain as they were, except that the affidavit is added to them and a record of the acquittal and the grounds for granting it. The whole dossier continues to circulate, as the regular official routine demands, passing on to the higher Courts, being referred to the lower ones again, and thus swinging backwards and forwards with greater or smaller oscillations, longer or shorter delays. These peregrinations are incalculable. A detached observer might sometimes fancy that the whole case had been forgotten, the documents lost and the acquittal made absolute. No one really acquainted with the Court could think such a thing. No document is ever lost, the Court never forgets anything. One day — quite unexpectedly — some Judge will take up the documents and look at them attentively, recognize that in this case the charge is still valid, and order an immediate arrest.' p177-178

Confessions of a good Arab [Aravi tov] [Hebrew]

'I grew up unwittingly into two opposing stories...' This is the mildest and most direct summary by Yosef Rosenzweig also known as Yosef Sherara, of his situation in life and in the life story which he writes while deciding between permanent exile or returning to Israel to face either a Jewish or an Arab bullet.

For Yosef Sherara or Yosef Rosenzweig is the son of Jewish mother Hava, whose parents Franz and Käthe fled from Nazi Germany for Palestine in 1936; and father Azouri, an aristocratic Arab, scholar, expert on the history of Arab-Jewish relations in Palestine and later prominent Communist (anti-Zionist) Party member, but also active for Jewish-Arab brotherhood. On his mother Hava's side, then, highly educated German Jews whose interest in Zionism was minimal until persecution forced them to see themselves as Jews, and then refugee status forced them to come to terms with their new land; and on his father Azouri's side, a committed, informed moderate, whose relatives had been dreaming lazily for generations of a pan-Arab 'Greater Syria' on the tranquillity of their scented terraced gardens that cascaded down to the sea from the slopes of the Carmel range, until, after profitable land deals with Jews at the collapse of the Ottoman empire, they found themselves after 1948 dispossessed, displaced and humiliated.

Yosef is therefore a 'freak', an historical mistake, whose life is divided against itself in advance. As such, he is already a 'professional traitor' before he begins any clandestine involvements, in Jewish Haifa and or Arab Acre. He has no place to call his own and is able only to dodge and weave across the Jewish-Arab borders which cut right through his only body and soul. So he twists the knife both ways, in attempts to heal his own wounds: he blames, and for long periods neglects, his patient father Azouri, and then the other hand he engages in an 'Arab period' touring the Soviet Union denouncing 'Zionist imperialists' and the robbery of the land of 'the peasant brothers'... Neither of these commitments, however, can encompass adequately Yosef's double blood. Moreover, the lies and distortions which he witnesses on both sides drive him underground where, again, he plays for both camps; for Arab organisations and for *Mossad* (the Israeli Secret Service).

This uncompromising and compelling work follows its protagonist's attempt to unravel how he came into being, the histories that join or fight within him, and hence something of the history of Arab-Jewish relations in the land of Israel from the turn of the century onwards. More than this, it is a profound meditation on political complexity, on the (opportunistic or coincidental) transformation of political movements into forms which they were never intended to inhabit and on the atavistic forces which nationalism can harness.

Written in a fierce and compact style, driven less by anger, self-pity or guilt — the Hebrew title, *Aravi tov*, translates simply as 'A good Arab', without the resonance of transgression and guilt which 'Confessions' introduces — than by a kind of dry passion, a passion to piece together, to reflect and understand.

The strength of *Confessions of a good Arab* is that it gives the Arab-Jewish conflict its true historical complexity, through the different experiences and thoughts of the characters, without filtering out those elements which don't fit neatly into the grid of a preconceived position. With this rigorous honesty with respect to both Arab and Jewish histories in Israel goes a taut, emotionally charged tale which manages to be gripping while never ever cutting political corners. This book doesn't allow the comfortable 'oh it is all too complex', or the cosy 'well they all have their rights and wrongs', it forces one to reflect and to question...

In the eyes of *The Nation*, Yosef Rosenzweig/Sherara is an affront, an affront to neat parcels of belonging and not belonging, deeply subversive and unsettling to the ideology of the unitary and homogeneous, and a searing expression of how 'in a tragedy there isn't one justice but two'. When the Nation can do something other than bludgeon this hybridity, it will be the time for nations again. Until then, this book will inflame, provoke and trouble you whichever borders you live on. S B

(Laila is Yosef's Arab lover — ed.)

'Laila sat and looked at me through weary eyes. She said, everything is harder because the devils haven't got any horns, the horrors are disguised as something almost human. Someone told me that the Syrians buried twenty-five thousand people alive in concrete — who cares? The Jews are playing the good guys on dangerous turf. New voices are emerging on the other side of the Jewish night and shouting that their blood is white as snow, people are returning from the oblivion of history with a dark, deadly racism, the catastrophe is waiting in the wings, in the centre of the stage the violence is sporadic, there's no one really to fight against, Fatah doesn't play according to my rules but I can't close my eyes to their anger, they've got justice on their side too, they're murderers but they murder so that I can hold my head up... Yosef, how are you going to survive?' p191

KANIUK
Yoram

His Daughter [Bito] [Hebrew]

Israelis have had to fight in many wars and produce soldiers in every generation. The toll this takes on individual, family and society is the real theme of this book.

Joseph Krieger is the father of Miriam, and *His Daughter* is about his search for her after she goes missing one January evening. Krieger is a famous (retired) brigadier, an Israeli war veteran. But his record is not without blemish, and many around him, including his daughter, hold him responsible for the deaths of others. Why has she chosen this particular moment to disappear? Who, in all the complex set of family, associates and fellow soldiers has played a part in this scenario? Is there a way that Krieger's military experience can serve him in the battle of wills now raging?

Yoram Kaniuk, who was born and grew up in Tel Aviv, reveals in his writing an exceptional honesty about the society he lives in. He focuses on the issues that make the Israeli situation unique in the world: in this case the state of war and war-readiness that is a constant in the life of every citizen.

This novel works primarily as Krieger's diary but it also replays a stream of confessions, as the spotlight falls on the different figures in the drama. There are his friends from childhood who formed the 'Three Musketeers' with Krieger; Reuben and the 'Chief of Staff' (he remains unnamed), whose lives have been interwoven in all aspects for so many years. There is his wife Nina who arrived in Israel after the war fragile and fragmented, for so long his only love although she could never be faithful to him. Then there are the military police and the television staff, Miriam's colleagues and a strange assortment of friends. As he inquires into the roles of Gideon and Naomi, of Sergeant Joy Rose and Hanoch Levi, of Noam Raphaeli and Jahash we see the complexity of this world, where army and civilian life are inextricably linked both in the present and in the histories they carry with them. The light of investigation shines on each of these characters and as it does its refraction reveals the possibilities of truth and falsehood, of self-knowledge and self-deception.

Kaniuk explores the different relationships of affection and lust, of brotherly, combative and parental love and the constant crossing of shadowy boundaries.

Krieger (whose surname is reminiscent of German *Krieg* or war) is perceived by some as 'the bitter poet of death', and this clearly represents an indictment on the way of life that requires soldiers at all times to be prepared for armed conflict, to sublimate all other feelings.

His Daughter is a taut drama of plot and intrigue. It is also a reflection of the price each person, career soldier or citizen has to pay in this complex society, the pattern of constant readjustment and adaptation, when life and death occur in such shattering ways. T L

'Naomi asked me why I had wanted to live in the house I'd grown up in since I was six. "It's never made any difference to me where I live," she said. 'Why is it so important to you?"

I said, "I never knew anybody who lived in the home they'd grown up in or were born in. That always bothered me. In France I met people still living in the house in which they and their parents and grandparents had been born. I was delighted. The idea of constantly migrating from one place to another troubled me. Your back was always to the wall, ready to make another exit. It offends me how rootless we are. Look how easily Israelis adapt to living in America or anywhere else. Every house here was built from scratch, there's no tradition, no real settling down, it's all temporary, just for the time being. To me a house is a declaration of loyalty, commitment, life. It's important to me," I told Naomi, who obviously wasn't expecting such a long sermon, but I was in quite a state; we were together and she, the second woman I'd ever been intimate with, so young, would she understand me? "It's important that I stay in touch, at every stage of my life, with who I once was. I always come back to the same bed in the same room. That gives me respite from all the battles and wars, from everything," and I added, "I'm falling in love with you, and that's dangerous. Today was a break-through for me." p156-7

KIŠ
Danilo

The Encyclopaedia of the Dead [Enciklopedija mrtvih] [Serbo-Croat Yugoslavia]

Kiš was a typically untypical Jew; born in Yugoslavia, familiar with Russian, Serbo-Croatian, Hungarian and French he stood at the crossing of languages and places that has often been the destiny of European Jews. He was also half-Jewish by descent —

an increasingly typical Jewish destiny — but it's clear from this book he was very fascinated by this part of his heritage.

The nine pieces in this collection are, appropriately for this author, wildly diverse in place and time but there is a common element of 'mythic truth'; a truth one can appreciate without being able to touch it literally or prosaically, since the events and situations are so distant or unusual. The writing is accessible yet often seems to arrive from profound reflection. It's the fiction of a scholar or philosopher, similar to that of George Steiner, Bertrand Russell, Claudio Magris (see *Babel Guide to Italian Fiction*) or Jorge Luis Borges.

The most perfect and surprising story here is *Simon Magus* which sympathetically explores the story of the 'magician' Simon mentioned — rubbished in fact — as an enemy of the early Christians in their *New Testament*. It's a rugged satire on Christian (and probably Communist) belief and history, funny and thought-provoking.

Last Respects disinters another historical 'loser', in this case a Hamburg dockside prostitute, Mariette, rescues her from the disdain of those who usually write the history books and celebrates her as a generous-hearted giver of love, affection and sexual healing to a generation of lonesome seafarers.

The title piece *Encyclopaedia of the Dead* is a Borgesian tribute to a life lived in a country (Yugoslavia) with, as they say, 'too much history'; too many changes of regime, too many invasions, revolutions, counter-revolutions, civil wars; it's an amusing and subtle story that asks questions about narrative, biography and the texture of the life we feel we live — what would be recorded of a life if *everything* could somehow be recorded? It's a story full of intimations and insights.

Interesting too in a sadder way is *The Book of Kings and Fools*, the lightly fictionalised story of the notorious anti-Semitic book the *Protocols of the Elders of Zion*, the best-selling forgery in which Jewish leaders supposedly announce their millennial campaign to enslave (and no doubt finally exterminate) the Christian world.

The final, elegant little story *Red Stamps with Lenin's Picture* invents a Yiddish writer in Soviet Russia, 'Mendel Osipovich', and is a commentary on creative passions and the political and emotional realities that surround and constrain them. R K

'They knew how to win over sceptics with flattery and promises, bribes and threats; and the more their power spread and their followers increased, the stronger and more arrogant they grew. They blackmailed families, sowed discord in the minds of individuals, hatched plots against anyone who expressed the slightest mistrust of their doctrine. They had their own firebrands and rabble-rousers, their own secret tribunals at which they pronounced maledictions and sentences, burned the writings of their enemies, and cast anathemas on the heads of recalcitrants. People joined them in ever-increasing numbers because they rewarded the faithful and punished the rebellious.' (p8 from *Simon Magus*)

'It took thirty years of research to pick up the trail of people who, though they had not lost their lives, had lost their names, cities, countries, even continents.' (*The Book of Kings and Fools*)

LASKER-SCHÜLER
Else

Concert [Konzert] [German Germany & Palestine]

The famous Viennese critic, Karl Kraus, called German-Jewish Else Lasker-Schüler 'the strongest and most impenetrable lyrical force in Germany' but this collection of charming and tender short prose pieces — reminiscent of the American avant-garde writer Djuna Barnes at her best — is highly 'penetrable', in fact enjoyable and often light-hearted. In pieces with titles like *The Sea*, *The Ginger Cat* and *The Inca Butterfly* an unusual and winning talent produces an elliptical but emotional vision of life.

Lasker-Schüler is generally seen as part of the Berlin Expressionist group of poets and painters. Her particular obsession was the attempt to leave the 'exile of everyday life' via the transfiguration of art. Exile from the consciousness imposed by everyday routine became real physical exile from Germany after Hitler's ascent to power and her move to Palestine.

As one can divine from the famous photograph of Lasker-Schüler dressed up as Oriental 'Prince Jussuf', the writer was fascinated by Middle Eastern themes, part of a reaching out from the secular rationalism of her German background towards the Jewish roots she saw as suffused with mysticism and exotic knowledge. Also in tune with current preoccupations is her mixing — again like Djuna Barnes or the Brazilian writer Ana Cristina César — of her real self and her literary self in her pieces, delighting in creating a seamless fabric of I, not-I and fantasy persona that perhaps mirrors more accurately than the fixed positions of narrator/author/character the actual way of human consciousness.

In the end though, this is simply the unique voice of a brilliant and unusual woman and a very enjoyable book; a translation that is a fine tribute to a person who represents so well the synthesizing and hopeful directions that Weimar culture of the 1920s and 1930s was taking in literature, drama, painting, film and music. Weimar Germany experienced a cultural renaissance soon dismantled and destroyed by the provincial nationalistic beasts that took the country over in 1933 and forced the likes of the gentle and sensitive Else Lasker-Schüler into exile or worse.

C C & R K

'When I ride back to Berlin from my lecture tours, I look out the train window, and my eyes leaf through the living picture-book of the world, and on my last trip home, it happened that the setting sun actually spoke with me. I was crying a little, but I was like a child, with a tear still hanging from its lashes. It was seen by the white sun, which I at first thought was the moon; it was already past twilight, and I was tired and sleepy from looking at the striped fields and the meadows' delight in flowers, and the trees marching along; the fir trees and poplars run with giant strides out of the way of the rushing train. I think they hate the sprinter, it frightens the birch brides and the harmony of growth, its breath makes the silver grasses in the fields dusty and their heavenly ally is happy to rain on the flag of grey and black sparks that blows from the train. I gazed into the pale white moon, into the little tent of peace. "It's the sun," said a fellow passenger. She understood the geography of heaven and earth better than I, because even before the train stopped, she knew where we would stop; she was familiar with even the smallest village. However, I asked the faithful, white-filled circle again: "Are you the sun? So light up my belief in this world in which I have to live, year after year, hour after hour with its sixty minutes; have to stay awake, subject of the most everyday chamberlain. And I would like to sleep a thousand times, if that were possible in a miracle minute." A frightened rabbit ran across the path, and for the first time I saw a deer in its natural habitat, with yellowy-brown branches on his head. He wasn't frightened either by the tempestuous insistence of my heart or by the speed of our machine, and I smiled questioningly at the white sun, which suddenly, in response to a magic word from God, turned into a glowing red ball and — fell into my lap.' p138-139

LEVI
Primo

The Drowned and the Saved [I sommersi e i salvati] [Italian]

In this internationally celebrated book, Primo Levi, an Italian Jew and a concentration camp survivor, leaves a harrowing testament. Most importantly he here accuses the German people of the collective crime of cowardice — cowardice in looking away from the system of human extermination set up in their name. He calls the whole existence of Nazi Germany 'a war against memory' and, for this reason perhaps, was moved to make the sacrifice of reliving his own memories of that period, an act that may have contributed to his sudden death shortly after the book's completion. From the chapter *The Grey Zone* one realises that the 'work' of the camps was huge, consistent and well-organised, and went on for years; it could not have been merely the enterprise of a few SS zealots.

Levi highlights something infinitely depressing: the — opportunism of German officers, functionaries and businessmen who simply didn't want to pass up the opportunities for promotion and profit that the concentration camp system offered them; many of these people later hid behind the excuse of being forced to obey, although they might well have sidestepped orders. Moreover, writes Levi, the ghastly glimmer of the 'drowned world' illuminates a wider one with similar mechanisms of irresponsible power. The (unpunished) political criminals of our times — the Chinese Government bullies in Tibet, the military torturers of Argentina, Chile or Guatemala, the mass-murderers of Rwanda or Bosnia — stand firmly in the footsteps of the Nazi pioneers of civilised barbarity.

Another part of the continuing significance of this book is that Hitler *did* permanently change the world: a hard fact to face for all the European survivors of fascism and World War Two, Jews and Gentiles alike. Two generations have grown up in a racially 'purified' Europe and must face and act upon 'the shame that the Germans never knew, the shame which the just man experiences when confronted by a crime committed by another.'

This is an important book not only because it documents the Holocaust but because so many fundamental questions are raised by the reflections of a man who was a witness and struggled to survive and, yet more heroically, to understand these events.

Levi tried to remember fragments of Dante in the death camp because 'they made it possible for me to re-establish a link with the past, saving it from oblivion and reinforcing my identity'. This search for cultural and psychological continuity in terrible conditions contrasts with the Europe that in 1945 sought to forget its past, immersing itself in dreams of building a socialist utopia in the East and a capitalist, consumer one in the West: two Brave

New Worlds suffering from the same amnesia, a disregard for an inheritance in equal proportion magnificent and ugly, half-Mozart, half-Hitler. If today's re-united continent is to retrace its steps, rediscover itself, accept and learn from its *whole* history, then the path leads through Auschwitz and Levi has written a guide. R K

'So I realised that the German of the Lager — skeletal, howled, studded with obscenities and imprecations — was only vaguely related to the precise, austere language of my chemistry books, and to the melodious, refined German of Heine's poetry that Clara, a classmate of mine, would recite to me.' p75-6

LEVI
Primo

If This is a Man & The Truce [Se questo è un uomo & La tregua] [Italian]

Primo Levi was a young, educated and inept member of the Italian resistance when he was captured by the fascist militia in the winter of 1943. He was identified as a Jew and shipped to Auschwitz. This book is an account of his time in hell until the liberation, and (in its second part) how he managed to make his way home in the chaos of post-war Europe.

It has already attracted so many superlatives — 'one of the century's truly necessary books', writes Paul Bailey — that the chief danger is that people will ignore it for that very reason, as they tend to do things which too many people say would be good for them. That would be a great pity, since it is not only a record of the ultimate expression of Nazism it is also a profound testament of and to all humanity. And it is beautifully written — as elegant, economical, and dispassionate as its subject-matter is horrific and emotionally overwhelming. The effect of this conjunction is uniquely poignant.

The immense camp where Levi and his fellow-prisoners suffered and mostly died never produced a pound of synthetic rubber, which was its ostensible purpose. Its real purpose was death. On one occasion, denied even an icicle to assuage thirst, he asked in his broken German, '*Warum?*' The guard replied, '*Hier ist kein warum*' ('there is no why here').

Everything about such a life was a deliberate denial of human dignity. Survival itself was largely a matter of chance, mitigated, for a few, only by falling on the right side of the ferocious law, 'to he that has, will be given; from he that has not, will be taken away'. Levi's dignity is therefore all the more authentic and moving for having been so dearly bought. No mere luxury, it was what he survived for, and what he has given to us.

The years since Levi's death have increasingly confirmed what he and his fellow ex-prisoners felt in post-liberation Vienna: 'not compassion, but a larger anguish, which was mixed up with our own misery, with the heavy, threatening sensation of an irreparable and definitive evil which was present everywhere, nestling like gangrene in the guts of Europe and the world, the seed of future harm.' No one should think that what has happened could not happen again; and for anyone who finds that an appalling prospect, this book is (as Levi puts it in his *Afterword*) 'a support and a warning'. It is also, by the same token, a reminder that literature itself is not an ornament of civilisation but integral to it. P C

'Monsters exist, but they are too few in number to be truly dangerous. More dangerous are the common men, the functionaries ready to believe and to act without asking questions...' p396

LEVI
Primo

Moments of Reprieve [Lilit e altri racconti] [Italian]

Like the *Drowned and the Saved* and *If This is a Man* this is one of the series of books Primo Levi wrote about his and others' experience of the German death camps. Levi strove, as all men and women with any social awareness must, to draw lessons for the future from this descent into scientific cruelty and morbid nihilism. In this particular book he chose to pick out stories he had witnessed or that were recounted to him of individuals who escaped, for a moment or for a lifetime, the Nazi extermination machine. Levi himself called these escapes 'breaches... in the black universe' and it is the unprecedented background of the camps that makes the lives and events he describes so shining.

There is the glitter of the ancient Lillith story told amongst desperate men (*Lillith*), a vision of the Hitler Youth being shown around the camp in late 1944 to see 'the enemy, the submen who were destroying Germany' (*Last Christmas of the War*) and the poignant story of Rappoport with his strange balance sheet of pleasure and pain (*Rappoport's Testament*).

Moments of Reprieve is a statement about the unspeakable and the unthinkable. However, horrified silence is a part of the barrier the Nazis built around their deeds, like the wire fences of the camps, but it is a barrier that still needs to be torn down and this makes Levi's subtle and thoughtful work of primary importance. R K

'A short time before,... we'd had the opportunity to observe close-up a singular school of fanaticism, a typical example of Nazi training. On some unused land next to our Camp, a *Hitlerjugend* — Hitler Youth — encampment had been set up. There were possibly two hundred adolescents, still almost children. In the morning they practised flag-raising, sang belligerent hymns, and armed with ancient muskets, were put through marching and shooting drills... But sometimes in the afternoons their instructors, who were SS veterans, would bring them to see us as we worked clearing away rubble from the bombings... They led them among us on a "guided tour" and lectured them in loud voices... "These that you see are the enemies of the Reich *your* enemies. Take a good look at them: would you call them men? They are *Untermenschen*, submen! They stink because they don't wash; they're in rags because they don't take care of themselves. What's more, many of them don't even understand German. They are subversives, bandits, street thieves from the four corners of Europe, but we have rendered them harmless; now they work for us, but they are good only for the most primitive work. Moreover, it is only right that they should repair the war damages; these are the people who wanted the war: the Jews, the Communists, and the agents of the plutocracies."... The child-soldiers listened, devout and dazed. Seen close up, they inspired both pain and horror. They were haggard and frightened, yet they looked at us with intense hatred. So we were the ones guilty for all the evils, the cities in ruins, the famine, their dead fathers on the Russian front. The Führer was stern but just, and it was just to serve him.' (p88-9 *Last Christmas of the War*)

LEVI
Primo

The Periodic Table [Il sistema periodico] [Italian]

The Periodic Table is an unusual and intriguing book in which Primo Levi's double vocation of industrial chemist and writer find themselves in happy alliance. In its twenty-one short pieces named after different elements of the periodic table (*Argon, Zinc, Carbon* etc.) he recreates both a personal and a collective story via the celebration of a particular craft — *chemistry*, the transformation of substances — which he sees as a special case of, a more strenuous version of, the profession of living.

Primo Levi was a Jew who only came to understand his Jewishness through the experience of persecution and, later found it hard to accept being defined as 'a Jewish writer'. His family in

Turin only observed the most important Jewish holidays. In this they were fairly typical of Italian Jews — at least from the time of the *Risorgimento* (the struggle for Italian unity in the nineteenth century) until Mussolini's imposition of the anti-Semitic 'Racial Laws' in 1938. Italian Jews tended to be highly assimilated and secular in outlook.

Three stories in particular; *Argon*, *Zinc* and *Gold* describe the heyday of the Jews in Piedmont, Levi's region in North West Italy, and the limbo into which they were relegated under Fascism. From the lyrical evocation of the tiny Jewish communities, comparable to Argon — a 'noble' gas present in the air in tiny quantities and which doesn't react with other elements — we go in *Zinc* to a portrayal of Italy on the eve of the Racial Laws and the anti-Semitic campaign in which the Jews were castigated as an 'impurity' in Italian society. However, as he writes;

'In order for the wheel to turn, for life to be lived, impurities are needed, and the impurities of impurities in the soil, too, as is known, if it is to be fertile. Dissension, diversity, the grain of salt and mustard are needed; Fascism does not want them, forbids them, and that's why you're not a Fascist; it wants everybody to be the same, and you are not.'

With *Gold* we move on a few years to 1943; Levi, captured as an anti-Fascist partisan, meets a fellow-prisoner, a common criminal, who is about to be released. He is a smuggler who is also a gold-panner. Levi on the other hand has lost his freedom and he senses the horor of an inescapable destiny to come.

Apart from the narrative, historical and psychological qualities it shares with other of Primo Levi's books, *The Periodic Table* is interesting for its transfer of a scientific discourse into a humanistic literary work and its unusual combination of personal recall with analytical lucidity, for all this and for its marvellous conciseness, it is a contemporary classic. C C

'There are the so-called inert gases in the air we breathe. They bear curious Greek names of erudite derivation which mean "the New", "the Hidden", "the Inactive", and "the Alien." They are indeed so inert, so satisfied with their condition, that they do not interfere in any chemical reaction, do not combine with any other element ... They are also called the noble gases — and here there's room for discussion as to whether all noble gases are really inert and all inert gases are noble. And, finally, they're also called rare gases, even though one of them, argon (the Inactive), is present in the air in the considerable proportion of one percent, that is, twenty or thirty times more abundant than carbon dioxide, without which there would not be a trace of life on this planet.

The little that I know about my ancestors presents many similarities to these gases. Not all of them were materially inert, for that was not granted them. On the contrary, they were — or had to be — quite active, in order to earn a living and because of a reigning morality that held that "he who does not work shall not eat." But there is no doubt that they were inert in their inner spirits, inclined to disinterested speculation, witty discourses, elegant, sophisticated, and gratuitous discussion. It can hardly be by chance that all the deeds attributed to them, though quite various, have in common a touch of the static, an attitude of dignified abstention, of voluntary (or accepted) relegation to the margins of the great river of life.' (p3-4 from *Argon*)

LIEBRECHT
Savyon

Apples from the Desert. Selected Stories [Hebrew]

Savyon Liebrecht was born in Germany and came to Israel in 1948, as the child of Holocaust survivors. The profound psychological difficulties that the survivors of the mass terror of the Holocaust endured has been the theme of several of her short stories. In her own words, she has engaged in 'breaking the silence that's been going on for 40 years'. As a child who grew up in a home where the Holocaust was not talked about the silence had the effect of 'triggering her creativity', because 'a child who grows up in such a home feels that questions are undesirable and so starts supplying her own answers.'

In *Morning in the Park Among the Nannies* she weaves the story of two middle-aged women who meet in a park and realise they share a secret past — they both were used and abused by the Nazis in the same camp when they were young — the narrator was kept as a seamstress, while the second woman was used, and given some protection, as the favoured whore of an officer. The ex-seamstress remembers the horrors that the pretty rabbi's daughter, then a young woman, endured in the camp. Now an older woman, her beauty ravished, she is employed as a nanny to the child of privileged Israeli professionals. She refuses to, or cannot, recognise the narrator who tries to engage with her in conversation.

Another major theme has been to create portraits of Israeli women from different religious and ethnic backgrounds. Her Jewish women identify with the minority Arabs and show solidarity with them, crossing the boundaries and trying to overcome ethnic differences. The story *A Room on the Roof* (also in the anthology *New Women's*

Writing from Israel, reviewed here) is perhaps the best example of this, while the title piece of this collection *Apples from the Desert*, deals with a different background clash when a deeply religious and conservative woman has to accept her daughter's flight from home into the arms of a free-thinking young farmer on a kibbutz.

Savyon Liebrecht is part of an important new generation of tough-minded, critical Israeli women writers, now beginning to be available in English, mainly thanks to the work of committed smaller publishers. M B & R K

'You gather your things, harness the little girl, get up and turn to the park gate. Again, a pace away from me, I see the ice-cold eyes surrounded by black haloes. The nannies fall silent, following you with their eyes as you pass us by. For a moment I seem to feel your glance lashing at me. Do I awaken a memory in you? An echo of German voices? The contact of flesh against your flesh? The fluttering of silk against your skin....The girl who had aged within days, the one who swept the marble tiles...' (*Morning in the Park among the Nannies*)

LIND
Jacov

Soul of Wood [Eine Seele aus Holz] [German Austria]

Imagine you are sitting in a train compartment opposite a cannibal. The cannibal opens his suitcase and inside you see doctor's instruments and a hammer, chisel, pliers, 'ordinary carpenter's tools', and you know what they will be used for. But what really strikes you is the salt cellar, the common glass sort you find in cheap restaurants, and your conclusion: 'He's stolen it somewhere... He's a thief'.

All the characters in Jakov Lind's very sharp and grotesquely funny collection of stories have this imperturbably logical and also moralising approach to situations which are horribly abnormal. The longest and most elaborate story here, the title piece *Soul of Wood*, is set in the Vienna of 1942 (four years after the annexation (*Anschluss*) of Austria by Nazi Germany), when the servant Wohlbrecht is entrusted with the care of the crippled son of a Jewish family before they flee, in return for receiving ownership of the Jews' apartment.

Wohlbrecht is a war-wounded World War One veteran, driven by a mixture of empty moral principles, social resentment, ignorance and received ideas fuelled by the constant quiet calculation of self-interest. The tale observes his terrifyingly average *Spiessbürger* (petty-bourgeois Philistine) mentality as he adapts and survives, disliking 'Adolf and his gang', but only because they and no-one else are getting all the loot, eventually becoming an assistant to the orderly who gives lethal injections to hundreds of Jews and Communists daily. In that job he puts on seventy pounds, grabbing cigars, cognac, meat and women while hunger and cold ravage outside.

Lind's chilling vision shows up both the pettiness and self-interest of his characters (which, in certain circumstances, can mean someone else's death sentence) *and* the cheerful, averagely helpful, averagely good-natured nature of your average man. This is one of the brilliant aspects of Lind's writing, drawing characters whom one would really quite like to loathe a bit more.

Wohlbrecht, for example, wakes up in 1945 to the realisation that he is on the wrong side; what he needs now is 'his Jew' back, to show that at least he tried to save one... With that native shrewdness and complacency which characterise most of Lind's characters, he calculates that while he may well have witnessed the needle being given to 20,000 Jews, a single individual Jew hidden at one's own risk, well, 'that would carry some weight. Any judge would get confused by that sort of thing'. There ensues a typically grotesque debate about how to lay claim to the Jew's skeleton... At the last moment, though, a streak of conscience and a surprise twist...

The tone of these stories is beautifully judged, hard-hitting and subtle, caustic and imaginative. They blend shocking with normal situations to say something about the normalisation of the intolerable (the 'banality of evil' in Hannah Arendt's famous phrase). Thus the apparently chaste Franz, in *The Pious Brother*, who takes pleasure in seducing and then rejecting women, using a 'frighten, comfort, frighten' recipe, and who recalls nostalgically his days as camp commander (after which he converted to become a Jesuit for 'divine mercy and grace'), when he 'held the life of others, especially women, in his hands'... Or the enraged father of a convicted criminal, in *The Judgement*, furious that the government is taking punishment out of his hands, since 'what do I care about the penal code. He has sinned against his seed'. Or the surreal Lithuanian immigrants in Sweden, who live with a dead horse, no clothes and much blood sausage (now where does that blood come from?...).

This is a great collection of tight, carefully written stories, both original and bold. S B

'Between three and four everybody falls into a dead sleep. You're educated, you should know that.

Yes, I know. But I got self-control.

Between three and four, said the man, rubbing the moustache that was yet to grow, all of us get locked away in our little cubicles, don't hear nothing, don't see nothing. We die, every last one of us. Dying restores us, after four we wake up and life goes on. Without that people couldn't stick it out so long.

I don't believe a word of it. You can't saw me up.

I can't eat you as you are, he said. Sawing's the only way. First the legs, then the arms, then the head. Everything in its proper order.

What do you do with the eyes?

Suck 'em.

Can the ears be digested or have they got bones in them?

No bones, but they're tough. Anyway, I don't eat everything, do you think I'm a pig?' p99

LINETSKI
Isaac J.

The Polish Lad [Dos poylisher Yungl] [Yiddish Poland]

First published in 1867 this extraordinary book, heavily based on personal experience, comprehensively trashed the 'miracle-working' Hasidic★ *Tzaddiks*★ of Poland. Linetski attacks Hasidism on all fronts; even the praying — 'the singsong accompanying the catechism was more interminable than the Diaspora'. One gathers from reading Linetski that Hasidim by the mid-Nineteenth century had declined from a pure and seeking religious enthusiasm to hucksterism, cynicism and greed on the part of its often hereditary religious leaders. Linetski describes a world of heavy schnapps-drinking, power-politics and the doling out of patronage to favoured connections, leading to all kinds of abuses — the disposal of unwanted wives in return for gifts to the Tzaddik for example.

Ribald and scandalous as all this is — and something of an antidote to I.B. Singer's sentimentalised version of Hasidism — there's also a lot of fascinating ethnographic detail here, with an abundance of superstitions, folkways and proverbs. Just one example; before a new baby is put in the cradle a cat is rocked in it, presumably to mislead the Evil Eye.

The Polish Lad was written at the height of the struggle for the soul of Polish Jews between the Maskilim★ and the Hasids but is far more than a propaganda text; its popularity, its keen sense of humour was such that it eventually became a sought-after book amongst Hasids themselves who could enjoy the descriptions of excess and the mickey-taking... The final chapter in fact argues for some compromise between modern, rational culture and the warmth, jollity and solidarity of the Hasids.

The pungent humour of *The Polish Lad* is sometimes reminiscent of the little-known masterpiece of Irish comic author Flann O'Brien (best known for *At-Swim-Two-Birds*) *The Poor Mouth* (translated from the Irish *An béal bocht*); hilarity that floats on a layer of knowledge and bitterness of the plight of a real people... R K

'When my mother first delivered me to the heder* conducted by Nachman "Slap" (as the boys called him), I was appalled by the squalor of the setting. Filth was everywhere; near the entrance were a round cistern and a mouldy slop pail on whose surface floated objects of the sort that were thrown at Haman's head. The panes of the narrow casement windows were thickly coated with a layer of frost etched with various graffiti, including the Star of David. Some of these were overlaid with a thinner layer, indicating that they were of relatively recent date; others were newly and superficially incised. Here and there a circle had been made in the rime, evidently by pressing a hot coin against its glistening surface. Water trickled down from the windows, along the walls, and onto the muddy earthen floor. Three infants, their skirts pinned up under their arms, crawled about in the mire.

A long, narrow, rickety table was held by twine and baling wire; its plank top was gouged, charred, and covered with ink stains. More planks, rough-hewn and studded with knotholes, were set on sawhorses to serve as benches for pupils of various ages, who sat huddled together with their backs against the dripping walls. The single tattered prayer book that did service as the text for ten pupils was swollen by the damp to three times its original thickness.

At one end of the table, a huge, battered wickerwork hamper over-flowed with pots and pans whose residues were being explored by a gray tom-cat, while its tail thumped against the head of a small child. Through an open door in one corner there was a glimpse into an adjoining room, where the melamed's* wife, her face clammy with sweat, and wearing a greasy cap, was shoving a poker into the oven.

Near the oven, our tutor held the place of honor: having shed the gabardine, he wore only his *tallit katan*, the four-cornered undergarment, whose ritual fringes were yellow with age; the dirty threadbare yarmulka that covered his bald head looked more like a potholder or a mustard plaster than a skullcap. In one hand he clutched a cat-o'-nine-tails, while with the other he scratched his hairy chest, which the unbuttoned and grimy shirt had left exposed.' p45-6

Family Ties [Laços de Família] [Portuguese Brazil]

Clarice Lispector is universally recognised as being the most original and influential Brazilian woman writer of her time. In feminist circles she is revered as an intensely feminine writer who articulates the needs and concerns of every woman in pursuit of self-awareness. Critics worldwide have found much to admire in her introspective writings, both fictional and non-fiction. Her obsessive questioning of human relationships and the social constraints which threaten rather than foster meaningful communication bring her to the conclusion that the problem of existence is that of language itself.

In all her work there is relentless self-questioning. Aware that she was speaking on behalf of all mankind, she was wont to say: 'I am so mysterious that I do not understand myself.' She saw the human condition as flawed, fragmentary and incomplete; the darker side of our nature as being compounded of fear, revulsion, cruelty and hatred. But once having recognised the inherent contradictions, she set about trying to reconcile freedom with restraint, humility with pride, solitude with the need to communicate. Strength had to be drawn from weakness, human reversals transformed into salvation. Despite her Ukrainian-Jewish background, Lispector identified completely with Brazil and, most of all, with north-eastern Brazil. Memories of her childhood, especially in Recife, evoked the authentic Brazil where traditions and folklore had been preserved. [G P]

However there also seems something classically Jewish in her 'strangeness' to the world, a level of delicate self-questioning that stems perhaps from a minority consciousness. Also we could cite her tremendous but unsentimental sympathy for the underdog as in her novella *Hour of the Star*. Above all there is a simultaneous refusal to take anything for granted while finding great pleasure in new worlds that is essentially 'Diasporic.' [R K]

Family Ties is a compilation of thirteen short stories, all linked by one theme: love. There is love and how it binds family members together, love and how it imprisons, love and love's cruelty, love and how it liberates or should liberate us.

Writing of love for Lispector is to write about the human condition. Each story is a profound journey into the psychology of her mainly female characters. Strong women, weak women, old women and young girls. Some men too; strong and weak; old and young. All of them seem to be on the verge of experiencing something new; plodding through their daily and often boring routines, set in their habits and habituated to the superficiality that surrounds them. But whether it is a blind man chewing gum, or a dead dog found in the streets, or a buffalo in a zoo, or the smallest woman on Earth in Equatorial Africa, these men and women are all susceptible to experiencing a breaking point in their consciousness.

Lispector brings the external world into the inner reality of each human being she encounters in her writings. And with words that so transparently transmit emotions she relates the intensity of this inner world when questioned, when shattered.

Thus the fifteen year old girl in *Preciousness* who is subjected to the sexual gaze of two young men in the street feels a huge change has occurred, something has been taken from her. The woman of *The Imitation of the Rose* focuses on a bunch of flowers and feels an intensity she has not known before. Should she give away these roses in their unbelievable beauty, or does she want to keep them for herself? The three young men of *Mystery in São Cristóvão*, on their way to a party, stop in a garden to break off a stem of hyacinth, but a white face behind the window stops them, scares them, makes them run away and a great mystery settles on this house.

Writing of love, Clarice Lispector draws us into another's inner self and so draws us into our own inner self. She does it by showing us that love, at the core of the human being and what links us one to the other, however strong it is, very rarely manages to deliver the spiritual liberty we expect of it. And families, as in the story *Happy Birthday*, end up being linked more by superficiality than by love.

In these short stories Clarice Lispector creates worlds that could be ours, worlds and existences that seem totally normal and yet are totally absurd, life that is real and surreal at the same time. She seems to be able write outside the usual social and political constraints with great feeling, wisdom, scepticism and warmth She writes about what is most real and what is kept furthest away from daily life. She questions, she shatters and she (re)creates. M C-L

'And she considered the cruel necessity of loving. She considered the malignity of our desire to be happy. She considered the ferocity with which we want to play. And the number of times when we murder for love. She then looked at her mischievous son, as if she was looking at a dangerous stranger. And she was horrified at her own soul, which, more than her body, had engendered that being so apt for life and happiness. And thus she looked at him attentively and with uneasy pride, her child already without two front teeth, his evolution, his evolution under way, his teeth falling out to make room for those which bite best.' (p92 *The smallest woman in the world*)

LISPECTOR
Clarice

Hour of the Star [A Hora da Estrella] [Portuguese Brazil]

The great Clarice Lispector's last book, published in the year of her death in early middle age. Her respected translator Giovanni Pontiero said she 'narrates from within'; a way of suggesting her astonishing ability to create intimacy with her readers, not through the gossipy divulgation of real or faked personal trivia, but an intimacy based on mastery of what she is saying combined with *heart*. Heart that is not just that engaging *Brazilian* humanness but, in her tenderness for children, animals, hurt souls there is something of her Jewish background too.

Hour of the Star, the story of poor Macabéa, a girl with no real talents, accomplishments or gifts — except her ability to accept humility and humiliation as if they were entirely natural things — is Clarice's testament for many reasons. Partly because it hits that fundamental question in Brazil and elsewhere; Do you care? Also because in it she succeeds so well with her ideas about writing and her ideas about life, about women's lives, about Brazil. In Macabéa, immortalized in a brilliant film directed by Suzana Amaral, she has created a character whose life was a kind of opposite to her own — Lispector herself was a successful writer and the beautiful, cosmopolitan wife of a diplomat — and she has used her sympathy and writerly talent in a marvellous piece of observation and creation.

Hour of the Star begins with a dialogue with the reader so that when the 'facts of the case' (as Macabéa's life and past is revealed) become known, the trust previously created makes them rebound in the reader's thoughts. Clarice Lispector does not write from a great distance but whispers in your ear and Macabéa, who is at one extreme of the human condition where 'sadness was a luxury' reaches us as all the more human for that.

Reading the book is not a sad experience as it is often appallingly funny; all Macabea's conversational tidbits and worldview are supplied by 'Radio Clock', a downmarket FM station that intersperses a constant stream of time announcements with the kind of desperate 'interesting facts' only Radio DJs know. *Hour of the Star* is quite possibly the best Brazilian book ever translated into English, appalling, delightful, accessible but radical and brilliantly accomplished. R K

[Macabéa is talking to her unpleasant, dismissive boyfriend, Olímpico]

'When she realized that her remark about the animals displeased Olímpico, she tried to change the topic of conversation:

"On Radio Clock they used a word that worried me: mimetism."

Olímpico eyed her disapprovingly:

"That's not a nice word for a virgin to be using. Why do you have to keep on asking questions about things that don't concern you? The brothels in the Mangue are full of women who asked far too many questions."

"Is the Mangue a district?"

"It's an evil place frequented only by men. This won't sink in, but I'm going to tell you something. A chap can still get a woman on the cheap. You've only cost me a coffee so far. That's your lot. I won't be wasting any more money buying you things. Is that clear."

Macabéa thought to herself: he's right. I don't deserve anything from him because I've wet my knickers.' p55

LITVINOFF
Emanuel

Journey Through A Small Planet [English Britain]

In this engaging book Litvinoff creates something rather more than a vivid memoir of his early years in the East End of London. It is a memoir, but the chapters work as well-crafted stories in their own right. In fact, more than half of the chapters first appeared in journals and anthologies, or were broadcast, before coming together in the present book.

What *Journey Through a Small Planet* offers that many other memoirs of the Jewish East End do not is an uncompromising, strong sense of the real hardships and family tensions created by overcrowding and poverty. There is no nostalgic or sentimental overlay in this book; no subtle rewriting of history to glamorise the East End crucible out of which many (but not all) of Litvinoff's fellow-Jews made their way with various measures of success. Instead his clear, unfussy prose gives weight and presence to a range of characters whose lives become important to the reader.

The first person narrator here emerges as neither hero nor

anti-hero, but rather as someone vaguely aspiring to a more fulfilling, creative way of life. He has to make his way in a difficult world while taking his first faltering steps into relationships with women, and into independence.

As well as describing the daily struggle to feed and clothe large families so crowded together the growing young man can find no space, physical or emotional to call his own, the narrative reaches out to the broader preoccupations and conditions of the world of these Jewish immigrants. Russia, its army, its Revolution, its dangerousness, has been a factor in many of their lives — the narrator's father, for one, was left orphaned.

The ideological oppositions of international socialism, communism and traditional piety reveal a Jewish world struggling to accommodate to modernity as much as to England and its curious class structure.

We are treated to the anomaly of the starving young Hasid* seeking refuge from the Salvation Army, while the narrator, atheistic, yet barely politicised, wangles a job and lodgings away from home from the Welfare Office of the Jewish Board of Guardians, only to lose it for allowing a trades union man to persuade him to insist on the 'rate for the job'.

We glimpse occasional, unsavoury, low-key anti-Semitism as well as its more threatening manifestations which simply add yet one more obstacle to the struggling young man. We see star-struck young Fanya seduced and abandoned by her glamorous Yiddish actor over from Chicago; we visit the furrier's workshop and Smithfield Meat Market. Yet everywhere Litvinoff maintains a sense of proportion, a wry humour and — most important of all —real compassion as he gives value and weight to these largely unrecorded lives.

The hardness of the world remembered here threatens at times to overwhelm the reader, but there are humour and affection as correctives, and we come away with a better appreciation of just what it took to *survive*, let alone to 'make good'. T H

'The Headmaster examined him for several painful seconds.

"What's the 'G.' stand for, lad?" he asked eventually.

"Giuliano, sir."

"Dad an ice-cream merchant, his 'e?"

"No, sir." Leoni's dark eyes flinched. "My father's a waiter."

The Headmaster exchanged an amused glance with Mr James...

My own name seemed a long time coming and I prepared for the shock of it by pressing my knees together to control their trembling. I knew with hopeless certainty I should never have come to this school. When the official letter from the London County Council offered me a place at the Cordwainers' Technical College it seemed a reprieve. Otherwise, at fourteen, like any other unsuccessful boy, I'd be dressed up like a man of forty sawn off at the knees and pitched into the turbulent labour market. The choices were few and gruesome... At the end of the week I'd buy my first packet of fags and have nothing to hope for but the Revolution.

In contrast, college was Greyfriars, Harry Wharton... Then I discovered that a cordwainer was someone who made boots and shoes. A boot and shoe college yet. But somehow, in a manner unforeseen, I retained a desperate hope that Cordwainers' might still lead to the cloisters of the elect.

The Headmaster adjusted his glasses to peer more closely at the register... "Lit – in – totinoff?" His head rotated in its starched collar as he surveyed the class. "Did I get it wrong?" He tried once more. "Lit – pot – sky – off, eh."

No-one answered...

"We are 'aving difficulties. Hi wonder, now, could it be that fine old Hanglo-Saxon name Levinskinoff?'"

MALAMUD
Bernard

The Assistant [English USA]

A book like the *Babel Guide to Jewish Fiction,* in its selection of authors, only some of whom are clearly identifiable as 'Jewish Authors', implicitly asks *What is a Jew?* Is it blood descent, is it religious observance, is it cultural heritage, is it just brute chance or is it being on a mission from God, being *Chosen* even.

Malamud was a writer of the era in which, in America, the old givens of Jewishness had for many faded; the Yiddish language, the regular observance of Jewish rites and even the anti-Semitism that makes a Jew feel an outsider who had better cling to his own for security. In *The Assistant*, one of his greatest works, he takes a radical, even shocking tack on what remains of Jewishness in his America.

In a dingy, failing corner food store in Brooklyn representatives of two generations meet in the persons of Morris Buber and Frank Alpino. Buber, as his wife drums into him day after day, is an economic failure and to fail like that in America is pretty grave. His little shop, despite his long hours and general tenacity, only brings in a pittance – not enough to get the bright but disillusioned daughter Helen through College to escape her parents' life of drudgery.

Frank Alpino, an Italian-American drifter, has, in many ways, even less going for him than the sick, desperate old Jew Morris Buber. Alpino is an orphan brought up in a harsh Catholic children's institution, from where he has graduated to becoming an unsuccessful petty criminal. It's clear that in his whole life he's never had a real relationship; with a friend, a woman, with the world of work or anything much at all.

However Alpino, in the most unlikely way, becomes Buber's assistant in the shop on, to say the least, unusual terms. He is drawn to this sad little family and wants to understand who and what they are. He starts off from a rational, 'realistic' vision of the Jewish condition; 'He read a book about the Jews... He also read about the ghettos, where the half-starved bearded prisoners spent their lives trying to figure out why they were the Chosen People'. Alpino, who has everything one needs to be a human *except* any humanity, comes, in a wonderfully cathartic progress of hopes and failures to a final understanding and sympathy for this unlikely, one might almost say *un-American,* hero Morris Buber.

Buber stands for and is a lovely example of suffering (Jewish) humanity; through him and with him — voluntarily sharing his fate — Frank Alpino becomes a *mensch.* The Sisyphean moral burden of Jewishness is passed on from one generation to another and what is good, what is fundamental, survives.

In *The Assistant* Malamud takes an intensely thoughtful stand on *What is a Jew?* For him to be a real Jew it is to accept the moral stance of the good Jew; because of having suffered — personally and through sharing the history of the Jews, rich in persecution and cruelty — one does not deliberately inflict suffering on others. And that really, for Malamud, is The Law.

His protagonist, the oppressed and beleaguered gentile Frank Alpino starts off 'Jewish' in his own past knowledge of suffering and, through the example of Morris Buber, he manages to cut away the vengeful, callous side of his nature that he had justified by the world's cruelty to him in the past. He thus becomes a morally self-controlled, righteous man and, at the very end of the book, is both symbolically and internally transformed.

The Assistant is a work of classic power and importance, illuminating the great issues and decisions of a life, in an exciting, engrossing narrative set in a small, intimate world. As it is written on Malamud's tombstone *'Art celebrates life and gives us our measure'*. R K

'The rabbi gazed down at his prayer book, then looked up.

"When a Jew dies, who asks if he is a Jew? He is a Jew, we don't ask. There are many ways to be a Jew. So if somebody comes to me and says, 'Rabbi, shall we call such a man Jewish who lived and worked among the gentiles and sold them pig meat, trayfe, that we don't eat it, and not once in twenty years comes inside a synagogue, is such a man a Jew, rabbi?' To him I will say, 'Yes, Morris Bober was to me a true Jew because he lived in the Jewish experience, which he remembered, and with the Jewish heart.' Maybe not to our formal tradition — for this I don't excuse him — but he was true to the spirit of our life — to want for others that which he wants also for himself. He followed the Law which God gave to Moses on Sinai and told him to bring to the people. He suffered he endured, but with hope. Who told me this? I know. He asked for himself little — nothing, but he wanted for his beloved child a better existence than he had. For such reason he was a Jew. What more does our sweet God ask his poor people? So let Him now take care of the widow, to comfort and protect her, and give to the fatherless child what her father wanted her to have." Yaskadal v'yiskadash shmey, rabo. B'olmo divro..."' p203

MALAMUD
Bernard

Stories [English USA]

Malamud is one of the unmissable Jewish writers and he is as effective with his short stories as in his novels. This is a standard collection of his work, with all the best stories. Most of them revolve around Malamud's great theme; the problem of poverty, including spiritual or existential poverty. His characters are generally losers, but losers who have not lost, or who manage to regain contact with, authenticity in their lives — in other words Mamalmud is the great Jewish existentialist.

One particular story here, *Idiots First,* pits all the compassion and indifference of the world against each other; a story about the real heaven and hell inside and around us. It is impossible not to be moved by it.

Another famous, potent story here is *The Magic Barrel* with its genuine whiff of humanity; a marriage broker, an isolated young man and the women he is offered as partners 'all past their prime, all starved behind bright smiles'. Then there is the tragi-comic masterpiece *The Jewbird* a celebration of the vulnerable, slightly ugly, well-meaning semi-unwanted person; except that in this case the person is a bird, a Jewish bird. If you only ever in your life read one Jewish short story...

Rembrandt's Hat is a relatively mysterious story for this author, but it is clear that Malamud, like Arthur Miller in *Death of a Salesman*, is interested in failure and in the brilliant promise *of a life not* achieved, in this story of an artist who won't exhibit his work.

Angel Levine returns to the theme of redemption from suffering through faith, in this case faith in something unlikely — a haunting, beautiful story.

In *The Death of Me* two immigrant lone wolves, a Pole and a Sicilian, work for a Jewish tailor, the situation turns into an unremitting quarrel, a feud between two desperate men with the well-meaning Jew in the middle. We sense that this is how Malamud sees the American Jews; as adjudicating the Gentiles' quarrels...

Read Malamud, the great American Jewish writer who, because of the mythic and universal quality of his stories, has stood the test of time better than any other, read him to know the real power of literature. R K

'Once after a momentary cooling rainstorm we sat on newspapers on a wet bench overlooking the river and Oskar at last began to talk. In tormented English he conveyed his intense and everlasting hatred of the Nazis for destroying his career, uprooting his life, and flinging him like a piece of bleeding meat to the hawks. He cursed them thickly, the German nation, an inhuman, conscienceless, merciless people. "They are pigs mazquerading as peacogs", he said. "I feel certain that my wife, in her heart, was a Jew hater." It was a terrible bitterness, and eloquence beyond the words he spoke. He became silent again. I wanted to hear more about his wife but decided not to ask.' (p100 *The German Refugee*)

MALAMUD
Bernard

The Tenants [English USA]

In Malamud's early fiction, Jews are typically represented more as archetypes than as concrete individuals. Early novels such as *The Assistant* and short stories such as *The Magic Barrel* tend to characterise their Jewish protagonists as suffering, hapless *schlemiel*s, whilst their apparently realistic plots can be seen as modern Jewish fables, often bringing in elements of the fantastic.

From this point of view, Malamud's short 1971 novel, *The Tenants*, comes across as a kind of self-critique; for rather than uncritically employ the archetypal Jewish narratives and characters of his previous fiction, he plays with and even satirizes them. The story of two writers — one Jewish, one black — living and working in the same run-down New York tenement block, *The Tenants* addresses the ways in which literature and culture contribute to our preconceived, stereotypical notions of 'Jewishness' and 'blackness'. At the same time, it is an apocalyptic lament over the parlous state of Jewish-Black relations in America, a theme that is still resonant today.

When Harry Lesser and Willie Spearmint first meet they seem to have clearly defined ethnic identities: Lesser is the Jewish humanist intellectual, the artist as dedicated craftsman and universalist made familiar by the likes of Bellow, Roth and Malamud himself. Spearmint, in contrast, is the 'soulful' black man, politically militant, aggressively sexual, a writer of instinct rather than craft. Rather than sustain these stereotypes, however, Malamud slyly turns them on their head. As their relationship develops, Spearmint, suddenly preoccupied with the demands of form, becomes increasingly like Lesser in his single-minded devotion to writing, whilst Lesser begins to turn his back on 'art' and embrace 'life', notably in the form of Irene, Willie's white girlfriend. Through this device of role-reversal, seemingly transparent racial identities are revealed as deeply unstable, vulnerable to change, as 'cultural constructs' rather than absolute realities. Some readers, however, may feel that behind this knowing attitude lies a rather conservative racial politics, particularly evident in the representation of Willie's black friends as pathologically hostile to both whites and Jews.

Dense with literary allusion, veering disconcertingly between reality and dreams, and employing the device of multiple, contradictory endings (including the surreal fantasy of a double inter-racial wedding jointly conducted by an African tribal chieftain and a Reform rabbi), this is Malamud's most experimental novel. Its spare prose and brutally compacted narrative convey a palpable sense of the racial and sexual tension, paranoia and claustrophobia of America's inner cities. J C

"'I'm writing the soul writin of black people cryin out we are still slaves in this fuckn country and we ain't gonna stay slaves any longer. How can you understand it, Lesser, if your brain is white?'

"So is your brain white. But if the experience is about being human and moves me then you've made it my experience. You created it for me. You can deny universality, Willie, but you can't abolish it."

"Bein human is shit. It don't give you any privileges, it never gave us any."

"If we're talking about art, form demands its rights, or there's no order and maybe no meaning. What else there isn't I think you know."

"Art can kiss my juicy ass. You want to know what's really art? I am art. Willie Spearmint, *black man*. My form is *myself*." p60 -61

MANDELSTAM
Osip

The Noise of Time [Sum vremenic] [Russian]

The Prose of Osip Mandelstam

Journey to Armenia [Putesestvie v Armeniju]

Osip Mandelstam may have been the single most brilliant Jewish writer of this century. Sir Isaiah Berlin, for example, spoke of 'the cascades of Mandelstam's glittering or tranquil images leaping out of one another, the historical, psychological, syntactical, verbal allusions, contrasts, collisions, whirling at lightning speed, dazzle the imagination and the intellect.'

It may be a surprise to find Mandelstam in a book dedicated to fiction as he established his literary reputation as a major Russian poet but his prose pieces — perhaps more satisfying than the poetry to read in translation — are quite unforgettable. Not exactly fiction, the prose pieces are often described as 'vignettes'. One of the most famous *The Noise of Time* recalls, from the vantage point of the turbulent 1920s revolutionary Leningrad a vanished, genteel Saint Petersburg of minor literary figures, grandparents and family trips. The description of this city, Mandelstam's greatest inspiration, a strange neo-classical pile all built at once, is affectionate but with a vivacity reminiscent of Louis Aragon's masterpiece *Paris Paysan*, (see *French Babel Guide*), itself a brilliant 'vignette' of a legendary city.

Part of *The Noise of Time* is a gentle, teasing section on what Mandelstam calls 'Judaic Chaos' by which he seems to mean, in his impressionistic way, the combination of a passion for life with a certain nervous over-eagerness. This story, like other places where he directly speaks of Jewish characters, reflects too the mixture of influences in an educated urban Jewish milieu in St. Petersburg, then the cultural capital of Russia. Under the heading *The Bookcase* he describes this part of the family's furniture as having descending shelves of Hebrew, German and Russian books; part of the 'chaos'; the lack of a single stable centre in the cultural universe he beheld. Isaiah Berlin's 'leaping images' are perhaps partly an attempt to find a way to write the complexity of his times and his (Jewish) place in them. Mandelstam was as much as anything a genuine, a fabulous cosmopolitan and his travel sections such as *Finland* in *The Noise of Time* or the separate short work *Journey to Armenia* reflect an enormous excitement about and awareness of the differences of the new people and places he encounters. One quickly loses oneself in his fantastically redolent worlds.

Another famous prose piece in both *The Noise of Time* and *The Prose of Osip Mandelstam* collections is *The Egyptian Stamp*, a child's vision with a force like the first part of James Joyce's *Portrait of the Artist as a Young Man*. Like Joyce he creates with minute localised references, the building-blocks of personal consciousness, even including the history of the associations we, child and adult, make to 'feel the world'; 'There is an obscure heraldry of moral ideas going all the way back to childhood: the ripping sound of a torn cloth can signify honesty, and the cold of madapollam cloth — holiness'.

In fact Mandelstam constantly, gleefully surprises with his uses of words and associations; a synagogue he sees as 'a Jewish ship' while as a boy he tells us he had a mania for collecting nails which he calls 'my spiky wealth'. There is the sense that Mandelstam — whose parents (amongst the first fully Russian-speaking Jews) spoke Russian in a stilted way, while he felt an immense freedom with Russian, a language free for him of what he called 'Jewish ruin' — the various mundane (and unhappy) associations of Jewish exclusion and persecution. Russian on the other hand was his beautiful toy, no more and no less than a wonderful plaything to spin out glorious worlds.

Bruce Chatwin, the great English travel writer (and much more than that) called Mandelstam's *Journey to Armenia* 'breathtaking elliptical prose'. In Armenia Mandelstam discovers amazing natural beauty on the island of Sevan and a cast of extraordinary characters wherever he goes. *Journey to Armenia*, particularly the first part, is a brief joy to read. The editor who published it in Stalin's Soviet Union was immediately sacked. Mandelstam, the Russian Jewish genius, was tipped into a Labour Camp in freezing Vladivostok to die. R K

'The Polish serving girl had gone into the church of Guarenghi to gossip and to pray to the Holy Virgin. That night there had been a dream of a Chinaman, bedecked in ladies' handbags, like a necklace of partridges, and of an American duel in which the opponents fired their pistols at cabinets of chinaware, at inkpots, and at family portraits.

I propose to you, my family, a coat of arms: a glass of boiled water. In the rubbery aftertaste of Petersburg's boiled water I drink my unsuccessful domestic immortality. The centrifugal force of time has scattered our Viennese chairs and Dutch plates with little blue flowers. Nothing is left. Thirty years have passed like a slow fire. For thirty years a cold white flame has licked at the backs of mirrors, where the bailiff 's tags are attached.

But how can I tear myself away from you, dear Egypt of objects ? The clear eternity of dining room, bedroom, study. With what excuse cover my guilt? You wish Walhalla? The warehouses of Kokorev! Go there for salvation! Already the porters, dancing in horror, are lifting the grand piano (a Mignon) like a lacquered black meteor fallen from the sky. Bast mats are spread like the chasubles of priests. The cheval-glass floats sideways down the staircase, manoeuvring its palm-tree length about the landings.' (*The Egyptian Stamp*)

MEMMI
Albert

Pillar of Salt [La Statue de sel] [French Tunisia & France]

Memmi's engrossing and startling book *Pillar of Salt* is the story of a young man growing up between Arab, Berber, Jewish and Franco-European traditions in mid-century Tunis, Tunisia and reveals like few others the living complexity of the Mediterranean civilisation that existed in North Africa until the early 1960s. We follow the painful trajectory of a survivor of that world during the period of its dissolution by the effects of a combination of colonialist, Arab nationalist and Zionist forces.

The book's protagonist had a tribal Berber (some Berber tribes are Jewish) mother, an urban Jewish father, was born in Tunis and educated at a school set up by French Jews to assimilate their North African co-religionists to 'European civilisation'. Emerging from this diverse background he says 'I cannot be simplified' and yet this is exactly the demand made in the twentieth century of so many individuals all over Europe and the Mediterranean.

Memmi's unforgettably moving book carries us inch by inch with him along the path of a conscious and intelligent youngster forced to continually renounce old parts of himself in exchange for others. While the *Lycée* [French High School] inducts him into the super-rational world of high French culture he returns home to the crowded den of a home that exists in a state of enormous ignorance of the modern world — bringing his *Prof.* home to meet Ma '(she) was not accustomed to shaking hands and caught hold of Poinsot's fingers, much as one grasps a kitchen utensil.'

Although Albert Memmi's life (until he emigrated in despair from Tunis to Paris, a city where he 'was doomed forever to be an outsider') has a setting and a history rather exotic for English-speaking readers, the book has universal qualities as it explores, sometimes tenderly, sometimes angrily, the common but often painful experience of cultural displacement. The displacement that is the experience of the petty-bourgeois or (God help him/her) *working-class* kid fighting for breath in the upper middle class atmosphere of a good university; the Polish Jew or Punjabi Sikh stranded on the street corner of an incomprehensible Englishness; even the young man marrying into a very different family. Crossing a cultural frontier permanently seems to be a transgression and one has to pay customs a pound of emotional flesh.

Anyone who in their own lives, personally or through their family or partner knows this experience will recognise immediately the sad, sweet, if finally triumphant, voice of Memmi.

The other side of this story is the lesson of the violated multicultural lands of the southern shore of the Mediterranean — particularly Algeria, Tunisia and Egypt — which were ethnically 'simplified' after independence by Nationalist politics and the emigration of cultural minorities. The lesson for those with ears is that we should protect our contemporary cultural mosaic in Europe, a continent (still) blessed with some cultural diversity...
R K

'Travel if you wish, taste strange dishes, gather experience in dangerous adventures, but see that your soul remains your own. Do not become a stranger to yourself, for you are lost from that day on; you will have no peace if there is not, somewhere within you, a corner of certainty, calm waters where you can take refuge in sleep.' p316

MICHAEL
Sami

Victoria [Hebrew]

This long novel by the Israeli writer Sami Michael recounts the lives of an extended family of Jews in Baghdad, tracing their fate from before the World War One, when Iraq was part of the Ottoman (Turkish) empire, to modern-day Israel where the grandchildren and great-grandchildren end up (during 1950-51, about ninety per cent of Iraq's Jewish community — about 150,000 people —moved to Israel).

Jews may well have existed for centuries in Baghdad, but so have floods, plagues, massacres and persecutions, such that, according to Michael, far from integrating into the surrounding cultures, these Jews 'huddled together in a cramped quarter, and most of them were born and grew up and grew old and died without ever leaving its confines'.

The confines in this novel are a squalid courtyard, around which the families live, and where the human occupants 'humbly recognise their transience' alongside the much more durable population of beetles, scorpions, snakes, mice and carriers of 'seasonal diseases and cyclical epidemics'. Across the generations, from the 'living foundation' and matriarch Michal downwards, a rigid hierarchy is in place: between the three brothers and their families (the always bankrupt Eliyahu and his family, 'excommunicated by the courtyard', live in the lightless basement), and between men and women (between the women, which wife has her stove nearest the doorway in the huge shared kitchen depends on her husband's prestige).

The novel focuses on the character of Victoria, granddaughter of Michal and daughter of vicious-tongued Najia and of brutish but ineffectual Izuri. If she is fat and therefore beautiful, and if the financial arrangements are acceptable to the two families, then Victoria, like other girls, is destined to be married off to a man considered eligible. This man could of course be like Victoria's sickly uncle Yehuda or like the good-for-nothing Eliyahu or even like her cousin Miriam's blacksmith, who jumps on her 'like a sledge-hammer' and in one of his beatings breaks her leg. So of course the prospect of marriage preoccupies Victoria... Not just marriage but of course sex, a subject which the girls of the courtyard hardly talk about, or if they do only shyly and with great ignorance, but of course they are obsessed by nothing else and since the courtyard is crammed with people living one on top of the other, mostly literally, everyone knows everyone else's business and information can be gleaned that way...

Enter Rafael. Rafael is a cousin of Miriam and Victoria, and both girls hope in their heart of hearts that they will become his chosen one. The novel's real focus is Victoria and Miriam's undying love for this supercilious, heartstoppingly attractive and spectacularly unreliable young man. For Rafael is different from all the rest, he emerges from the basement (he is a son of the wretched Eliyahu) in a European suit, he reads books (those of the men who know how to read don't bother), and disappears mysteriously for long stretches of time. He is in contact with the developing world of the Middle East, and returns with tales from the Lebanon. He treats his surroundings in the courtyard with a disdain and distance which makes him very attractive indeed to every single woman there (except for Najia who loathes him, but precisely because he is so seductive).

Victoria, after years of lusting, suppression of lusting, waiting and uncertainty will one day be singled out for Rafael on one of his visits back to the courtyard. She will then go through what everyone has been waiting for — sex (Rafael is a more considerate husband than most) and childbirth — and will subsequently experience the rounds of sickly children, beatings and of course Rafael's instant infidelity.

Edifying it is not: 'Ghosts, jinns, Evil Eyes, magic spells, miracles, and dreams that told the future' are the daily nourishment of the women (who receive no education at all and are unable to read and write). They spend their time hatching spiteful jealousies over attractiveness to men and worrying about whether they will conceive a boy this time (girl children are 'another catastrophe', sometimes left out to die on the flat roofs). They spy on others, look out for signs (usually of desire or sexual activity), and get shouted at by brothers, fathers and husbands.

Not to mention the beatings, roughhousing and rape. Not to forget the incest — a seemingly blissful father-daughter couple on the rooftop — and older men sleeping with girls hardly ten years old, adultery which is really *de rigueur* for any self-respecting husband, and a few irrelevancies like World War One (a great trauma for the conscripted Jews who had never borne arms or strayed further than across the river), the arrival of running water and the growing prosperity of the families of the courtyard (Rafael succeeds with his exercise-book factory, and he and Victoria will eventually move from the courtyard to a new house which is 'an anonymous door in a long row of doors')...

This is a gutsy tale, where smash-and-grab lives are described in all their violent, raunchy earthiness. These lives may be mercilessly dismal and impoverished, but they seethe with straightforward angers, lusts, cravings and loathings. Although the novel has an interesting narrative structure (flashbacks and anticipations of the future), what the reader will remember is the steamy, dark and claustrophobic world of the courtyard, where almost anything can happen... S B

'Eliyahu's children, emaciated from their long hunger, had invaded the kitchen and they were snatching the food straight from the boiling pots and devouring it in blind greed. One of them choked on a bone and vomited. They chewed with their mouths full, they burned their snatching fingers. The girls lifted their skirts shamelessly and shovelled pieces of lamb and joints of chicken and scalding rice into their dresses. Their hands dripped with oil, gravy ran down their chins. And Najia was beating their backs and slapping their faces, ready to rip off their sleeves in her fury as she struggled to rescue the pieces of meat into which their nails were digging, while the children, frantic with greed, ignored her. Pots overturned. Bare feet were scalded by the steam. In the end the children fled, their mouths and pockets crammed with meat and rice.' p50-1

MICHAELS
Anne

Fugitive Pieces [English Canada]

Some books you don't get over, rather they get all over and into you, take you over. *Fugitive Pieces*, a highly acclaimed first novel by the Canadian poet Anne Michaels, which won several prestigious literary prizes in 1997 is just such a book.

Jakob Beer, silent witness to the murder of his family from within the wall cavity of his family's apartment in Poland, a seven-year-old who eluded the Nazis by burying himself in mud by day, roaming for food at night, is picked up by the erudite and cultured Greek archaeologist Athos and taken to a remote Greek island. Athos supplements the penury and confinement of Greece under Italian then German occupation with a gentleness and spiritual fullness in which the young boy grows. The pair then move to Toronto where Jakob marries while carrying on his involvement with archaeology, poetry and music. In the last part of this book we hear of Ben, son of concentration camp survivors, who is so struck by Jakob's personality that after Jakob's death he begins to re-trace his footsteps.

Simple, really, as is Jakob's dilemma which is summed up: 'To survive was to escape fate. But if you escape your fate, whose life do you then step into?' Having only fragmentary memories of his family and especially of his fifteen-year-old sister Bella, what influences do the events and destruction have which he never saw but which were the most important moments of his life? The book uses the metaphor of archaeology and of different archaeological times — 'slow persuasion and catastrophe', carbon dating (which takes the moment of death as the starting point), slow accumulation, remote causes — to explore memory, personal history and how after-effects of events live on in the present.

Another major theme is music: the lost sister Bella was a young pianist (and Anne Michaels herself writes music for the theatre). As the title *Fugitive Pieces* suggests, the fugue is the form which might best fit this book: multiple voices, brought in at different times, overlapping, interweaving and recurring but never synchronised. This is how the self is viewed, and the work of mourning (voices emerging suddenly into the fabric of the present), an endless creative dialogue which Jakob also carries on with and through his two great loves — Alex and Michaela.

This beautiful, resonant book carries the reader along with a powerful momentum, and is written with a poetic intensity which leaves one wanting to begin again as soon as one has put it down. One of its most striking and original aspects is the way in which memory, loss and joy are given a truly physical quality, 'we feel our phantom skin buckling', we live out an 'evolution of longing', even languages, strange new languages (Greek and English for Jakob, after his early Yiddish and Polish) are like foreign foods, mouthed carefully, 'suspicious, acquired tastes'. While this book has some remarkable things to say about the Holocaust, about destruction and responsibility (a moral act could be as little as 'eyes looking away or blinking, while a running man crossed a field'), about history and memory, it also celebrates living as a tactile and sensuous activity, endlessly flavoursome and to be savoured. The blend of grief and delighted love which runs through this writing is profoundly moving in a rare way, and takes us on a journey both compelling and very intimate. On no account to be missed. S B

'I was surprised to discover not everyone sees the shadow around objects, the black outline, the bruise of fermentation on things even as light clings to them. I saw the aura of mortality like a snake that sees its prey in infrared, the pulse-heat. It was clear to me as cut fruit turning brown on the plate, a lemon peel shrivelling to scent.'

Bitter Herbs [Het bittere kruid] [Dutch]

The opening sentence of *Bitter Herbs* simply states: 'It began one day when my father said: "We'll just go and see whether everyone's back."' What this 'it' refers to, is never explained. There is no need to. The book never mentions that the uniforms and the boots belong to German soldiers or that 'the stars' are yellow stars of David, but it doesn't take the reader long to realize that what is being described is the persecution of Dutch Jews in occupied Holland during World War Two.

Bitter Herbs tells this story through the eyes of a young girl. Her age is not specified, but she must be about eleven or twelve when the war begins. She doesn't always understand what is going on around her, and asks few questions. Her father remains grimly optimistic, refusing to believe the rumours they hear — or is he hiding his fear from the children? When the first restrictive measures affecting Jews are announced, the family complies. When the girl's elder brother Dave is called up for the labour camp, he makes himself ill and gets off. But the noose tightens. The girl's sister is rounded up during a raid in Amsterdam. The parents receive orders to move to the Amsterdam ghetto. Despite the restrictions the girl goes to join them. When the police come to take them away, the girl escapes and manages to join her brother Dave and his girl-friend who are now in hiding. She bleaches her hair. As the three of them move on to another safe house, Dave's girl-friend is arrested and Dave gives himself up to be with her. Alone now, the young girl sits out the war in a series of hiding places. The Epilogue is set after the Liberation, when the girl goes to visit an uncle who cannot bring himself to accept that virtually the whole family has been wiped out and keeps hoping against hope that they will return. The uncle's wife, who is not Jewish, thinks he is crazy, but the girl understands him perfectly.

This is a slight book, barely a hundred pages divided into twenty-two short chapters, bearing out its subtitle: *'A little chronicle'*. It is not hard to see why it has become one of the most moving and celebrated accounts of Dutch Jews during the Nazi occupation. Its innocuous, sparing style leaves much unsaid, but the reader knows what to fill in. The reticence and seeming naivety give the account its stark emotional force. Although the book is based on the author's own experience, it ends up being much more than autobiography. As the epilogue suggests, *Bitter Herbs* is also the story of Jews in the Netherlands who tried to become 'Jewish Dutchmen' but whose suffering made them realise they were Dutch Jews too. Theo H

'They must have had a master key.

They were standing in the room before we could stir. Two tall men, wearing light raincoats.

"Fetch our coats, will you?" Father said to me. Mother finished her cup of tea.

With my coat on, I lingered in the hall. I heard my father say something. One of the men said something in reply. I could not make out what it was. I put my ear to the door of the room. Once again I heard my father's voice, and again I could not make out what he said. Then I turned round and walked through the kitchen, into the garden. It was dark. My foot struck against something round, I must have been a ball.

I shut the garden door softly behind me and ran down the street. I did not stop running until I arrived at Frederiksplein. There was no one to be seen. Only a dog, nosing along the house fronts.

I crossed the square. It was as if I was alone in a deserted city.' p77

MINCO
Marga

An Empty House [Een leeg huis] [Dutch]

In some ways this is the sequel to Minco's *Bitter Herbs*. Whereas the earlier story dealt with a Jewish family whose members were being picked off one by one by the Nazis in wartime Holland, here we see the sole survivor's attempts to adjust to life after the war. In terms of style and presentation, however, the two books have little in common. The story line in *Bitter Herbs* is simple and chronological, although no dates are mentioned. *An Empty House* is built around three specific dates: Thursday 28 June 1945, Tuesday 25 March 1947, and Friday 21 April 1950.

On the first of these dates the first-person narrator, a Jewish girl called Sepha, is returning to Amsterdam after a month in the country. She meets Yona, who has also been in hiding. Sepha is going back to her boyfriend Mark, Yona has no-one waiting for her. That same evening Yona is in hospital, having fallen into a canal — or did she jump? Two years later we find Sepha in southern France. She has left Mark, who is now her husband, to think things over. Mark turns up, but they don't really talk. Sepha is still in touch with Yona. Another three years later Sepha and

Mark are together again in Amsterdam, although Sepha remains restless and sleeps around. The couple plan to move into a new house. News reaches Sepha that Yona has died: she fell from a train — or did she jump?

This basic story line is complicated, and very much enriched, in two ways. One is the use of flashbacks. While the main story is told by Sepha in the past tense, it is shot through with scenes from the past, told in the present tense, as if for Sepha the past is more alive and immediate than the present. The transitions occur suddenly, from one sentence to the next, and cover life in hiding during the war, the relationship with Mark, and the pre-war years. They help us to understand the nature of Sepha's trauma, her desperate attempt to regain some sort of balance.

The other way in which *An Empty House* gains in complexity and depth is the subtlety with which it suggests that Yona may be Sepha's double. Yona, after all, appeared out of the blue with her backpack, her features resemble Sepha's when Sepha looks in Yona's cracked mirror after the latter's death. But while Sepha tries to shake off the unbearable weight of the past, Yona carries her burden of guilt with her everywhere, until she can no longer cope. Whether or not Sepha's strategy will prove any more successful is left open at the end. Theo H

'I began to put the photographs into some sequence, following chronological order as far as possible so that I could see her growing older. Then I looked at the self-portrait. It didn't look like her at all. But it was already becoming too dark to see it properly. I pulled open the cupboard drawer and found an exercise book under a pile of papers. I took it out. It had a hard brown cover. There was a large letter Y with the Star of David around it on the label. The Y was drawn with black ink, the Star in pencil. Perhaps it was a diary. She might have written in it just yesterday, this morning. At last I'll get to know what had gone on inside her, what her intentions had been when she left here. But I didn't open the exercise book. I replaced it under the papers and closed the drawer.

What had she expected from me when she came to me this morning? Hadn't I given her a chance to say what she had wanted to say? Had she for the umpteenth time wanted to make me feel that I was no less free of guilt?' p149

Tell me a riddle [English USA]

This collection of four short stories from the 1950s shows the enormous versatility of Tillie Olsen as a writer, her sensitivity to idiom, and her passionate involvement with the living language of those whose worlds she depicts. Whether in the jangled conversations of sea-dog Whitey with his old friends in *Hey sailor, what ship?*, or the mounting euphoria of a black gospel meeting in *O Yes* ('The music leaps and prowls. Ladders of screaming. The voices in great humming waves...') or the terse words of Eva, embittered by a life of drudgery ('Vinegar he poured on me all his life; I am well marinated; how can I be honey now?') in *Tell me a riddle* — whatever themes Olsen treats, the language is rich and powerful, bearing the still warm imprint of the worlds it comes from.

These worlds are the worlds of America during the Depression, tales of poverty and the reproduction of poverty across the generations, of the slow entrenchment of racial divides, of age and social neglect, and above all these are tales of the impassioned but thwarted and impoverished lives of cleaners, shoppers, cooks, workers, mothers and wives: women. In *I stand here ironing*, a mother contemplates the string of constraints and necessities which have brought distance between herself and her eldest child, a gifted young girl with an already cold and windswept heart. The young mother had to work by day, then by night, the child was taken into care, no welfare, no daddy (who left fed up of 'sharing want'); and the child's reserve at school, 'dark and thin and foreign-looking' in an age enthralled by chubby blondes. The mother muses on the impossibility of calculating the damage, but notes that a life is there which goes on as best as it can ('so all that is in her will not bloom...but in how many does it?'), with its hopeless constraints but with its robustness too.

The emotionally most intricate story is the title novella, *Tell me a riddle*, about the bursting apart of an old woman's world, a world shared with her husband for forty-seven years. She has laboured, toiled, she has humiliated and denied herself over her working life to secure food and clothing for her husband and children, isolated by enforced domesticity and with no time for a social life or for reading. When her working life is over, the weight of these burdens erupts into the present, not so much in bitterness as in a determined pursuit of what now she desires, the last possible opportunity to have the life which could be hers...

This couple though are destined to remain in exile, immigrants from Russia, torn from their Jewish roots ('Tell them to write: Race; *human*, Religion; *none*'), alienated from their all-American grandchildren ('Commercial's on; any Coke left?') and bred — ironically enough in the context — on revolutionary ideals of progress '*with flame of freedom in their souls/and light of knowledge in their eyes*', which could never be exercised because of isolation, hunger and hard work, even to the 'hard work of dying'. Even before Eva falls ill, her question is already trenchant: 'Where *is* my home?'.

This could all be most miserable. What is very special about this writing, though, is that the characters, however socially marginalised, are given a tenacious individuality by Olsen. They remain resolutely in their own worlds, both mentally and verbally, fiercely thinking and fiercely feeling, mature, survivors. S B

'Outside in the garden, growing things to nurture. Birds to be kept out of the pear tree, and when the pears are heavy and ripe, the old fury of work, for all must be canned, nothing wasted... And her one social duty (for she will not go to luncheons or meetings) the boxes of old clothes left with her, as with a life-practised eye for finding what is still wearable within the worn (again the magnifying glass superimposed on the heavy glasses) she scans and sorts — this rag for rummage, that for mending and cleaning, and this for sending abroad.

Being able at last to live within, and not move to the rhythms of others, as life had forced her to: denying; removing; isolating; taking the children one by one; then deafening, half-blinding — and at last, presenting her solitude.

And in it she had won to a reconciled peace.' p79-80

OPATOSHU
Joseph

A Day in Regensburg [A Tog in Regensburg] [Yiddish USA]

Opatoshu, born in Poland in 1887, lived most of his life in America but his writing is a real bridge between two worlds; an intellectually self-sufficient, largely self-enclosed Jewish world and the wider world of today where Jews are one minority group amongst others.

Opatoshu adopts a fascinating perspective in this book, an overview of the history of (Ashkenazi) Jews in Europe from the early Middle Ages through the sixteenth century and into the twentieth. The most ambitious part of this is the title story, the novella *A Day in Regensburg*, which is a tale of Jewish life in the ancient city of that name in the twelfth century or so. Although perhaps a little clumsy — there is a whiff of Hollywood Historic about it — it is still a fascinating glimpse into an interesting period. If this early Medieval period was a rather glorious time for Jews in Germany, *A Sabbath Afternoon* shows Jews in the process of being forced out of Germany a few centuries later and captures the kind of tense and over-heated atmosphere amongst a people under siege. The protagonists of *A Sabbath Afternoon* are preparing to sell everything off and move to harbour towns in readiness for a messianic transference to the Land of Israel. It's the atmosphere of the Ghost Dance Society hundreds of years later in America when another people — the Plains Indians — also embraced fantastical solutions (magical bullet proof shirts to fight the US Cavalry) and a false Messiah when under terrible pressure from outside.

Opatoshu then takes us to a happier time in Jewish history in *Ben Sira's Grandson* set in ancient Alexandria, the great Greek-speaking city of pre-Islamic Egypt. We hear something of the Delta and Gamma quarters of a city that was at one time one third Jewish.

There are also stories set in seventeenth century Poland, *In the Jewish District of Vienna* set in late-medieval Vienna (which was a considerable centre for Talmudic studies) and in the Polish-Russian borderlands shortly after the Russian Revolution, showing the disruption to traditional Jewish culture this created. *The Mute Hungarian* is a grim story of Jewish partisans fighting the German mass-murderers in World War Two. Another story from this period is the excellent *Meyer Balaban*, brief but burning-hot in its anger at the destruction of Jewish Poland, in which Opatoshu takes us, in the person of an elderly Jewish historian, to the freshly smoking ruins of the Warsaw Ghetto in 1944.

Joseph Opatoshu, on the showing of this book, was more of a worthy craftsman than great artist as a writer, but the breadth of these visions of Jewish history in Europe, Egypt and America over more than a thousand years makes it a fascinating read, and, at his best he is well able to transmit the emotional reality of his rich material. R K

'Eleazar ben Jeshua entered the Gamma quarter. Though fewer Jews resided here, Gamma, had three synagogues, one where Egyptian Jews worshipped, one for Roman Jews, and one for the Macedonians, whose ancestors had helped build Alexandria. Indeed Alexandria was truly a Jewish city, every third inhabitant being a Jew. Of the city's one million two hundred thousand souls, some four hundred thousand were Jewish. That is not to say that the remaining eight hundred thousand were Egyptian. There were people in Alexandria from all over the world. But none of the other groups could compare with the Jewish one, which was the largest and richest.

Every year the Jews of Alexandria celebrated the eighth day of Tebet, the anniversary of the translation of the Hebrew bible into Greek.' (*Ben Sira's Grandson* p204-5)

OZ
Amos

The Hill of Evil Counsel – Three Stories [Givat Ha-Eitzah Ha-Ra] [Hebrew]

In *The Hill of Evil Counsel* Oz, a major Israeli writer, has summoned to life the period of transition immediately prior to the end of the British Mandate in Palestine in 1948 by presenting three interconnected novellas, each narrated by a different protagonist from the same neighborhood in Jerusalem. Juxtaposed to the contemporary Zionist thrust for a Jewish State their intimate desires and awarenesses expand in a vision of volatility, intrigue and rites of passage. At the same time the myth of the hero, arising to redeem the nation, is explored in a refreshing manner

The opening novella, *Hill of Evil Counsel*, follows the impact British rule in Palestine had on the lives of one family, as seen through the young, puzzled eyes of Hillel Kipnis living in the outlying suburb of Tel Arza, Jerusalem. The main action depicts the events and impressions between the opening scenario, a celebration of Allied victory at the Edison Cinema in Jerusalem in 1946, and the May Ball, a very British affair, taking place several weeks later. Dr and Mrs. Kipnis are invited to the second event by virtue of the doctor leaping to the assistance of a fainting Lady Bromley at the first. During this timeframe their son tries to explore and decode the strong emotions and circumstances surrounding him. The reader is introduced to Dr Kipnis, a veterinary rather than a medical doctor. He has brought with him from his original life in Silesia and in Leipzig in Germany a sense of wonder at the physical and geographic environment of Palestine, plus a need for solitary pursuits. His wife, an immigrant from a much more sophisticated society in Warsaw seems to regret all that is pioneering and basic and unworldly in her life in the

Land of Israel.

Frequently left to develop his own imaginative world, Hillel must also contend with Mitya, the militant socialist living as a boarder in their house, as well as Lyobov Binyamina and her aunt Madame Yabrova, his exotic, mysterious neighbours and sometime child-minders. Conflict abounds: mixed responses of disdain and awe towards the British and their stranglehold over Palestine, plus a sense of being unwittingly seduced by their ceremony and achievement, their 'otherness'. Highlighted in every episode is Hillel's initiation into the world of political intrigue and physical maturity, as well as his intuitive concerns regarding his mother and father. The overwhelming sense of the novella is sadness and trepidation as everything around the young boy is destined to change.

The second novella *Mr. Levi* develops the fascination and total commitment of another young boy, Uri Kolodny, towards the cause of ridding Palestine of British authority. Clearly another facet of the one persona, Uri inhabits the same neighborhood as Hillel. He suffers less from any conflict between his parents in their relationship than from an innocent passion and zeal in the furthering of the political ambitions of Ephraim Nehamkin his mentor whom he serves valiantly as 'lieutenant'. The plot concerns his attempt to interpret the clandestine actions and events around him, with all the poignant perseverance of a precocious youngster.

The final novella represents a complete change of perspective. It takes the form of letters from an ailing Dr Emanuel Nussbaum to his onetime love, Mina. Intuitive in another mode, it contains the doctor's reflections on his past life and the people he had contact with in his medical and social world. It is most successful when it too turns towards the young Uri, his anguishes and relentless efforts in the 'cause'. Uri visits the dying doctor, hoping to be able to carry forward his supposedly Trojan work in the field of bomb making. Representing the end of an era, the end of one type of philosophy and culture, this section sums up the moment of transition in the life of a nation.

We have a strong sense that this represents a pivotal point in the life of the young Amos Oz too: his mother was to die by her own hand when he was twelve years old. He then chose to leave Jerusalem altogether and embrace another kind of society, growing up instead on a kibbutz. It was at that time moreover that he changed his surname from his native 'Klausner' to the adopted name of 'Oz', meaning 'strength'. T L

'While my father and Ephraim were absorbed in their game of chess, my mother would sit at the piano, with her face toward the window and her back to the room. Ephraim looked at her not longingly, like the heroes in the pictures, but with an expression that resembled dismay. I myself was dismayed at their silence. At that time, distant sounds of firing could be heard almost every evening in Jerusalem. Father chewed mint leaves: he was always afraid of having bad breath. Ephraim smoked so much that sometimes his eyes watered. Mother played the same *étude* over and over again, as if she had made up her mind never to move on until she had received an answer. Outside the wind touched the trees as if pleading for silence. But there was silence anyway.

On the sill of the deep-set window that faced north, my battlefields were laid out. Corks, pushpins, silver foil, matchboxes, and empty cigarette packs were battleships, troops, and tanks. I conducted cunning mopping-up operations by the army of Bar Kochba and Marshal Budënny against the Nazi storm troopers. By the middle of the summer holidays my Maccabees had conquered Athens, breached the walls of Rome, burned its palaces and razed its towers, and reached on to besiege Berlin and London. By the time the winter rain and snow made the roads impassable, we would force them to surrender unconditionally.

It was Ephraim who outlined the strategy.

"Always attack on the flank," he instructed me, "always from the desert, from the forest, from the mountains, always from where you are least expected."

His eyes glowed as he spoke, and he could not keep his hands still. He would add in a whisper, "Only don't trust them. Never trust them. They're all thirsting for our blood.' (*Mr. Levi p73*)

OZ
Amos

The Panther in the Basement [Panter BaMartef] [Hebrew]

Amos Oz has worked with many narrative voices in his impressive body of work. In this latest book he returns to the childhood persona he presented with such poignant strength in *Hill of Evil Counsel*. The title immediately strikes a chord: animals of prey haunted the author in his childhood consciousness, jackals prowled in the wadis around his native Jerusalem, and they are a motif of the early short story collection *Where the Jackals Howl*. However in this slim volume, a novella rather than a novel, the panther of the title pertains to a Hollywood film of the period, starring the screen hero Tyrone Power. It is the period immediately before the end of the British Mandate in 1948, when Proffy (short for

Professor, nickname of the young pre-adolescent protagonist) is attempting to carve out a role for himself in the wave of political and national change sweeping the country. Hillel and Uri in the earlier collection of novellas [*The Hill of Evil Counsel*]were faced with similar challenges and similar family set-ups. In this work, written some twenty years later, Amos Oz is examining the question of loyalty and betrayal as experienced through the intense, probing and precocious mind of Proffy, clearly a vision of 'the artist as a young man'.

In the opening scene Proffy is charged by his friends and teammates with 'lowdown treachery' in the struggle against 'Perfidious Albion' (England). This sets the tone of defense, in his own imagination, of all the possible crimes of betrayal he could be accused of: towards his original friends, at once tormentors and accomplices; towards his father, whom he at once respects and despises; to Yardena, delightful older sister of his friend Ben Hur, whom he has glimpsed undressing from his balcony look-out. The most significant charge regards Sergeant Dunlop, the soft-faced British policeman with whom he strikes up a conspiratorial relationship, aimed at teaching one another their respective languages — Modern Hebrew and English. The body of the work explores this association, and the possibility of befriending one's 'enemy' once intimacy and co-operation are attained. This issue reverberates into the modern-day scenario of the possibilities of peace between Arab and Jew, of whom Amos Oz is such a staunch supporter.

We must question why Amos Oz has returned to this moment in time and experience, after the wealth of works exploring adult issues and relationships written in a far more modern, even post-modern vein. Is it an existential need to re-evaluate that moment when the new State was born? For on the national level hope was unlimited, yet on the personal level for Oz, shortly before his mother's death and his migration to live permanently on Kibbutz Hulda, so much was to change. T L

'I knew by heart all the neighbourhoods, villages, hills, and towers that were visible from my look-out post. In the Sinopsky Brothers grocery, in the queue at the clinic, on the Dorizons' balcony opposite, in front of the Shibboleth news-stand, people would stand and argue about the borders of the future Hebrew State. Would they include Jerusalem? Would they include the British naval base at Haifa? And what about Galilee? And the desert? Some hoped that the forces of the civilized world would come and protect us from being murdered by bloodthirsty Arabs. (Every nation had a fixed epithet, like a first name with a surname: perfidious Albion, tainted Germany, faraway China, Soviet Russia, rich America. Down on the coast there was bustling Tel Aviv. Far away from us, in Galilee, in the valleys, was the labouring Land of Israel. The Arabs were labelled bloodthirsty. Even the world had several epithets, depending on the atmosphere and the situation: civilized, free, wide, hypocritical. Sometimes people said: "The world that knew and said nothing." Sometimes they said: "The world will not stay silent about this.")

In the meantime, until the British pulled out and the Hebrew State finally emerged, the grocer's and the greengrocer's opened at seven in the morning and closed at six in the evening in time for the curfew. The neighbours — the Dorzions, Dr Gryphius, ourselves, Ben Hur and his parents — gathered at Dr Buster's because he had a radio. We listened in gloomy silence to the news on the Voice of Jerusalem. Sometimes, after dark, very softly, we listened to the clandestine broadcast of the Voice of Fighting Zion. Sometimes we stayed on after the news to listen to the appeals for missing relatives, in case they suddenly mentioned a relative murdered in Europe who turned out to have survived after all and had managed to make his way to the Land of Israel or at least to one of the DP camps that the British had set up in Cyprus.' p14–15

OZ
Amos

My Michael [Mikha'el sheli] [Hebrew]

Amos Oz is the Israeli fiction writer best known outside the country, acclaimed for his incisive short novels which address almost every facet of Israeli society, and reach back into the time before Independence. Born in Israel, a committed kibbutznik and secularist active in the 'Peace Now' movement, he manages to weave between the personal and wider social and political events with extraordinary deftness, lucidity and humour.

My Michael, Oz's prize-winning novel of 1968, runs from the days of the British Mandate in Palestine through the upheavals of the War of Independence and new statehood to late 1950s Israel. The political backdrop is also the backdrop of a place, Jerusalem: rationing, food queues, corrugated iron and unlit streets are the constant features of this hostile and windswept city, which Oz has elsewhere described as a 'city of outskirts' and which in this novel has the glum strength of presence of a human character. Apart from Jerusalem, we also see the extraordinary, exhilarating diversity of Israel: Aunt Jenia who, like so many, is still most at home in Polish and German, the terse debates about the new

State ('Instead of being a light to the nations we have become just one of the nations'), the secluded secular kibbutz in the North whose concerns are farming and chickens, and the workers' estate in the new sun-drenched town of Holon with a constant breeze from the sea: all this and much more is Israel, diverse, evolving, fiercely debated and shadowed by conflicts old and new, internal and external.

The conflicts are also internal in the sense of psychological. The focus of this absorbing book is the growth — or stunting — of the relationship between Hannah and the Michael of the book's title, she a young, pretty, dreamy student of literature, he a contained and inexpressive geology student. They marry, live in a poor and gloomy religious quarter of Jerusalem (although not particularly observant themselves), have a child Yair and then a second one, proceed down life's paths together, and scrimp and save for, among other things, the first ever volumes of the *Encyclopaedia Hebraica*. And yet, while nothing particular happens, this is an immensely stirring story of the inscrutability or perhaps elusiveness of love, the different deceptive masks it can wear and the small misjudgements or confusions which can determine the course of a whole life.

Narrated from Hannah's point of view, the novel charts briefly her emergent love (the way Michael handles a teaspoon with his fingers is the clinching image for Hannah) and then her gradual, bewildered loss of self over the years to the point of breakdown, described with calm understatement as 'a pane of glass which grows progressively more opaque, despite frantic polishing'. The elegant and often funny stylistic characterisation of her viewpoint is extremely telling as Hannah interweaves the retrospective story of her life with vivid cascades of people and places in her dreams and in the feverish excitements of her fantasy life.

Hannah's fantasies, which recur throughout the book, are rooted in the tense and sinister atmosphere of the British Mandate, with British destroyers parading the coast, curfews, Arab gangs and Jewish saboteurs involved in silent and deathly guerrilla conflict. In Hannah's fantasies, these political realities are a source of deep and brooding fear, but are also sifted for their sexual content of strong men, torture, discipline and humiliation, while she herself takes the part of cruel princess or erotically subjugated victim. The psycho-political residue of her childhood under the

Mandate emerges above all in the repeated motif of the Arab twins ('Halziz'; Halil and Aziz) with whom she used to play as a child. This pair, in her politically imprinted fantasy, are both menacing and arousing, forever lost — or repressed? — as companions, but never going away. This odd alliance is Oz's remarkable figuration of Arab-Jewish relations.

Not only are we shown how political events filter down into fantasy, but also the chilling ways in which patterns of behaviour and even patterns of desire (supposedly so personal, individual) drip down from generation to generation — Hannah's desire for studious and incommunicative Michael springs in large part, it is suggested, from her love for her dead father, who so admired scholars; and this pattern is shown to be a straightforward recipe for disaster.

Above all this book is a heartrending commentary on all those who, in an environment which is tough and full of conflict, mistake care and helpfulness for love; Michael never in any sense behaves badly to Hannah, but his punctilious, dutiful considerateness, his clinically measured care is as deathly an injection to Hannah's spirit as the chaotic, scary and abusive life of her fantasies would be if they were real. Hannah's incomprehension of her present life — 'the power of loving is dying' — is the awful toll of her emotional blindspot. A fascinating and humbling read. S B

'Yair is particularly interested in two subjects: the engagements in the War of Independence and the network of public bus services.

On the former subject Michael is a mine of information. He points with his hand, identifies features in the landscape, draws plans in the dust, demonstrates with the help of twigs and stones.

I, too, listen and learn. How little I knew about the battle for Jerusalem. The Germans and Greeks abandoned the German and Greek Colonies. New people moved in to take their place. New men, women and children moved into Jerusalem. That would not be the last battle for Jerusalem. So I have heard our friend Mr Kadishman say. I too can sense secret forces restlessly scheming, swelling and surging and bursting out through the surface.

Yair imagines war as an extraordinarily complex game, which displays a whole fascinating world of system and logic. My husband and my son both see time as a succession of equal squares on a sheet of graph-paper, which provide a structure to support the lines and shapes.

Yair knew the makes of the buses operating on each route by heart. He enjoyed explaining the reasons for the use of the different makes: here a steep hill, there a sharp or a poor road-surface. The child's style of explanation closely resembled his father's. Both of them made frequent use of such words as "thus", "whereas", "in conclusion", and also "remote possibility".

I made an effort to listen to both of them quietly and attentively.'
p187-8

OZ
Amos

Don't call it night [Al tagidi laila] [Hebrew]

This recent novel by Oz focuses on a small new town in Israel built on the very edge of the Negev desert, near to where Oz himself lives, and on the life of a couple there. They are Noa, a Hebrew literature teacher at the local school, who has just launched an absorbing new project to set up a drug rehabilitation centre, as a consequence of the mysterious death of one of her pupils, and her partner Theo, fifteen years her senior and in his sixties, who has more or less abandoned his brilliant town planning business and seems to eye with mute negativity the sudden energy which his partner is finding.

This is the basis for a vivid and humorous analysis of the couple, set against the patterns of the life and crazy characters of this small, far-flung town, the melting-pot world of 'New Israelis'. While the busy little town and the awesome desert are important figures in this work (evoking the history of Israel from early Pioneers to modern town-dwellers, a history which both Theo the town planner and Noa the Hebrew literature teacher represent and contribute to) it is the manoeuvres of Noa to assert herself which take the foreground in this book. Noa's thoughts and feelings and above all the *pace* of her life are portrayed with great perceptiveness as she battles energetically against her sense of inferiority with respect to Theo (whom others call a 'national treasure'); and as her thoughts are increasingly occupied by the strange young boy who died striving for words (he had written good literature essays) and for life, as Noa herself is now doing, challenging her relationship with Theo, bidding for a new start.

This is a beautifully told tale, intertwining the perspectives of fiery Noa and controlled Theo, sometimes on the very same event, so that the differences between the two are shown up, often quite hilariously. Oz also conveys the wealth of perception, feeling and calculation which familiar activities can contain. For example, there is a risible shopping episode when from Theo's slightly cautious opinion on a dress — we can never be sure just how undermining he is being — Noa infers that he does not support her drug clinic project, and, forgetting that she used the word first, accuses him of discouraging her in her ideas by describing the dress as 'folksy'. The writing moves so smoothly from such finely observed sparking to the arguments of the two stylists in the *Champs-Elysées Hairdressing Salon* or to the bad jokes of compulsive womaniser Muki, that these perceptions are woven into a picture of the society at large.

Despite the trip-wires which this couple, who know each other so very well, set for each other, the book also celebrates the moments of tenderness which suddenly spring between the pair when free of irritation and suspicion. Unlike the earlier *My Michael* (also reviewed here), it is not bleak but a warm and witty vision of old love, like the desert ancient, yet still edgy, potentially destructive but also with a beauty all its own. S B

'At the Entebbe falafel stand a Bedouin in his fifties is buying shawarma in pitta. The shawarma is a new venture, and Avram is happily explaining to the Bedouin that it's still running in. If it goes well, in a couple of weeks' time we'll try grilled shish kebab. Meanwhile a haughty white cat with tail erect prances past Kushner's bitch who had a litter of pups a couple of days ago. The bitch chooses to feign sleep, but opens one eye a slit to observe the extent of the insolence. Cat and bitch alike behave as though the whole situation were beneath their dignity.

At a quarter past eleven a small funeral cortège passes by the lights, only a handful of mourners, mainly elderly Ashkenazim. From his invariable stool in the doorway of Bozo Shoes, Pini Bozo asks who has died and how, and Kushner the bookbinder replies that it is old Elijah, Schatzberg the chemist's senile uncle, the doting old fool who kept escaping and sitting in the post office all day long; every five minutes he used to join the queue and when he got to the counter he'd ask, When's Elijah coming, and however often they chased him away he always came back.

The cortège is in a hurry. The pallbearers are almost running because the Sabbath is approaching and they still have a lot of preparations to take care of before sunset. With all the commotion the corpse, covered in a yellowing tallit, looks as though it is writhing in agony. A fair-haired, sparsely bearded religious youth hurries at the head, rattling a tin can and promising that almsgiving saves you from death. Theo reflects for a moment and concludes that it is a moot point.' p58-9

Bloodshed and Three Novellas [English USA]

Bloodshed, after which this second volume of Cynthia Ozick's stories is named is the shortest piece here, and is both formally the most concise and, with respect to content, the most challenging. Whereas in her earlier collection, *The Pagan Rabbi*, Ozick had been concerned very much with paganism and idolatry in its contemporary manifestations, and had recourse to what many readers may find a quite taxing imaginative fantasy, here she makes rather less extravagant sorties into the 'supernatural'.

The novella *Usurpation (Other People's Stories)* is perhaps the exception here. In *Bloodshed*, however, we follow Bleilip who has arrived by Greyhound bus in a new Hasidic* community to visit a young relation who has given up the very way of life that Bleilip in a sense embodies; the familiar secular Jewish-American world. She has married a young Hasid who takes Bleilip along to the Study House where he meets the Rebbe, the spiritual leader of this sect. All around him are survivors of the Holocaust, and the Rebbe himself carries the physical scars of perverse medical experiments carried out on him in the camps. The whole second half of the story revolves around Bleilip's encounter with the Rebbe, and this in turn takes place in the context of the Rebbe's exposition of the Talmudic laws of *Yom Kippur**, and more specifically, of the sacrifices (bloodshed) and the sending off of the scapegoat to its death in the wilderness. Bleilip is confronted with a challenge to his idea of himself as a Jew, and we, like him, are invited to contemplate and to re-evaluate our notions of the 'barbarity' of animal sacrifice in the light of the twentieth century's record of human bloodshed.

This is a story of many levels, likely to haunt the reader's memory and invite reading and rereading. Ozick manages the quite remarkable achievement of integrating the modern short story into a more traditional Jewish literary genre of rabbinic study. Elsewhere in the collection, however, the reader is treated to Ozick's continually unpredictable and witty story-telling in which the familiar is revealed in most unfamiliar ways. T H

'He was addressing Bleilip — he pointed a finger without a nail.

"Who are you? Talk and look! Who?"

Bleilip spoke his own name and shook: a schoolboy in a school-room. "I'm here with the deepest respect, Rabbi. I came out of interest for your community."

"We are not South Sea Islanders, sir, our practices are well known since Sinai. You don't have to turn your glance. We are not something new in the world."

"Excuse me, Rabbi, not new — unfamiliar."

"To you."

"To me," Bleilip admitted.

"Exactly my question! Who are you, what do you represent, what are you to us?"

"A Jew. Like yourselves. One of you."

"Presumption! Atheist, devourer! For us there is the Most High, joy, life. For us trust! But you!..." (*Bloodshed*)

OZICK
Cynthia

The Cannibal Galaxy [English USA]

Like much of Ozick's fiction, *The Cannibal Galaxy* is simultaneously absorbing narrative and philosophical allegory — indeed, her exceptional power as a writer lies in just this effortless fusion of the roles of storyteller and thinker. As in all of her writing, the central theme is the condition of physical and spiritual exile which defines the modern, and especially post-Holocaust Jewish experience.

Joseph Brill, a Parisian astronomy student and son of a pious Jewish fishmonger, is hidden in the cellar of a convent during the Nazi occupation. Here, he reads the work of Edmond Fleg, a French-Jewish thinker who inspires the project which will occupy the whole of his post-war life: a school founded upon the fusion of the two great civilizations — Western and Jewish — he absorbed as a child. Abandoning his graduate astronomical studies in Paris, he moves to America, and in an unnamed lakeside area of the Mid-West opens the Edmond Fleg Primary School.

The novel centres on Brill's curious love-hate relationship with Hester Lilt, woman of ideas and mother of Beulah, one of the school's pupils. Over the eight years her daughter spends at the school, Hester relentlessly strips away the layers of illusion which have blinded Brill to his failure as thinker and teacher. The school's 'Dual Curriculum', far from the utopian interweaving of cultures he had once envisaged, has become little more than an empty slogan, mired in the quicksand of test-scores, pushy parents, and mediocre teachers more concerned with class discipline than intellectual cultivation.

Hester's criticisms of Brill are couched obliquely in the form of the essays she sends him and the lectures she invites him to. Two of her ideas have particular significance for Brill. The first is embodied in her metaphor of 'the cannibal galaxy', 'megalosaurian colonies of primordial gases that devour smaller brother galaxies'. The metaphor awakens Brill to the cannibal galaxies in which his own dream of cultural fusion has been swallowed; for whilst he remained in the darkness of the convent cellar, Europe devoured his fellow Jews, just as now a terminally 'middling' middle America swallows up both cultural inheritances.

Hester's second idea relates more specifically to her daughter. At the heart of her thought is the idea that silence and invisibility are not 'nothing', but potentialities to be recognised and drawn out. This is the truth that Brill and his teachers are blind to in Beulah Lilt. Incapable of seeing beyond the brute reality before their eyes, the little girl is for them merely a 'low achiever'. Many years later, Brill is tormented by the belated recognition of his own blindness when Beulah becomes a celebrated painter, whose canvases apparently depict nothing, yet conjure up in the imagination an infinite number of associations. Her paintings, in fact, express artfully her mother's thesis that in 'nothingness' lies endless possibility. This is the profound truth which animates Judaism, with its belief in 'creation out of nothing', and which Brill has gradually forgotten along with the rest of his aspirations.

Ozick's novel would appear at one level to be a cautionary parable about the dangerous seductions of assimilation. Yet her writing is always far from crude moralizing, because it is itself implicated in the very condition of assimilation she is exploring. If Ozick's plots have something of the character of the simple Jewish homily, her style — breathlessly inventive, steeped in the modern Western tradition — does not. Few other writers draw out so vividly and subtly the complexities of living between cultures. J C

'Two worlds split him. A school that teaches Chumash and Rashi and Gemara is called a yeshiva; its head is called the Rosh Yeshiva. Whereas he, in his mock-Sorbonne, was a Principal and ran a Dual Curriculum. It could be done and yet it could not be done. Rather, it could be done only in imagination; in reality, it was all America, the children America, the teachers America, the very walls of the chair factory America. Egalitarianism — the lowest in the lead. And therefore all things lost to any hope of the patrician, himself the betrayer of Edmond Fleg.' p61

The Pagan Rabbi and other stories [English USA]

This collection comprises seven stories originally published separately over a period of ten years up to 1971; it constitutes a natural introduction to the exceptional, imaginative world of Cynthia Ozick's storytelling and marked the arrival on the scene of a new phase in Jewish-American fiction.

Unlike earlier writers Ozick is not concerned with the anxious accommodations of acculturating Jews finding their feet and their place in the new world. Ozick's characters inhabit a Jewish world which is geographically in America, which is linguistically English, (an English stretched to accommodate Jewish ways of thought, perceptions and cultural reference), and which is historically a contemporary development of the millennia-long Jewish experience. The tone is set in the story entitled *The Pagan Rabbi* which opens the collection. The narrator, the classmate, from a rabbinical seminary, of a brilliant rabbi who has hanged himself in a public park, visits the suicide's widow. His motives are a mixture of curiosity about his former companion and interest in the woman herself. From her he learns that Rabbi Isaac Kornfeld, her husband, had become a pagan. She gives him her husband's notebook to read in which Isaac plots his spiritual development and apostasy. Set naturalistically enough, in a familiar, contemporary world, the story dramatises the profound and ancient opposition between Judaism and the worship of the world. Ozick's story boldly presents the lure of paganism, which today we rarely refer to by that term, preferring a variety of humanistic, ecological and New Age concepts.

The effect is one of a giddying departure from the familiar everyday world into a heightened consciousness of the 'soul' of the world.

These are not stories for the faint-hearted or the unadventurous reader. Nor do they offer reassuringly familiar views of the Jewish world, such as those of I.B.Singer or Leo Rosten or even the more angst-ridden versions of Saul Bellow or Woody Allen. Instead the reader is surprised by stories in which what we might ordinarily think of as the miraculous or supernatural flow 'naturally' out of the everyday world. Lying at the heart of these stories are issues which have provided the contestants in Judaism's spiritual battleground for many centuries, i.e. Classical

Greek or Hellenistic ideas. In these stories they are unexpectedly 'real' and contemporary and initially familiar.

Such a piece is *The Dock Witch* in this collection, a woman who visits the departing liners in the New York docks, ostensibly the wife of a rather drab drugstore owner, but revealing herself in the course of a number of encounters with the narrator at the docks as a Siren-like creature in whose hands a washboard becomes a lyre, but whose final metamorphosis is into Undine, a water-spirit. As such she leaves the narrator and her husband, who knows her as Sylvia, by becoming the figurehead on an old sailing ship among others visiting the East River. T H

'The druggist's glance hopped from ship to ship.

Then I — too shy of what I sought to look so far — spied her: she hung nearly over our heads, she was an eave shadowing our heads, her hair streamed backward over her loins, her left hand clasped a lyre, her right hand made as if to pluck it but did not, her spine was clamped high upon the nearest prow. Although her eyes were wide, they were woodenly in trance: I had never known her in so pure a sleep.

"Undine!"

"Sylvia!" mocked the druggist.

"She doesn't answer."

"She won't," he responded with satisfaction. "You can go on home now, buddy."

"She won't answer?"

"Use your eyes, buddy. Does she look like she will?"

I saw the long and delicate grain in her thighs, the nodules in her straight wrists, the knots that circled and circled about her erect and exact nipples...

I flung back my neck and shouted up: "Undine"

A figurehead does not breathe.' (*The Dock-Witch*)

PEREC
Georges

W or The memory of childhood [W ou le souvenir d'enfance] [French France]

Perec was a renowned literary experimentalist, famous for his novel *A Void* which is written without recourse to the letter 'e'. Using this kind of constraint can make books turn out extremely strangely but in *W* even the more sceptical reader might start to see the point of such experiments.

Unlike much of his work, which has a light-hearted, irreal

tone, almost an extended joke by a very literate man, *W* is an exploration of very real and serious material.

It is an especially bold venture because Perec juggles and teases the bare facts and private memories of his own childhood to form a sort of autobiography that ends up as tremendously original and valid. His material is drawn from a tragic childhood; he was the son of Polish Jews in Nazi-occupied France; first his father died in the fighting during the Nazi invasion and then his mother was rounded up by French gendarmes and shipped off to a German death camp.

The boldness is in applying his extreme scepticism and creativity as a (distanced and aloof) writer to the facts of his own life and background. In the course of telling his story he disputes with and refutes his own memories; of school, of the farm where he found refuge, of relatives. The memories he has to interrogate are of course very sad ones; he shows great courage in examining in the light of mature reflection the roots of his own self.

The halting, fragmentary approach to autobiography in *W* is profoundly educational and will stimulate the reader in their own reconstruction of that essential part of their lives shrouded in the distant personal past.

What increases the impact of *W* is that interleaved with the 'childhood memory' is another seemingly unconnected story; a Utopian fantasy of a society based around sporting competition, a society in fact that take the idea of sport as a way of life and a moral project in itself to absurd and ghastly limits. It is a rather good satire of both Communist and Fascist authoritarianism as well as the darker aspects of the kind of bureaucratic carrot-and-stick democracy of 'The West'.

The moment where the two stories connect is shocking and brilliant. While one story is the personal testament of suffering the other is an acute analysis of the cultural and political roots of that suffering. This is a book written in the writer's own blood, and can only be admired and respected (and enjoyed). R K

'As for me, I would have liked to help my mother clear the dinner from the kitchen table. There would have been a blue, small-checked oilcloth on the table, and above it, a counterpoise lamp with a shade shaped almost like a plate, made of white porcelain or enamelled tin, and a pulley system with pear-shaped weights. Then I'd have fetched my satchel, got out my book and my writing pad and my wooden pencil-box. I'd have put them on the table and done my homework. That's what happened in the books I read at school.' p70

(from the autobiography strand)

'But even the most senior Athletes, even the doddery veterans who clown on the track in between races and are fed rotten vegetable stalks by the hilarious crowd, even they still believe that there is something else, that the sky can be bluer, the soup better, the Law less harsh; they believe that merit will be rewarded, that victory will smile on them, and be wonderful.' p140 (from the sport Utopia strand)

PERETZ
Isaac Loeb

The I.L.Peretz Reader [Yiddish Poland]

Selected stories of I.L.Peretz

Sholem Aleykhem popularised Yiddish writing more than any other writer, but I L Peretz (1852–1915) raised its literary status more than any other writer of his generation, and perhaps of subsequent generations as well. His great contribution was to fix Yiddish into the matrix of modern European culture, to adapt to prevailing literary influences and to produce a literature for the Jewish world of Eastern Europe that was undergoing radical modernisation.

The dilemma for Peretz, and the Jews in general, was that Europe both welcomed Jews and rejected them and that in turn Jews were attracted and repelled by what was on offer. The same world called for assimilation on the one hand but saw the spread of Pogroms* in Russia and the rise of anti-Semitic movements throughout the rest of Europe.

Although he later cared for and sought to influence his public, Peretz claimed that he began writing 'for my own pleasure and only according to my mood'. Eminent writer on Yiddish Ruth Wisse said that he turned to literature as a result of his dilemma, and turned his dilemma into literature. He was very dissatisfied with the limitations of the Yiddish language. In his early poem *Monish* (1888) for example, in which a handsome and brilliant young scholar sells his soul for fame, fortune and sex, Peretz complains that Yiddish lacked a vocabulary for the erotic.

Peretz developed a compressed, shorthand style, his sentences often unfinished. His style was direct, often didactic. His characters were more agents for his moral and social purposes, vehicles for expressing his ideas rather than for the display of the human condition or elaborated for their own sakes. He rejected humour, because it dissipated anxiety rather then harnessing it to social reform. Later on, occult elements entered his work, because here he believed he was drawing on elements of Jewish folk culture, and his work and personality became the battleground for warring forces of modernism and Jewish tradition. When he did deal with Jewish religious values, however, he sought to humanise them, and they were expressed with irony and scepticism.

The transcendent impulse was used as another means to improve the real world. Hence one of his most famous stories, *Bontshe the Silent*, can be interpreted in radically different ways. Bontshe is a worker who has led a bleak life, exploited and abused by his employers and his family, but who never complains. When he dies, however, he is immediately received into heaven, and even the Devil's Advocate is reduced to silence by the example of Bontshe's life. Bontshe is asked by the divine powers to name his reward, and all he asks for is a buttered roll to be provided every morning. Was Bontshe the holy fool, saintly Jewish martyr, uncorrupted even when faced with the delights of the next world? Or is he a revolutionary worker who knows that even the demand for the most basic needs will upset the prevailing order? Is he the oppressed human being who failed to articulate his needs during his life and is therefore unable to do so after his death? In that case there is no reward in the hereafter for the suffering in this life, and all should not be accepted as 'God's will.'

Peretz criticised Jewish society for its treatment of women. In his poem *The Three Seamstresses* which later became a popular song he depicts the oppression and the anger of the three women. Again, in the story *A Woman's Fury* published in 1893 he exposes a sexual division of labour, where the woman had to bear the physical burden of caring for the children and providing a livelihood, whilst the man bore the relatively weightless spiritual burden of religious duties and study.

Peretz was himself imprisoned for revolutionary activities in 1899 but nevertheless expressed his suspicion of the socialist future in his essay *Hope and Fear* published in 1906; 'There will be no empty stomachs, but souls will go hungry.' After his imprisonment, and absorbing neo-Romantic influences from European literature, he was drawn to Hasidism*, with its supernatural and mystical elements. For him Hasidic values themselves were spiritual and democratic, accessible to ordinary people, even if the actual Hasidim of his day he considered corrupt and obscurantist.

Sometimes these positive values had to be used even in revolt against God himself if he colluded in human oppression. In his play *The Golden Chain* (1906) the Hasidic Rabbi refuses to accept the end of the Sabbath, as this represents the world of freedom which is denied him and his followers in the workaday world. In consequence, he is replaced by his son and authority is restored. Later stories originally collected as *Hasidic Stories* in 1908 and *Folktales* in 1909 were based on traditional stories and seemed simple on the surface, but with a clear ideology underlining them — the ethic of liberalism replaced the divine imperative, Jewish morality triumphed over Christian authority and the powerless triumphed over the powerful. Emotionally, however, Peretz himself seems to have become increasingly seduced by the traditional values he sought to reject intellectually, and his writing inevitably lost some of its cutting edge. Nonetheless, for the 25 years before his death in 1915, when he lived in Warsaw, he was at the centre of the web of contemporary Jewish intellectual life.
B D

'Here on earth the death of Bontsha the Silent made no impression at all. Ask anyone: Who was Bontsha, how did he live, and how did he die? Did his strength slowly fade, did his heart slowly give out — or did the very marrow of his bones melt under the weight of his burdens? Who knows? Perhaps he just died from not eating — starvation, it's called.

If a horse, dragging a cart through the streets, should fall, people would run from blocks around to stare, newspapers would write about this fascinating event, a monument would be put up to mark the very spot where the horse had fallen. Had the horse belonged to a race as numerous as that of human beings, he wouldn't have been paid this honor. How many horses are there, after all? But human beings — there must be a thousand million of them!

Bontsha was a human being; he lived unknown, in silence, and in silence he died. He passed through our world like a shadow. When Bontsha was born no one took a drink of wine; there was no sound of glasses clinking. When he was confirmed he made no speech of celebration. He existed like a grain of sand at the rim of a vast ocean, amid millions of other grains of sand exactly similar, and when the wind at last lifted him up and carried him across to the other shore of that ocean, no-one noticed, no-one at all.

During his lifetime his feet left no mark upon the dust of the streets; after his death the wind blew away the board that marked his grave. The wife of the gravedigger came upon that bit of wood, lying far off from the grave, and she picked it up and used it to make a fire under the potatoes she was cooking; it was just right. Three days after Bontsha's death no one knew where he lay, neither the gravedigger nor anyone else. If Bontsha had had a headstone, someone, even after a hundred years, might have come across it, might still have been able to read the carved words, and his name, Bontsha the Silent, might not have vanished from this earth.

His likeness remained in no-one's memory, in no-one's heart. A shadow! Nothing! Finished!' (*Bontsha the Silent*)

PERUTZ
Leo

By Night under the Stone Bridge [Nachts unter der steinernen Brücke] [German Austria & Israel]

Leo Perutz was an immensely popular writer of the 1920s and 30s who was largely forgotten after his enforced emigration (he was Jewish) to Palestine after the *Anschluß* (the union of Austria with Nazi Germany in 1938). In the 1970s and 80s he was republished, and many new translations have recently appeared.

After his enforced emigration from Vienna in 1938, nothing by Perutz appeared until *By Night under the Stone Bridge* in 1953, subtitled 'A novel from old Prague'.

It consists of fourteen chapters, each of which is a novella complete in itself, using stories and legends of the Prague of Emperor Rudolf II (reign: 1576–1612). From the various novellas a story emerges, involving the most famous characters of sixteenth-century Prague: Emperor Rudolf himself, who was more interested in alchemy and art than in ruling, Rabbi Loew, with whom the legend of the *golem [a kind of Jewish version of Frankenstein – ed.]* is associated, and Mordechai Meisl, the fabulously wealthy Jew who financed Rudolf's art collection. But the real subject of the novel is Prague, especially the Prague ghetto, the destruction of which in the name of urban renewal the young Perutz observed as a schoolboy.

The linking story is the love of the Emperor for Esther, the beautiful wife of Mordechai Meisl, whom he saw when riding through the Jewish quarter. He calls Rabbi Loew and describes the woman, whose image will not leave him in peace. When the Rabbi replies that she is the wife of a Jew and cannot be his, Rudolf threatens to expel the Jews from all his lands. To protect the Jews, the Rabbi uses magic to fulfil the Emperor's desire: he plants a rose and a rosemary bush on the banks of the Moldau, under the great stone bridge, and says a magic formula over them. The two plants intertwine, and every night the Emperor dreams he is in Esther's arms. But, although only fulfilled in dreams, their love is still sinful, and the Lord sends the plague to the Jewish ghetto, until Rabbi Loew pulls up the rosemary bush and throws it into the Moldau.

Around this love story, which he weaves from a few delicate threads, Perutz has painted a lively picture of the Bohemian capital at the beginning of the seventeenth century, just before the religious wars were to deprive it of much of its glory. The ghetto, palaces, streets and squares are thronged with soldiers, beggars, minstrels, clowns, alchemists, nobles, among whom historical figures such as the astronomer Kepler and the young Wallenstein (a famous General in the Thirty Year's War) appear. It adds up to a portrait of a civilisation at its vigorous peak, with, behind it, constant reminders that the tragic end of Rudolf was the harbinger of the disasters and destruction of the Thirty Year's War. M M

'Young Waldstein (Wallenstein, ed.) smiled, his gloom had vanished, and he couldn't help thinking of Johannes Kepler, who had told him that not Mars but Venus was going to preside over his adventure.

"As the loveliest of all women has been pleased to choose me as her lover," he began, taking her hand...

"Don't misunderstand me," the loveliest of all women interrupted. "For one night," she said, freeing her hand and starting to fumble with her dark violet dress. "For one night only, captain, please note. Because I want to be free to do what I choose with myself. But that one night will be worth a hundred to you."

"If," said young Waldstein, without showing much disappointment, "if you have decided to make me your lover for tonight why will you not show me your face, so that I may caress it?"

"Because," said the lady, still fumbling with her dress, "I am more concerned than you think with my reputation...You can ask anything of me tonight, but the mask stays on."

She threw back her head, dropped her arms, and the dark velvet dress slipped to the floor.' p101

PRAGER
Emily

Eve's tattoo [English USA]

In 1989 the Communist government in Poland falls, Hungary opens its borders making it possible for East Germans to escape to the West, the Berlin Wall crumbles, Germany is on the verge of reunification, and Eve, on her fortieth birthday, has the camp number of an Auschwitz victim tattooed on her arm.

Eve's Tattoo is the story of Greenwich Village columnist Eve and her act of remembrance for victims of the Holocaust. In the ephemeral culture of late 1980s New York, where art and commerce are often indistinguishable, at least in the fashionable artistic circles in which Eve socialises and works, the concerns of Europe, present and past, are viewed from a safe and cynical distance. For Eve's coterie of friends and acquaintances historic events are experienced via cable television, with an accompanying aestheticising and anaesthetising effect

Her act of remembrance shocks those she meets into a recognition of the relevance of the Holocaust to their lives. The Holocaust acts as a historical anchor for the current European political and social upheavals. Perhaps more importantly in the book's schema, the Holocaust is made relevant to America as well as to Europe.

By tattooing *500123* on her arm, Eve identifies with a Holocaust victim she names Eva. Eva is a composite of identities, an amalgamation of different people Eve has researched, each with a personal history that leads to internment and death in Auschwitz. Relating these versions of Eva, Eve turns herself into a living memorial, re-humanising victims that might otherwise be remembered only as the Nazis wished: "What responsibility do you and I have to a mound of skeletons in a mass grave murdered before we were conceived? None. But to the people those skeletons once were? Infinite." Literally possessed by Eva's identities Eve creates a painful consciousness of the Holocaust in a culture where history usually only happens on television and where it is too easily digestible and forgotten. Making it difficult to forget for some, for others, she unearths past lives perhaps too difficult to remember.

Significantly, only one of Eva's identities is Jewish, a woman hiding in Berlin with her baby, who is eventually discovered and sent to Auschwitz. The others find themselves on the other side of citizenship as they resist the Nazi regime in their own personal ways, but with fatal consequences meted out in the gas chambers. 'Eva the doctor' subverts the sterilisation programs and performs illegal abortions. 'Eva the Catholic charity worker' works with dispossessed Jews and protests against the euthanasia programs. 'Eva, the eccentric old spinster', saves the pets of deported Jews only to sell them back to the SS as thorough-bred pedigrees.

Finally, Leni Essen, discovered to be the real owner of the tattooed number, is, ironically, an enthusiastic Nazi. A working-class widow who sought to climb the social ladder through ignorant but fervent and proud conformity to the regime. Only when the SS arrest and hang her teenage sons for their subversive political activities does she resist. Stabbing the SS officer (whom she happens to be dating) overseeing their executions leads to her arrest. A bureaucratic mix-up sends her to the gas chambers. Eva's various crimes against the state are gender-related. Eva collectively feels the machinations of the state foremost as a woman as the state seeks to control her body through its definition of female citizenship.

By examining the Holocaust through the context of gender Prager is able to examine the relationship between women and the nation-state — a relation that allows an implied comparison with late 1980s America. Prager implicitly suggests that, when it seeks to control the bodies of women by dictating abortion and motherhood rights, the state, wittingly or unwittingly, follows a totalitarian precedent. This introduces a dimension of the book that is not without controversy!

While the idea of a living memorial to the Holocaust is a worthy concept, which is, by definition, difficult to forget, Prager also introduces a comparative dimension to discussions of the Holocaust. Is it really possible to empathise with the victims of the Holocaust, as Eve believes she can? Can we really, fully understand their experiences and compare them with our own? Embodying Holocaust victims as Eve does suggests that she has given herself some kind of historical ballast in an age when identity is very much determined by fashion. Perhaps memories of the Holocaust are needed to anchor and counterbalance the ephemeral and superficial American culture of the 1980s.

Eventually the tattoo is erased during surgery following a serious accident that befalls Eve the columnist. This is not the exorcism of Eva from Eve, but a register of the temporary nature of memory itself. Whatever liberties Prager's book seems to take she recognises at least that no memory can be completely recreated and that we cannot totally possess and appropriate the experiences of others. R C

'Eve looked down at the number on her forearm and then up at the party around her. The drunken starlet was perched on the knee of a novelist in his mid-forties who was talking loudly about his absent wife. Moluk had arrived and the first novelists were genuflecting before him as he spoke delightedly about a black kid who tried to sell him crack and with whom he talked Kafka.

In the corner, the fiction editor was hovering over a celebrated literary couple like a giant crow over a shiny bauble. The female of the couple was saying, "So I went to Fred Segal to try and get something to wear to the Oscars. I felt I was representing the literary community and I should look smart, no? But all they had were bras studded with spikes. So militaristic, this modern sexuality." The fiction editor laughed uproariously, as did the development women, who, when they heard the word Oscars, immediately homed in like pigeons to their roost. Eve ran her finger over the tattoo and began, "Eva Berg was a gynaecologist in Berlin when the Nazis came to power, a gynaecologist and obstetrician."... "Eve had obtained her degree at the height of the suffragette movement in Weimar Germany. She had thought she would dedicate her life to the eradication of certain female diseases that she was studying in the laboratory adjacent to her office. She had planned on it, in fact. So it came as a great shock to her when the Nazis got in, and, in 1933, stripped women of the rights they had won, outlawed birth control, instituted a whole raft of invasive laws, and made the performing of abortions a treasonable offense. Through no fault of her own, Eva, an upstanding citizen, suddenly became a fighter on the female front lines.'" p63-4

PRESSBURGER
Giorgio

The Law of White Spaces [La legge degli spazi bianchi] [Italian Hungary & Italy]

These five stories, set mainly in the poverty-stricken, sometimes chaotic Budapest of before and just after World War Two, form a series of reflections on illness and its resonances in our feelings. This is an unusual theme for literature and one that gives the stories a fresh, revelatory force.

The title piece shows a doctor afflicted with a disease that makes his memory slip away from him literally word by word until he comes to believe that meaning really resides not in words but in the white spaces between words... The strange tale *Vera* illustrates a similar disturbance of outer and inner worlds. As in much of Pressburger's writing, a lot of the main action takes place out of frame. In this sense Pressburger's work is like that of S.Y. Agnon, another Jewish writer also originally from Mitteleuropa. Agnon was described as having 'a deliberately restrained tone of narration'. This restraint, this delicacy in the face of individual tragedy and the general loss of war and social dislocation also marks Pressburger's tone. Both writers' work is set against the background of a world that no longer exists; their writing and their memories are, practically speaking, all that remains of it. Perhaps it is this great sadness, indirectly reflected in their stories, that makes the stories more than they appear to be at first glance. R K

'He was a swift worker; no one else could set as many ens per hour as he could. Typographical errors were unknown to him. He could decipher the most garbled manuscripts. And no spelling mistake ever escaped him, no matter how deeply buried in the work of some poet or novelist. He would sit at his machine for thirteen, fourteen hours a day. With his pliers he would pull the tiny pieces of lead, each one embossed with a letter, from the packed wooden cases, and from there slide them into position in lines of type. The thoughts enclosed in each symbol by his own two hands danced before his eyes; and no messages born in dark rooms would find their way in the hands of other people into sumptuous buildings.' p155

PRESSBURGER
Giorgio & Nicola

The Green Elephant [L'Elefante verde] [Italian Hungary & Italy]

Like *Homage to the Eighth District* and *The Law of White Spaces* also by the Pressburgers this book emerges from memories of a poor Jewish Budapest in the period from the end of the First World War to the end of the second — which doesn't at all convey that behind its simple storytelling is a profound and rather magical reflection on life and on the burden or gift of parental expectations.

This charming novella, told mainly through a child's eyes, is secretly an essay on a strand that has deeply marked exceptional Jews throughout the last few centuries; the messianic, utopian, far-seeing urge that often possesses them; something born out of the combination of the notion of a Chosen People, their relative sophistication in a world of ignorant peasants and feckless aristocrats and the actual limitation on what Jews were allowed to do in a universe of hostility and discrimination. A yearning for a better, holier, richer, wider life thus became deeply ingrained and the dream of the Green Elephant that is the keynote of this book seems to be a beautiful literary reflection of the rich and felicitously mad idea many Jews have had that the world will/can/must change for the better.

The writing of *The Green Elephant* is in a peculiarly exalted vein and as sweet and pungent as a *heimishe* pickled cucumber and well reflected by the marvellous jacket design by Graham Peake. Our glimpse into District Eight — a substantially Jewish area of pre-war Budapest — develops into a *Kaddish* (the Jewish prayer for the dead) for Europe's Lost Tribe, an elegiac, fanciful and beautiful tribute. A book about twins, written by twins an honest parable about the desire *not* to be chosen of the exceptional and gifted person who resists the responsibility that exceptional intelligence, subtlety or beauty demands. R K

'The young couple went to live in Kun Street, near the Teleky market, in a single alley-like room which stretched from the railings overlooking the court-yard on the inside of the house to the external wall on the other side, into which was set the only window. It was a poor dwelling: the only thing that made it bearable was the knowledge that the other Jews of the Eighth District were no better off. The wedding bed was a present from Rachel's mother. There was little else in the way of furniture: a chest of drawers, a table, one or two chairs and a radio with a green-lit dial completed the set-up. A cupboard in the middle of the room gave them somewhere to store their kitchen uten-sils. The kitchen stove just sat inside the door; its red glow lit up the room in the cold winter evenings as the couple rested after a long day's work.' p47

PROUST
Marcel

In Search of Lost Time [A la recherche du temps perdu] [French France]

This long novel is about a young man growing up in Paris in the last years of the nineteenth and the first years of the twentieth century, how he discovers art and artists and how he becomes a novelist. But it is also a wonderfully rich and often very funny book about French aristocratic society, its hangers-on and its servants, about love and its torments — both heterosexual and homosexual — and about solitude, the passing of time and the approach of death.

We meet Marcel as a boy, at his great-aunt's house at Combray in the French countryside. He is a sensitive boy, always longing for his mother's goodnight kiss, but very aware too of the places and people around him. (In many ways the book follows Proust's own life).

In one direction from their house — the 'Guermantes way' — lies the house of an ancient aristocratic family; in the other — 'Swann's way' — lies the house of a family friend, Swann, who is rather looked down on by Marcel's middle-class family, but is actually a close friend of the Duchesse de Guermantes and a member of the smartest Parisian society.

Another figure who looms up in the young Marcel's life is the family servant, Françoise, who can sit weeping buckets over the account of a disease in a medical encyclopaedia while the kitchen-maid is presently lying suffering agony from that very same condition. This is a tragi-comic example of the disturbing disconnections in life that begin to haunt Marcel and that one day his novel will set out to overcome.

There is a flashback now to Swann's life as a younger man and his love-affair in Paris with a beautiful courtesan, Odette. We realise that the real Odette is totally different from the Odette that haunts Swann's imagination — another failure of connection, and one that presages Marcel's own later experiences in love.

On holiday at Balbec, on the Normandy coast, Marcel starts to make acquaintance with the Guermantes' world and is soon absorbed by the fascination and brilliance of so many of the people he meets. There is the Duchesse de Guermantes herself, who has become queen of *Le Faubourg*, or aristocratic quarter of Paris through her wit and the dashing parties she gives. But she is completely heartless — one night when she is going out she cannot stop to talk to Swann, who is dying, but comes back again instead to change her shoes. Another striking figure is the mysterious, snobbish Baron de Charlus, whose homosexual leanings are dramatically revealed to Marcel one afternoon. We get much intriguing gossip about the Guermantes circle. Then there are the aspiring outsiders like Madame Verdurin, with her artistic salon and her extravagant raptures over music. Marcel meets the fictional counterpart of musicians like Debussy, various Impressionist painters and writers like Sainte-Beuve.

At Balbec, Marcel also meets and falls in love with Albertine, one of a group of young cyclists on holiday there. Their love affair goes through many complicated vicissitudes, with Marcel thinking all the time that he does not really know her or understand her feelings, and fearing with acute jealousy that she is also having lesbian love affairs.

Marcel becomes obsessed with feelings of separateness and loss. Time slowly erodes his life away until one day, years later, he tastes a little cake, a madeleine, that has been dipped in tea. Suddenly he remembers how his aunt would give him just the same thing when he was a child — and with it, a whole wealth of memories floods back. He begins to see how he can write the book he has always dreamed of writing, in which all his experience — the passion and joy, the comedy and the pain — can be restored and brought together. It will represent the conquest of time. In its pages, Swann's way will link up for ever with the Guermantes way. Marcel's book is, of course, the book, so elaborate in style and so abundant in life, that we have been reading. D M

'And as soon as I had recognised the taste of the piece of madeleine soaked in her decoction of lime-blossom which my aunt used to give me, immediately the old grey house upon the street, where her room was, rose up like a stage set...In that moment all the flowers in our garden and in M.Swann's park, and the water-lilies on the Vivonne and the good folk of the village and their little dwellings and the parish church and the whole of Combray and its surroundings. taking shape and solidity, sprang into being, town and gardens alike, from my cup of tea.' *(In Search of Lost Time Vol. 1)* p54-55

(The Duc de Guermantes is talking to the dying Swann while the Duchess is changing her shoes before they leave for a party.)

'"Besides, I tell you frankly, I'm dying of hunger. I had a wretched luncheon this morning when I came from the train...Five minutes to eight! Ah, women! She'll give us both indigestion before tomorrow. She's not nearly as strong as people think." The Duke felt no compunction in speaking thus of his wife's ailments and his own to a dying man, for the former interested him more, and therefore appeared to him more important...' *(In Search of Lost Time Vol.3)* p690-691

A note on the Jewish Proust

If you read Proust's *In Search of Lost Time*, you may get an inkling of why few people realise that Marcel Proust was Jewish: the novel returns recurrently to the notorious 'Dreyfus Affair' and its effects on French society and we learn of the particular shape of anti-Semitism in turn of the century France. From the enormous scandal of the Dreyfus Affair we can perhaps infer why the French Establishment might have hesitated to declare that Proust, writing from the 1890s until his death in 1922, was at once France's most exceptional and in some ways most French prose writer *and* a Jew.

Alfred Dreyfus, a French army officer from Alsace and son of a Jewish manufacturer, was accused in 1893 of treason (passing information affecting national security to Germany). He was court-martialled and sent to Devil's Island for life. It eventually turned out that the Chief of Military Intelligence, no less, had forged the documents which convicted Dreyfus and that the French War Office had knowingly suppressed evidence incriminating another officer. The case was retried (in a military court) and Dreyfus was again declared guilty but then pardoned by the new French President and allowed back to France, but with his life and reputation to all intents and purposes destroyed.

The Dreyfus Affair was the O.J.Simpson trial of the 1890s in that everyone from duke to doorman had an opinion as to whether Dreyfus was guilty or innocent. The issue divided France along new lines, with significant effects. Proust's book focuses on the small and large treacheries of Parisian high society at this time, charting Swann's gradual marginalisation as he, a highly cultured, highly assimilated Jew, gets turned away first from the *salon* of the Prince de Guermantes, then from that of the Duc de Guermantes. Swann, as a Jew, is of course pro-Dreyfus, and through attitudes to him is revealed one of the key contradictions of anti-Semitism: how, muses the Duc de Guermantes, can this man who yearly sends me the best port in the world and who is so cultured and respected, fall into the 'aberration' of openly declaring Dreyfus' innocence? More French than the French and yet 'an unpatriotic outsider', that is the paradox which inflames this particular anti-Semitism.

Proust, with his characteristic interest in inversion and instability, charts how *l'Affaire Dreyfus* gave rise to a social mobility which had not previously existed. Whether one was bourgeois or aristocratic — previously the prime social markers — became less important than one's alignment in *l'Affaire* — as long as one was nationalist and anti-Semitic, one had access to the most illustrious circles. Then of course the tide turns, as it always does in Proust, and *dreyfusisme* becomes a social accessory. So the Dreyfus Affair redraws the map of social hierarchy and political influence in ways that are irreversible in France, and for a time tingeing other political positions with a *dreyfusard* or anti-*dreyfusard* character.

Quite apart from the dissection of the Dreyfus Affair at numerous points in the novel, Proust's Jewish heritage shows in his position as both insider and outsider, spectator and actor, particularly acute at social commentary for never fully belonging. This marginality perhaps makes him particularly aware of the instability or volatility of political factions, of tastes, of the self and of sexuality. Few characters in *In Search of Lost Time* and few actions ever simply subsist without some surprising displacement or inversion: the Baron de Charlus surprisingly frequents a bourgeois rather than an aristocratic salon, the reason being that he is stalking Morel; lesbianism surfaces throughout the novel; motivations are never what they appear; even the intimacy of a kiss (Marcel and Albertine) is progressively deferred as face moves closer to face but at the same time the possession of the other is lost in a mass of detail of skin and looming shapes. In all this, Proust is a true modernist, following psychology and social commentary to their limits whereupon they become something quite other, unknowable, volatile, infinitely intricate. S B

RABON
Israel

The Street [Di gas] [Yiddish Poland]

Amongst the greatest European novels of the century is Norwegian Knut Hamsun's *Hunger*, the gripping story of a man struggling from one day to the next in a world that grudges him his merest existence. Israel Rabon's book was influenced by the widely-translated Hamsun and is no mean tribute to it. It is the highly-readable story of an unemployed ex-soldier in 1920s Poland, at that time the heartland of Yiddish literature. The Poland Rabon presents us with is largely his home town of dreary industrial Lodz, a textile centre with important Jewish and German populations. He shows us Łodz as a wasteland badly affected by World War One and inhabited by despair and fierce mutual enmity between its Polish, German and Jewish citizens.

The classic experiences of 1920s Depression literature are all here; sleeping in damp basements, being recruited as a strike-breaker, parading the streets clothed in advertising boards, ending up in the municipal poor house... Like Hamsun's *Hunger* Rabon's *The Street* has the desperate authenticity of lived — and long and tiresomely lived — direct experience. *The Street* is a book giving us the unvarnished truth, the smell and texture of the Poland of the badly-off. The scenes in the poor house ('Beggar's House') are familiar from George Orwell's masterpiece of vagabondage *Down and Out in Paris and London*; the outcastes, the elusive stories of work available, the rumours of plenty in the next town or the one after that, the ways of getting around 'the system' so as to obtain extra soup or be able to keep out of the cold for a little longer...

The picture fills out with descriptions of Rabon's experiences in the Russo-Polish war of 1921-22, also described by another Jewish writer, Isaac Babel, but from the Russian side, while another of the book's characters — a circus strongman — has lived and fought through Bela Kuhn's Hungarian Revolution, a short lived Communist regime of 1919, and provides a fascinating coda of both romantic adventure and political savagery.

The Street is not yet an established Yiddish classic and has only quite recently (1985) been translated into English. It's subject matter is very far from the sentimental *Yiddishkeit* (Yiddish Jewishness) or the Chagall-painted 'Shtetl-land' Yiddish literature is assumed to contain. In fact it demonstrates that there was by 1928 an emerging urban, fully modern and complete literature only snuffed out, as was Rabon's life, by the German war criminals. R K

'As a matter of fact, Fabianik was German.

His mother, Stepha, had lived with a German noncommissioned officer during the occupation of Poland, and it was he who had fathered the boy.

The poor child was hated by everyone. But he was most particularly detested by the old shoemaker.

Fabianik, a weak child with a narrow chest and a large round head perched on a long slender neck, was the butt of the children's most casual anger. They cursed him, tormented him and beat him. It was a dreadful sight to see the children or the old man mauling him with hands, fists, belts, sticks — anything within reach. Always he was called the Schwab — the Swabian — rather than Fabianik. If something was lost, it was the Schwab who had taken it. If something was broken, it was the Schwab who had done it. By the time he was three Fabianik had learned not to cry, as if he understood that tears would do him no good. Child though he was, he accepted that it was his destiny to be beaten, cursed, and tormented for no better reason than he was a Schwab, a German. The boy endured silently and calmly the blows that came his way and though his eyes might plead for compassion, there was never a trace — not so much as a gleam — of a single tear in them.

Because the children were ashamed to play with him, he acquired the habit of being alone. Isolated from them all, he had his secret dark corners where he made dolls out of bits of dough, where he kneaded animals and people out of clay. If the children intruded on his hiding places and disturbed him or stole his nests of animals, he pretended to ignore them and, without scowling, went quietly off to find some other hiding place where he began again to collect dough and clay with which to make his collection of lions, horses, people, and cats. Not the slightest trace of pain or sorrow in his dull, immobile face; in his soul every impulse of protest, of resistance against torment, had been uprooted.

I had occasion to notice that Fabianik avoided sunlight. He was drawn to the dark. To shadows. To whatever was veiled and obscure. He avoided the clear light of the day, as if he feared he might be noticed—seen. And Fabianik was not supposed to be seen. Was supposed to keep his distance. Because he was a Schwab.' p13-14

The Apprenticeship Of Duddy Kravitz [English Canada]

Following from an earlier American tradition of *The Rise of David Levinsky* by Abraham Cahan, *The Education of Hyman Kaplan* by Leo Rosten and *The Adventures of Augie March* by Saul Bellow, *The Apprenticeship of Duddy Kravitz* chronicles the emergence, here in a comic vein, of its young hero from Montreal's Jewish ghetto. Born on the wrong side of the tracks with a rusty spoon in his mouth and the spark of rebellion about him, Duddy races across those tracks and rebels against all forms of silver-spooned authority. In his persistent drive towards entrepreneurial triumph he frequently has to retrace his steps, double-cross his friends, and trip up anyone who stands in his way, lest he himself be tripped up by a society that blocks his path at every turn.

Captivated by his grandfather's dictum that 'a man without land is nobody', Duddy's obsession to own land leads to his possession as if by a *dybbuk**, by the wandering soul not only of his uncle and grandfather, but of all his ghettoised European ancestors denied ownership of land. With this guiding force underpinning his every act, Duddy leaves an ignominious school career behind and lunges with vulgarian force towards entrepreneurship and economic power.

Beginning humbly by fleecing guests with a roulette wheel while working in a Catskills mountain resort, Duddy enters the film business, employing a gin-soaked director to record Montreal's various barmitzvah celebrations. The ensuing films, studies in comparative tribal initiations, complete with African circumcision ceremonies, are declared 'a most edifying experience' by a bemused Rabbi and with the money earned from this venture, Duddy pursues the real estate around a magnificent lake with dreams of running his own resort.

Diversifying all the time, from pinball machines to film rental and distribution, Duddy gains control of the land with the help of Yvette, his Polish girlfriend and Virgil, an epileptic simpleton. It is in respect of these latter relationships that the book asks its most serious questions and intrudes upon the same territory as Saul Bellow's *Seize the Day*. In his sustained exploitation of both Yvette and Virgil, Duddy's once noble quest is rendered ignoble as Richler forces us to consider what happens when success is measured by material gain only rather than by considering morality, ethics and the state of one's soul.

Richler has here created the Jewish-Canadian novel. As Canadian and Jewish, he is a doubly alienated minority writer who is forced to be more caustic in his mockery of the majority. As a Jew he is barred from a rigidly stratified society of Canadian Gentiles and as a Canadian, he is denied acceptance in the Jewish-American mainstream. What Richler creates then is a Jewish-Canadian comedy of cultural revenge. The lineage of his characters does not go back to the 'little man' of the *shtetl**** who cowered before hostile Cossacks but to the rogues of Isaac Babel's *Odessa Tales*, whose vulgar physicality and bold defiance of the law shocked fastidious Jews and Gentiles alike. Richler's urban comedy, with its unbuttoned candour, schoolboy irreverence and gutter literalness, ridicules the faithful and taunts the squeamish. Uncovering the venal within the venerable, it exposes the earthly fallibility of the seemingly virtuous. A G

"'Why didn't you have time for me?"

"Because you're a pusherke. A little Jew-boy on the make. Guys like you make me sick and ashamed."

"You lousy intelligent people! You lying sons-of-bitches with your books and your socialism and your sneers. You give me one long pain in the ass. You think I never read a book? I've read books. I've got friends who read them by the ton. A big deal. What's so special in them? They all make fun of guys like me. Pusherkes. What a bunch you are! What a pack of crap-artists! Writing and reading books that make fun of people like me. Guys who want to get somewhere. If you're so concerned, how come in real life you never have time for me? It's easy for you to sit here and ridicule and make superior little jokes because you know more than me, but what about a helping hand? When did you ever put yourself out one inch for me? Never. It's the same with all you intelligent people. You never take your hand out of your pockets to a guy like me except when it's got a knife in it. You think I should be running after something else besides money? Good. Tell me what. Tell me, you bastard. I want some land, Uncle Benjy. I'm going to own a place one day. King of the castle, that's me. And there won't be any superior drecks there to laugh at me or run me off. That's just about the size of it.'"

RICHLER
Mordecai

Solomon Gursky Was Here [English Canada]

Richler's ambitious novel is a sprawling, international and multidimensional affair. In it we follow the fortunes of the Gursky family, a Canadian-Jewish family the origins of whose considerable fortune lie in the Prohibition days of contraband whiskey-smuggling. Its richness derives from the improbable juxtapositions that result, as his ineffably Jewish characters struggle, and more often than not flourish, in the *milieux* of the nineteenth-century exploration of the Arctic wastes; in the indifference, alternating with anti-Semitic hostility, of French Canada; and in the jaded aristocratic salons of contemporary London. But their vicissitudes — even when the result of their own susceptibility to ambition, lust, and reckless extravagance — are instantly recognisable as universal human propensities. This is what justifies Richler in gloriously defying the straitening conventions of political correctness (as he rarely loses a chance of doing).

When such earthiness is then brought into contact with moments of mysticism, the result, rather than diminishing the merely human and quotidian, is to humanise mystery; in fact Richler's novel shares this power with the best of 'magic realism', and its unlikely cast and setting only heightens the effect. It's also often desperately funny! P C

'...without warning an exasperated Mr. Bernard strode toward him, unzipped his fly, yanked out his penis, and shook it in his son's face. "I want you to know, you whore-master, that in all my years this has only been into your mother, God bless her," and zipping up again, tearful, adding, "and to this day she has the only c*nt still good enough for Bernard Gursky. Respect. Dignity. That you still have to learn. Animal."' p265

ROSTEN
Leo

The Education of Hyman Kaplan [English USA]

An hilarious look at both teaching and learning the English language, this book manages to convey all of the frustrations, contradictions and misnomers of English through the lens of Hyman Kaplan, the enthusiastic immigrant student who, with his thick Middle-European accent, somehow contrives to learn without making progress and in so doing turns the tables by rendering his long-suffering teacher, Mr. Parkhill, speechless.

Rather than a sequence of events, the plot follows Kaplan and his classmates through an academic year, each chapter acting as a single lesson on the elements of language: vocabulary, pronunciation, tenses, verbs, comprehension. It is Hyman Kaplan's numerous interjections and enthusiastic suggestions, however, which turn what would be an ordinary evening class into a study in consistent misunderstanding and malapropism. Hyman Kaplan's charm is that, while his answers are not always correct, an essential hysterical truth which it is hard to deny lies behind his mistakes.

For instance, when asked to name the opposite of new, Kaplan replies 'second-hand'. When asked to decline the verb 'to fail' his reply is 'fail, failed, bankrupt'. His refusal to be interrupted which infuriates the bewildered Mr. Parkhill point to a casual indifference on Kaplan's part. Why should he follow the usual maxims of conversation? Kaplan has his own plans for conquering America!

Every new idea introduced by Mr Parkhill is examined in fine Talmudic detail by the unsatisfied Kaplan. When learning about homonyms he interrupts his distraught teacher to inquire 'how eet ees possible thet Mary's littel lemb hes fleas as white as snow?'. Kaplan takes on the full moral force of the language he is learning. In one memorable episode a fellow student's life story is interrupted by Kaplan's polemic against citizenship and the U.S. immigration service. Although presented as the immigrant everyman, an unmistakable Jewish pattern lurks in Hyman Kaplan's thought patterns. Even his comments on history are attempts to Judaize American icons. On the *Gettysburg Address* he remarks: 'Abram Lincohen vas soch a schlemiel telling all the pipples ver he liffd!'.

While it remains a classic of linguistic anomalies, the book is actually about a relationship; between pupil and teacher and the simple fact that both, in the end learn from each other. The former begins to understand the glorious complexity of the English language, while the latter learns that communication between human beings relies more on passion and positive intent than just plain speech. As for the reader, it is an adventure back into the classroom and a reminder that while we take the mother tongue for granted, many of our immigrant ancestors could not. Hyman Kaplan is an undoubted link to those ancestors and a delightful rejoinder to those who forget we all have to start somewhere. A G

'Mr Kaplan rubbed his chin."In voibs, vhat does de beginnis cless nid? Just de prazant tanse, de pest, an' de future. Dat's enof for a lifetime!"

Mr Parkhill tried to repress his dismay."You mean you would erase all of the tenses except past, present and future?!"

"Mit' plashure."

"But so many of the other tenses and moods — are so valuable!"

"Bendages are weluable too," mused Mr. Kaplan,"if you are bliddink. But if you are not bliddink, iven in a finger, vhy bendage op de whole hend?"

Mr Parkhill gazed with falling affection and failing pride upon that impressive aggregation: the staunch "shall have's, the bold "shall have beens". He felt awful.'

ROTH
Henry

Call it Sleep [English USA]

This is the famous New York immigration epic written by a poor young Jewish hopeful in 1934. The family language in this story of a lad growing up in squalor is a charming English version of the Yiddish Roth's Bronx family actually spoke. The poet Baudelaire famously said 'genius is childhood recollected at will' and Roth really seems to have a perfectly convincing, even an enthralling recall of his childhood consciousness. A total recall that he transmits to us with a striking command of language, for example watching his mother in the kitchen; 'There was a pause while she emptied the dishpan into the sink; the grey water muttered down the drain.'

In fact the tender relationship between mother and son, protecting each other from a harsh and irascible husband and father is the delicate heart of the book. Also in the family equation is the outrageous and funny Aunt Bertha, with her ironic take on the wonders of America. She and David, the Henry-Roth-as-a-boy figure are very recognisably Jewish characters; he clever but anxious — a loner; 'he neveh hengs oud wid nobody' — she sarky and rebellious.

It was clearly in what is currently called a 'dysfunctional family' that Roth's talent and story emerged; his emotional development has only three notes; dreamy adoration of his mother, fear of his harsh anti-social father and, above all, anxiety. Roth even reaches back into childhood to describe the 'birth of anxiety' in his soul and, after a set-piece family argument between father, mother and aunt where all kinds of terrible grudges and hatreds going back years get an airing David is left 'feeling himself caught as if in talons of stress'.

Call it Sleep, sixty four years after first seeing the light of day remains a sustained and fascinating child's vision of what is, in a way, the childhood of America. The effort of distilling it on the page (and criticism from his literary comrades in the Communist Party for its emotiveness) left the young Roth blocked as a writer until old age when, after years of completely different work, including being a duck farmer he started to write again. R K

'Hurt, David had turned away and gotten out his box in the pantry in which he saved both the calendar leaves he collected and whatever striking odds and ends he found in the street. His mother called them his gems and often asked him why he liked things that were worn and old. It would have been hard to tell her. But there was something about the way in which the link of chain was worn or the thread on a bolt or a castor-wheel that gave him a vague feeling of pain when he ran his fingers over them. They were like worn shoe-soles or very thin dimes. You never saw them wear, you only knew they were worn, obscurely aching.' p35

ROTH
Joseph

Job. The story of a simple man [Hiob, Roman eines einfachen Mannes] [German Ausria]

The Biblical story of Job is one of the most puzzling and challenging books of the Bible: Job was 'perfect and upright, one that feared God and eschewed evil', as the Good Book has it. Yet God made him suffer terribly. Why? No answer. In the Western tradition Job is a paradigm of undeserved and incomprehensible suffering and something of an outrage to our earthly sense of justice.

Joseph Roth's version has the Biblical Job transposed to turn-of-the-century Russia, where Mendel Singer lives crammed into his one-roomed hut with wife Deborah and four children. Pious and God-fearing, like any number of Jews of the *shtetl* * Mendel Singer ekes out a living teaching the Torah — and does not complain.

But then the disasters start, and the story of a modern-day Job bewildered before his God serves as shorthand for the story of the Jews of Russia (but maybe also for the history of the Jews across the ages): unjustly persecuted and exiled, impoverished and weighed down with personal grief.

The sufferings start with very private ones; the loveless, ugly relation between Mendel and his wife, shackled together in 'faithful enmity' or, as Mendel experiences it, 'a disease bound to him by day and by night'. By the end of this short novel the sufferings have grown to tragic proportions with a mounting series of calamities: the sons are drafted (until the mid-1850s Jewish boys could be conscripted into the army at the age of twelve), Mendel's beautiful daughter Miriam spends her evenings with the feared and hated Cossacks, the youngest son Menuchim is epileptic and therefore shunned... Finally the family, deserting the sick Menuchim, head for New York — where further misery awaits them.

Roth's prose has a lyrical quality which seems distilled out of suffering, and which lends a calmness to a book which would otherwise be a writhing cry of despair; it reads like a colourful nightmare narrated the morning after, shadowed by the emotions of the night but having passed beyond them.

Nowhere is Roth's literary craft more evident than in how he makes palpable a character who hardly takes up any page space at all: the abandoned epileptic child Menuchim, presumed dead and, more gruesomely, presumed burnt alive, helpless in a house fire back in Russia. Roth depicts how loss and guilt follow Mendel and Deborah around, besetting them when they least anticipate it (Mendel, improbably, thinks he hears the whimpering of Menuchim in a back alley, Deborah feels something is missing but can't quite define what), and how therefore from the very start their new world is unbearably haunted by the old.

This is, then, a Job who *has* sinned. All the more poignant, then, the final, moving sections, so carefully yet unobtrusively prepared for: we are at a Passover Seder, when unexpectedly through the door opened to Elijah (a harbinger of redemption) — something stirs. Like a light touch which says everything will be all right, Mendel's world is transformed for ever — and we are left facing the wide blue of the sea and the bright white sands of America's West Coast where Mendel has — literally and figuratively — been transported. S B

'Mendel remembered the ageing grey snow that edged the wooden pavement of the sidewalks at this time of year in Zuchnow. He remembered the crystal icicles which hung from the faucets; the sudden, soft rains which sang in the gutters of the eaves the whole night long. He remembered the distant thunder rolling far away behind the fir forest, the white rime which tenderly decked each bright blue morning. He remembered Menuchim, whom Miriam had stuck into a roomy vat in order to get him out of the way, and he remembered the hope that at last, at last, in this year the Messiah would come.

He had not come. He did not come, thought Mendel; he will not come. Let others await him. Mendel did not.' p200-1

ROTH
Philip

Portnoy's Complaint [English USA]

If Franz Kafka set out to present an external labyrinth of unknown enemies in *The Trial*, then *Portnoy's Complaint* adds a further chapter by exploring the internal labyrinth of ethics and sexuality the Jewish male must navigate. Part comedy but mainly psycho-tragedy, Philip Roth built this book, his defining novel, on a monologue of such extraordinary venom that the reader is continually blown off-balance by the force of its intent.

In telling the story of his sexual and other frustrations to his psychoanalyst, thirty three year-old Alexander Portnoy explodes into a cruel, obscene and comic fantasy. Roth is brutally satirical in his dissection of the 'all-devouring Jewish mother', ascribing Portnoy's abuses of and perverse desires for women to her suffocating intensity. His onanistic evocations are vulgarly provocative; in particular, Portnoy's employment of the family dinner as sexual stimulant is breathtaking in its daring. It is only with Dr. Spielvogel's final statement 'Now ve may perhaps to begin' that we understand the vital necessity of Portnoy's catharsis. As Roth himself predicted, his book aroused a storm of protest, but increased his reputation, both at home and abroad

Accused of self-hatred and anti-Semitism, Roth claims affinity with Kafka in suffusing a world of punishing and harsh realities with ironic self-awareness and comic derision. Roth's humour should not be mistaken for romance however — it reaches no happy ending, only a cessation of pain. Part of that pain is the comedy itself: the reader laughs until it hurts, not innocently, but at the protagonist's expense. Sometimes described as ungenerous and immoral, *Portnoy's Complaint* invites the raised eyebrow and then makes the raised eyebrow its target. It remains one of the most important works of modern Jewish literature because of its compelling suggestion that the Jewish psyche is a broken jigsaw of familial relationships. The constant challenge, implies Roth, is to fit the pieces together. A G

"'Good Christ, a Jewish man with parents still alive is a fifteen year-old boy, and will remain a fifteen year-old boy till they die!... Doctor! Doctor! Did I say fifteen? Excuse me, I meant ten! I meant five! I meant zero! A Jewish man with his parents alive is half the time a helpless infant! Listen, come to my aid, will you — and quick! Spring me from this role I play of the smothered son in the Jewish joke! Because it's beginning to pall a little, at thirty-three! And also it hoits, you know, there is pain involved, a little human suffering is being felt, if I may take it upon myself to say so.'"

ROTH
Philip

Zuckerman Bound [English USA]

The Ghost Writer

Zuckerman Unbound

The Anatomy Lesson

The Prague Orgy

Following the publication of Portnoy's Complaint, his uproarious anatomy of Jewish familial and sexual dysfunctionality, Philip Roth was confronted by angry criticism from various prominent American-Jewish individuals and institutions. The charge was 'Jewish self-hatred' — Roth's personal alienation from and bitterness towards his own people had induced him to mock and denigrate the cherished cornerstone of Jewish life.

Common amongst these critics was a blindness to the difference between Portnoy and Roth, between autobiographical experience and fictional creation. For Roth, the attacks set in train a series of ideas about the complex relation between life and art, which became the springboard for much of his subsequent writing, and in particular the Zuckerman 'trilogy and epilogue' written between 1979 and 1985, later published as Zuckerman Bound.

These four books, originally published separately, cohere to form a single work whose recurring theme is 'the unforeseen consequences of art'. Centring on Nathan Zuckerman, a fictionalised version of the author, each novel is clearly grounded in, and yet at some distance from, Roth's autobiographical experience and calls into question the boundaries between art and life. In each book, Zuckerman is made to confront the troubling real-life consequences of writing fiction, and in particular to recognise how intricately his anxieties about writing are tied up with his Jewish identity.

In *The Ghost Writer*, the first of the trilogy, Zuckerman recounts his visit to the great, elderly Jewish writer 'E.I.Lonoff' at his New England home. There, Zuckerman discovers that Lonoff has effectively sacrificed the pleasures and distractions of life for the austere demands of art, to the misery of his non-Jewish wife, and the frustration of his would-be mistress Amy Bellette, an aspiring and beautiful young writer. Towards the end of the novel, Zuckerman appears to uncover Amy's secret: that she is Anne Frank, who survived Auschwitz and took refuge in America, only to discover that her *Diary* has become a publishing sensation. Realising that the world 'needs' her death, that her survival would render her diary meaningless, she keeps her identity secret even from her father.

Bellette, of course, is not Anne Frank; in inventing this phantom biography, however, Roth provocatively exposes how Anne Frank's memory has become a kind of collective fiction, a generalized symbol of Jewish loss rather than an individual story. It is because of this symbolism that Zuckerman becomes infatuated with Amy; if she really is Anne Frank, their marriage would surely exonerate him from the accusations following publication of his first stories, that he is 'heedless of Jewish feeling' — for 'who dares to accuse of such unthinking crimes the husband of Anne Frank?' The stories of both Lonoff and Amy Bellette, then, reveal the strange and unpredictable ways in which life and art can slide into one another, especially for the Jewish writer, for whom their relationship is always fraught with guilt and anxiety.

The same guilt and anxiety haunt Zuckerman in *Zuckerman Unbound*, which centres on the personal crisis induced by celebrity after the massive success of *Carnovsky*, a thinly veiled version of *Portnoy's Complaint*. Two events in the novel intensify this crisis: firstly, being stalked by Alvin Pepler, Jewish victim of 1950s quiz show scandals, who threatens to kidnap Zuckerman's mother and finally accuses him of having 'stolen' his life. And secondly, being charged by his brother with having accelerated his father's death by satirizing 'his' family in *Carnovsky*. Once again, Roth shows us the web of guilt in which the Jewish writer, torn between duty to his people and to the creative process, is entangled.

The third novel, *The Anatomy Lesson*, is an intensely funny study of writer's block, caused by a mysterious pain in the upper body that cripples Zuckerman's ability to think or write. Searching obsessively for the cause of his pain, he identifies it in the psychic and physical imprisonment brought on by his own writing and especially by the neurotic tension brought on by charges of Jewish self-hatred. His solution is to liberate himself from writing by moving to Chicago and enrolling in medical school. As a doctor, he can become an unambiguous force for good in the world, and so eliminate the painful self-doubt of the writer. The move to Chicago, of course, turns out to be a hilariously miserable failure...

Roth's 'epilogue', *The Prague Orgy*, introduces us to the bizarrely distorted forms of sexual and creative 'freedom' produced by the political repression of writers in Communist Prague. It extends to a broader context the continuing preoccupation with the mutual entanglements of Jewish life and writing explored in the trilogy.

Consistently funny and inventive, intellectually challenging yet highly readable, *Zuckerman Bound* is a fascinating journey through the world of the secular Jewish writer and his contradictory commitments. A G

'Her first time in hospital, the doctors diagnosed a minor stroke, nothing to leave her seriously impaired; four months later, when they admitted her again, she was able to recognize her neurologist when he came by the room, but when he asked if she would write her name for him on a piece of paper, she took the pen and instead of "Selma" wrote "Holocaust", perfectly spelled. This was in Miami Beach in 1970, inscribed by a woman whose writings otherwise consisted of recipes on index cards, several thousand thank-you notes, and a voluminous file of knitting instructions. Zuckerman was pretty sure that before that morning she'd never even spoken the word aloud. Her responsibility wasn't brooding on horrors but sitting at night getting the knitting done and planning the next day's chores. But she had a tumor in her head and it seemed to have forced out everything except the one word. That it couldn't dislodge. It must have been there all the time without their even knowing.' (*Zuckerman Unbound* p324)

RUBENS
Bernice

The Elected Member [English Britain]

With *The Elected Member* Bernice Rubens won the UK's leading fiction award, the Booker Prize, in 1970. The novel tells a disturbing and moving story with that vivid blend of pathos and black humour which characterises Rubens' best writing. There is an imaginative inventiveness at work in *The Elected Member* which allows her to tell the story of a prodigiously high-achieving immigrant Rabbi's son, his breakdown, his mother's overwheening ambition and the resulting collapse into nightmarish dysfunction of the whole family but without for a moment slipping into stereotypes or losing our sympathies.

That this family is Jewish is not merely circumstantial. But the family's extraordinary relationships and their development through painful crises into kinds of redemption, through suffering and growing self-knowledge, speak to human sympathies that are not at all exclusively Jewish. The novel does not allow itself to be confined by the claustrophobic atmosphere created by the immigrant, ethnically unadaptable outlook of the parents' old-world Jewishness. Themes of psychotic breakdown, forbidden sexual relationships, deceptions and self-deceptions are played out in a rapidly paced narrative which is full of surprises, heart-stopping shocks and numerous moments of irresistible comedy.

Rubens quotes R.D.Laing's *The Politics of Experience* at the start of the novel: 'If patients are *disturbed*, their families are often very *disturbing*.' But although from the opening paragraphs of the first chapter we are introduced to the son Norman's hallucinations, Rubens is not offering a study in pathology or psycho-social dynamics. The experience of each of her characters is given its weight and reality, and the dynamics of the family remains a compelling drama, in which our sympathies settle and shift and rarely completely abandon any one of them. T H

'All those great expectations, they'd had of him. All that infant prodigy stuff, with him in short trousers till his beard started to grow, and her in those white socks to clinch the illusion. She didn't want to think about it. She felt guilty of the part she inevitably played in her brother's madness, and the part played indeed by the whole family. Norman and his whole life had been an event for them all, it was something that had happened to *them* and had ultimately nothing to do with Norman at all. Norman might be in an asylum, but it was they, the two of them around the table, who were in crisis, because their event had gone sour. They had elected Norman for their scapegoat, each in their own way, her father, her mother, her sister and herself, and now the backlash was on them. Norman was in a nut-house, asserting his rights, the right not to have been chosen. For a moment she saw Norman alone, without sisters or parents, and she saw him whole and sane.'

The Street of Crocodiles [Sklepy cynamonwe] [Polish]

Schulz, a Polish Jew writing in Polish rather than in the Yiddish, Hebrew or German also used by various Polish-born Jewish writers, was the great poet of small-town day-dreams. His *Street of Crocodiles* is a benignly humorous version of the Sicilian Vitaliano Brancati's dark *The Lost Years* [see *Babel Guide to Italian Fiction*]. What these two off-the-beaten-track writers recognisably have in common though is the use of fantasy to enrich and subvert the fixity and boredom of provincial life. In Brancati's hilarious book we see the launching of short-lived and quixotic projects for individual or municipal 'improvement' while with Bruno Schulz we witness an inspired transformation of all the ordinariness of life into a magical realm. Such is Schulz's genius that we simultaneously receive a cleansing and a re-vivification of our perceptions because he helps us sense that 'The whole of matter pulsates with infinite possibilities'.

Ever-present in the little corner of Poland called *Drohobycz* is the problem of 'conquering the days' as Schulz reveals the pure and suffocating density of time in small towns. But it is this heavy weight of time that leads eventually to Bruno Schulz's marvellous vision; Diane Arbus, the great American photographer, summarised her method; 'as the Chinese say, through boredom one reaches fascination'. With Bruno through Drohobycz one reaches (funny) Nirvana.

Perhaps appropriately for a Jewish writer 'escaping the ghetto' by choosing to use Polish as his medium, Schulz takes us out into the wide Polish forests where we meet animal as well as human characters. The most memorable animal in *The Street of Crocodiles* is the puppy Nimrod in the story of the same name. *Nimrod* is about a puppy and about life itself as this happy, exploring little animal embodies Schulz's philosophy of existential joy.

Cinnamon Shops (which gave its name to the original title of this collection) is about an unforgettable winter night full of light and snow and intimations of spring, while in *The Street of Crocodiles* colourless provincial-modern squalor ('The old, shaky suburban houses had large hastily constructed portals grafted on to them which only on close inspection revealed themselves as miserable imitations of metropolitan splendour.') is transformed through

Schulz's soaring, comic fantasy. A dreary tailor's shop in the low-rent district becomes a highly inventive brothel, a place of 'shiny dark eyes shooting out sudden zigzag cockroachy looks'. One discovers though that this story is more than a vignette when it reaches its quite pointed ending; 'the women of the street of crocodiles are depraved only to a modest extent, stifled by thick layers of moral prejudice and ordinary banality.'

This is a simply a life-enhancing book of wonders from 'the black parliaments of saucepans' in permanent session in the attic (in *The Gale*) to a new and useful 'thirteenth month' invented in a Borgesian kind of way for *The Night of the Great Season,* to the mysterious highly-coloured flocks of birds that inhabit some of the stories and are symbols of free flight, fantasy and perhaps Jewish wandering.

Do not fail to discover and celebrate the marvellous Bruno Schulz, who was, sad to say yet another Jewish martyr to German brutality. R K

'In July my father went to take the waters and left me, with my mother and elder brother, a prey to the blinding white heat of the summer days. Dizzy with light, we dipped into that enormous book of holidays, its pages blazing with sunshine and scented with the sweet melting pulp of golden pears.

On those luminous mornings Adela returned from the market, like Pomona emerging from the flames of day, spilling from her basket the colourful beauty of the sun — the shiny pink cherries full of juice under their transparent skins, the mysterious black morellos that smelled so much better than they tasted; apricots in whose golden pulp lay the core of long afternoons. And next to that pure poetry of fruit, she unloaded sides of meat with their keyboard of ribs swollen with energy and strength, and seaweeds of vegetables like dead octopuses and squids — the raw material of meals with a yet undefined taste, the vegetative and terrestrial ingredients of dinner, exuding a wild and rustic smell.' p11

SCHULZ
Bruno

Sanatorium Under the Sign of the Hourglass [Sanitorium pod lepsydra] [Polish]

Born and raised in the predominately Jewish section of Drohobycz, a small town located in south-eastern Poland, Schulz later studied lithography and drawing at a school in Lwow before returning to Drohobycz and taking a position as an art teacher in a secondary school for boys. He was a gaunt, reclusive man who devoted most of his leisure hours to writing and drawing: however, initially, he wrote only for himself, since his timidity precluded him from seeking publishers and his fragility could not have sustained rejection.

Schulz finally found his way into the Warsaw literary establishment by way of Zofia Nalowska, a prominent Warsaw novelist, who read a collection of Schulz's stories sent to her by a mutual friend. In 1934, at the age of forty-two, his stories were published as *The Cinnamon Stores* (Sklepy cynamonwe) since retitled *The Street of Crocodiles*. Once he was finally accepted by both the Polish literati and publishers, Schulz published his second and final book *Sanatorium Under the Sign of the Hourglass* (Sanitorium pod lepsydra) in 1937.

John Updike has said of *Sanitorium* that 'the pages are crowded with verbal brilliance'. Updike's description is not arbitrary; each word, line, and paragraph in Schulz is a prayer to metaphor, to the unequivocal power of the colour within an image which at one and the same time can delight the senses and appall the heart.

Sanitorium is neither a novel nor a collection of short stories; rather, it is an anthology of tales made up of prose poems each with its own diction, meter, and melodic fluency, and each capable of standing on its own as a model of the form. The tales bear the structure and discipline of a novelist like Flaubert and the poetic vibrancy of Baudelaire. They are also the creation of a painfully sensitive human being.

Isaac Bashevis Singer wrote of Schulz that 'he wrote sometimes like Kafka, sometimes like Proust, and at times succeeded in reaching depths that neither of them reached'. Schulz's prose is sometimes reminiscent of the work of Franz Kafka, a writer whom Schulz both admired and translated. Like Kafka his work is unified by the person of a narrator who is the somewhat ethereal 'I' of the author. The narrator relates his experiences in a provincial town, much like Drohobycz, where everything is distorted, mutated, altered by his fantasies. Some of the adventures disclose certain incongruities of nature: properties of time, space, and matter. Because of its fluidity, matter was a constant wonder for Schulz as was space: that constant, unchangeable mass of emptiness.

There doesn't seem to be a line in *Sanitorium* that doesn't either bask in metaphor and convolution or make the reader question the sense of reading at all. Schulz challenges the reader with so many images, symbols, and metaphors that one can almost fault him for it; but what a magnificent fault to have!

Among all the rich and fecund images, Schulz seems constantly consumed with the idea of *dusk* and all that dusk connotes. In the title tale, the setting is inundated with blacks and grays, with darkness and ink and the all-pervasive dusk.

An extra feature of *Sanitorium* is the inclusion of thirty sketches which complement the text. The sketches, like the prose, emphasize the fear that Schulz had for what was nameable yet at the same time unknown...

In fact Schulz can be unnerving, over and above the beauty of each passage there lies an omnipresent uneasiness, a heaviness which reminds the reader that beauty is transient and is lost in the absorbing chill of the universe... M A

'When the tree roots want to speak, when under the turf a great many old tales and ancient sages have been collected, when too many whispers have been gathered underground, inarticulate pulp and dark nameless things that existed before words—then the bark of trees blackens and disintegrated into thick, rough scales which form deep furrows. You dip your face into that fluffy fur of dusk, and everything becomes impenetrable, push across the dull humus—and suddenly you are at your goal, on the other side; you are in the Deep, in the Underworld.' (*Spring*)

SCLIAR
Moacyr

The Strange Nation of Rafael Mendes [A estranha nação de Rafael Mendes] [Portuguese Brazil]

Scliar, a descendant of Russian-Jewish immigrants from the beginning of the century, has, since the early 1960s, led a dual career as a medical practitioner in Porto Alegre, capital of the southern state of Rio Grande do Sul, and as Brazil's leading Jewish fiction writer. This is his seventeenth book, originally published in 1983, and is his most explicit, if ironic, investigation into the history of the Jewish contribution to the making of Brazil — a still neglected subject shrouded in ignorance, despite evidence that the immigrant Portuguese population during colonial times was disproportionately Jewish (or converted New Christian*) in its composition.

The idea of a crypto-judaic identity at work beneath the surface of Brazil's chequered evolution is the central theme of

The Strange Nation of Rafael Mendes, which embraces a panoramic stretch of history and myth from Jonah's encounter in the belly of the whale, through the Diaspora to the Iberian peninsula and beyond to the South American New World.

In a characteristic blend of fact, speculation and fantasy, Scliar weaves his account of the Mendes dynasty, whose wanderings are driven in part by the dream of magical wealth, the Gold Tree, in part by the vision of a mythical country that bears more than a passing resemblance to a paradisiacal Brazil — 'a beautiful bay with waves lapping on the pure white sands of the beach, coconut trees, brightly coloured birds wheeling in flight, a gloriously blue sky, a country inhabited by friendly people (bronze-skinned men, women and children, their faces painted in gaudy colours, their long black hair adorned with feathers).'

Most of all, though, it is the perennial 'perplexity' of the Mendes nation, caught between the impulse to adventure, the wisdom of caution and restraint, and the dilemma of the Jewish condition, endlessly called to serve yet hounded by paranoia and suspicion. Such is the fate of the physician Maimonides, who discovers the cholera responsible for the illness of the sultan Saladin, but is forced by the palace conspirators to collude in his death. Or of the Rafael Mendes, a descendant of New Christians, who foresees in a dream the execution of Tiradentes, the leader of an eighteenth-century revolutionary movement, but is disbelieved by those around him. Or of the doctor Rafael Mendes, appointed to a sinecure by the populist Vargas regime of the 1930s, and who becomes innocently embroiled in a scandal concerning an Indian land occupation, a mysterious epidemic, and a media campaign against the regime.

Something of an anti-epic, then, this unwritten history is a healthy antidote to other, more triumphalist accounts of nation-building, one in which the Mendes line plays a, by turns, unwilling, accidental or unheroic part. And when it finally does comes to light, it illuminates the life of its most recent protagonist against a background of renewed chaos and crisis, the Brazil of the mid 1970s, as the euphoria of the Economic Miracle is beginning to crumble. Only now is it revealed to an unsuspecting Rafael Mendes, the junior partner in a collapsing finance company, in the form of two notebooks left to him by his father, who had mysteriously disappeared to Spain at the time of the Civil War. Rafael reads the notebooks on the eve of his arrest for collusion in embezzlement, as he finds out that his wayward daughter has been having a secret affair with his best friend, the Jewish company director Boris Goldbaum ("Goldtree"), and that together they are plotting their escape to Paraguay.

One of the book's many ironies is that the pursuit of the mythical Gold Tree has led the last unwitting heir of the Mendes dynasty to an understanding of its foolish futility, in the shape of his failed business partner. With his life falling to pieces about him, surrounded by betrayal, the perplexed Rafael, one of a long line of perplexed Mendes, all at once discovers his own fantastic ancestry, his Jewishness no less, and is freed from 'the perplexity of generations' in order to confront his destiny, a wiser man. D T

'He feels fine; now he feels fine. His head light, his forehead cool; fine. And thus he drifts off into drowsiness; and in this twilight between sleep and wakefulness, it seems to him that all of them are there, standing around the bed — Jonah and Habacuc, Maimonides and Rafael Mendes, all the ones named Rafael Mendes. In silence they look at him. Suddenly he realizes. All of them have the face he saw in the mirror a while ago; all of them are him, he is all of them. Now he understands the *Notebooks of the New Christians*; they are his father's legacy to him — Rafael is no longer beset by doubts. Instead of solutions, fantasies; instead of answers, imaginary possibilities. The perfect message from a perplexed individual, concludes Rafael — and then the figures begin to vanish, and he falls asleep.' p296

SHABTAI
Yaacov

Past Continuous [Zichron devarim] [Hebrew]

What is it that, with you or without you, just keeps on going? With a tireless drive, oblivious to joy or wreck, to which one can't but submit? Shabtai would surely answer: life, with its catalogue of deaths too, or perhaps just time. This force ever pushing onwards is Shabtai's theme in his remarkable first novel, which in Hebrew bears the title of *Zichron Devarim*, 'Recollection of things', with more than a wink at Marcel Proust's epic on time lost, remembered, written and regained.

Past Continuous takes an unforgettable sweep through 1970s Tel Aviv, following the lives of three friends in their forties — Caesar, Goldman and Israel — first in their attempt to attend a funeral (the funeral of Goldman's father: they turn up at the wrong cemetery), and secondly as they mix with friends and relatives at the house of the bereaved. Here the linear progression of the novel diverges to a myriad of criss-crossing stories, as we encounter the friends' sisters, aunts, great-uncles, mothers, lovers, fathers, cousins and their various histories, contentments, bitternesses or madnesses. The book ends nine months later, with Goldman's suicide and the birth of an unwanted child from Israel's lover Ella; life rubs up against death — one of the novel's major themes

In between the beginning and end, where we all live, is Shabtai's racing prose, driven by an extraordinary rhythmic energy, taking in a vast network of life stories as they press into the present. The Jews of the generation of Goldman's parents come from the complicated polyglot worlds of Jewish Europe, and additionally experience the transplantation to Palestine. Each character is bearer of their own unique life events, and these are never solely individual and psychological: for example Manfred, who as a Zionist pioneer became a communist and as a communist rejected Zionism and returned to France in the 1930s, and then as a disillusioned communist devoted himself to the study of Christian demonology; or Uncle Lazar, whose childhood was spent in a luckless village which changed hands from Poland to Russia to Germany. Lazar's emigration to Tel Aviv was followed by a profound and poisonous rift between himself and his brother over the right classificatory system for their respective stamp collections — by country or by subject? Shabtai shows here his keen sense of the small matters which can, hilariously to outsiders, carry immense weight in our lives.

Meanwhile Grandma Clara throws her Yiddish-Polish-Russian curses at the 'heat and the people and the taste of the water and the rabbi and the prices and the shape of the houses and the howling of the jackals...'. *Past Continuous* has a full inventory of mesmerising and complex tales, trajectories and characters.

These are, according to Shabtai, the ingredients of Tel Aviv in the 1970s. But the land of Israel is changing, it is no longer the land of the pioneers, and the new Israel grates against the old: in the background are rocketing property prices (overshadowing the old socialist ideals), there is nepotism and corruption in the Labour Party, ongoing struggles over land, peace and the Palestinians, and the rise of the political Right under Menachem Begin, who took power the year the novel was published, 1977.

Faced with these changes, the generation of the pioneers engages in passionate argument. Caesar, Goldman and Israel, however, educated, bohemian middle-class *Sabras**, internalise these rifts and crises in the form of a sense of alienation and rootlessness, so that a huge question mark hangs over 'Life' and its value(s). All three men are unfulfilled and on edge: Israel prevaricates over just about everything (where to live, what to do, whom to love), Caesar bounces restlessly between at least three lovers, always stretched somewhere between regret at the absence of permanence and a desire for detachment, and Goldman the one-time lawyer moves disconsolately between Taoism, dieting, cosmology and his Bullworker™ exercise machine. Life is, as Caesar puts it, a 'swinging suicide'.

An extraordinary, unique book, to be relished, as Shabtai (who died young) would have it, with a kind of exhausted jubilation. S B

'...and Besh approached the table, still shouting... announced that life was so idiotic and false and perverted that on the one hand it mesmerized him and fascinated him to such an extent that he would never abandon it, on the other hand he would never abandon it because he wanted to annoy it by his presence, and on the third hand he would like to tear it to pieces and set it on fire, and then he said that he would sell the present and the future and the world to come and eternity for one plate of the fish soup that his mother used to make, and that she was without a doubt one of the wonders of the world and like his brother in Australia she had also regarded herself as a German, but unlike his brother she had been so convinced and so consistent in this belief that she had held to it until the Nazis finished her off and maybe even now — in the form of smoke or something, because according to the law of the conservation of matter nothing in nature was ever lost — she still believed in her Germany and she was sure that it was all some terrible mistake, and he burst out laughing again...' p143-4

SHAHAR
David

Stories from Jerusalem [Hebrew]

Take the first sentence of the first story, *The Fortune teller*, and you will get a feel for how this collection of stories from the 1960s and early 1970s by the Israeli David Shahar treats the reader: 'As will become readily apparent, it's not the fortune teller that I want to talk about here, but my uncle Kalman'. Even that is disingenuous, though, since nothing in these deceptively simple and calm stories is 'readily apparent'.

Shahar's stories look at first sight like memoirs, told in the first person, often involving tales of life in Jerusalem either from childhood or as a young man, tales of family and neighbourhood, departure and return: pharmacists, plumbers, Arab, Jewish and British government officials, doctors, mediums and (maybe) fortune tellers. Take a closer look and you see that the main theme or character seems to slip away (as above, where the fortune teller in fact plays a trifling role), moves into something completely different. At the same time you notice that the chain of apparently accidental events has a pattern to it, not psychological but mythical or mystical, involving curious coincidences, doubles, repetitions, strange workings of destiny...

The story *Uncle Zemach* is a case in point. It *is* actually about Uncle Zemach who, like many characters in Shahar's stories, has shunned the world of work in favour of less straightforward paths (painter, musician or simply lethargic advocate of 'philosophical laziness'). But then Uncle Zemach reforms and studies law abroad, returning to Jerusalem with a wife and a sober attitude, unlike his oddball brother Lippa who earns his living playing violin in a cafe. Gradually though, something happens to Zemach: a prestigious and hard-working lawyer, he resigns from his job over a petty quarrel, begins teaching his nephew to draw, sees ghosts, and busies round his sister helping her choose her dress and sort out the lunch menu.... Uncle Zemach is shown to revert to eccentric family ways for reasons which neither he nor the reader readily understands...

So alongside realistic descriptions of life in Jerusalem we find a world of spirits, phenomena belonging to the 'fourth dimension' and surreal transformations: we read of a perfect water droplet incarnating 'the great calm of life in its essence and its nothingness', out-of-body experiences, 'double doorways' into the past and the future, and reincarnated Knights Templars or Christian Crusaders. In relation to this strange world, Jerusalem takes on the role of a stage set, 'the permanent reassuring decor of an old, familiar play into which a man sinks in order to exorcise his own being'.

The mythical, spiritualist aspect of Shahar's stories contributes forcefully to the uncanny feel of these tales, their seemingly arbitrary and unpredictable unfolding (the woman in the title *The woman with the familiar spirit* is introduced only at the end of the story), their unemphatic tone — to the point of flatness — and their uncertain genre (memoir, autobiography, fiction?). But this is also why they are so intriguing, retaining a quiet power to dwell in the mind and, literally, to enchant. S B

'I push back the chair, propel myself toward the door, and peep through the slit in the blind. The plants are silent in their pots. I don't return to the table, but walk up and down the room with tense, jerky steps before sitting down in an armchair. Now it fills the whole room. The tension in the air is freezing the room into a motionless silence. All solid substances are solid only because of a supreme tension. The floor of the room and its ceiling, the walls and the bookshelves and the books themselves and the table and chairs and copper utensils are solid and firmly fixed in their places only by virtue of this supreme tension. If it should slacken even for a second they would all melt and begin to drip and soon evaporate in whitish tongues of steam. I must fight to the end. If I allow it to reveal itself I'll be sucked out of this solid substantiality like water swallowed into a pipe or air sucked up into the mouth of a pump.' p113

SHALEV
Meir

The Blue Mountain [Roman Rusi] [Hebrew]

The story of the *Second Aliya** migration to Israel of enthusiastic pioneer groups from Eastern Europe is vividly brought to life in this novel. These pioneers, their contributions to the settlements and villages in Israel, their willfulness and contradictions, are the leitmotif of the story. This is reinforced by the narrator, Baruch, grandson of one of the three founding fathers of a settlement in the Jezreel Valley. He grows up surrounded by the intimate memories and experiences, more compatible and comfortable himself with the past than the future. As a result he decides to establish a cemetery, 'Pioneer Home', for all the Second Aliya participants both in Israel and abroad, that will nestle under the Blue Mountain of the title.

The tale of those who are eligible to be buried there, plus those who are not, fills this entertaining, tender novel. With wit and empathy Shalev presents us with some highly varied personalities, including Meshulam Tsirkin 'the scholar', intent on creating his own unique tribute to the Pioneers, who contests most of Baruch's decisions. Baruch himself, orphaned at a young age, is brought up, nurtured, educated, initiated by his devoted but eccentric grandfather. His world is enriched by the lively, philosophic Pinness, second of the trio who established the village, and teacher of all the generations of its children. The story abounds with agricultural detail, the very warp and weft of existence at that time. Life-cycles of the children and grandchildren of the pioneers, their loves and lusts, are interwoven with the life-cycles of the animals, insects and flora growing in abundance.

The novel unfolds according to the seasons and sensory, tactile timeframes; oftentimes the links to the world of nature are more significant than the human relationships. Uncle Ephraim and his Charolais bull, lovingly nurtured which he, unbelievably, carried on his strong shoulders almost everywhere; Rilov and his beehives, producing his exotic, seductive honey; Grandpa, with his passion and intuition for his prolific vineyard. Baruch recalls events through these associations, as he builds a picture of the intertwining relationships, especially of his Grandfather and Grandmother Feyge. The history of the Workingman's Circle, three men plus Feyge who first came to this valley, unfurls through a series of flashbacks and insights: did Grandfather really love her, and if so, why did he continue receiving letters, by stork (!) from Russia? What happened to the personalities who left the village, never to return, or to Shifris, whose arrival was still awaited continually? How did Rachel teach Ephraim to walk silently, like 'a cat on sand'? And how would cousins Yosi and Uri resolve their relentless desire for the womenfolk of the village?

By arranging this formal tribute to the Pioneers, Baruch must also acknowledge the passing of time and a particular way of life. How he adapts to this, with an equivocal and nostalgic glance backward to his forbears, combined with a forward glance to the future, filled with trepidation, forms the impact of this captivating story. Meir Shalev, born 1948, has turned towards a significant stage in Israel's social history, the Second Aliya of 1904-1914, and brought it to life with astonishing realism and understanding. T L

'The two old men drank a dozen glasses of tea, ate a pound of olives, and at 3.00 a.m. Pinness announced that he was going home and that if he ever found the Casanova, "he'll rue the day he was born."

He opened the door and stood facing the darkness for a moment. Then he turned around and said to Grandfather that he felt heavy at heart because he had just thought of the hyena.

"The hyena is dead, Ya'akov," said Grandfather. "No one knows that better than you do. Relax."

"Every generation has its enemies," said Pinness darkly as he left.

He made his way home through the warm thicket of the night, treading upon "the thin crust on which our life has been established," and thinking, I knew, of the menacing creatures of havoc that hatched and swarmed ceaselessly around him, bursting in his somber nightmares like the bubbles of a foul, unruly past. He could sense the silent squat of the mongoose and see the blood-spotted face of the wildcat padding on its silken-pawed rampage of murder and plunder. Mice gnawed at the farmer's labors in the fields of grain, and beneath the checkered carpet of plowed field, stubble, and orchard, waiting for the first signs of Doubt, growled the most legendary beast of all, the great swamp imprisoned by the founders. Far in the west he saw the orange-glowing lights of the big city beyond the mountain, with their seductive glitter of exploitation and corruption, of easy money, carnal baubles, and lewd winks.'

SINGER
Isaac Bashevis

Collected Stories [Yiddish Poland USA]

Justly I.B.Singer is the most celebrated and successful Yiddish writer ever. The variety and the breadth of his production make him a real reference point on Polish Jewry in different periods and circumstances, including that of American emigration. More than that, and the main reason for his success, is that his writing is a joy to know.

All Yiddish fiction is in some way a bridge between two worlds; the isolated world of East European Jewry, closed up for hundreds of years in its own particular culture, and the modern world in which Yiddish novels and short stories were written and read. The Yiddish story started off by giving a modern spin to the folk tales saturated in pious moral truths and the superstitious yarns about Dybbuks* and Demons. I.B.Singer, in both his personal history and in his work seems to perfectly embody the idea of Yiddish literature as a bridge.

Singer's father, by whose life and surroundings he was immensely influenced, was a Hasidic Rabbi, immersed in the old pious culture that both disdained secular culture and reached out to miracles and magical goings-on; held to be signs of God's presence. His mother was more rationalistic and sanguine as was his brother Israel Joshua Singer, a leftist Yiddish writer [see this *Babel Guide*]. He himself set out on a career in the modern world of Warsaw publishing before emigrating to New York where he wrote regularly for a Yiddish newspaper and then to a far wider audience.

I.B.Singer seemed to live and share the consciousness of both the antiquated world and a quite modern one. Some of his stories preach a ferocious sexual moralism for instance while in others he is quite casual about adultery. His stories are generally set either in the modern milieu of 1930s Warsaw coffee houses,

New York newspaper offices and Miami apartment complexes or in the seventeenth, eighteenth or early nineteenth centuries — but about which he writes as if that was yesterday.

This anthology of Singer stories chosen by the author himself from his twelve books of translated stories is a solid and widely-available collection. The stories bear out the Singerian manifesto he posts in his introduction 'Genuine literature…has the magical power of merging causality with purpose, doubt with faith, the passions of the flesh with the yearnings of the soul.'

Of the forty-seven stories here, some are already covered in this *Babel Guide's* reviews of general Jewish or Yiddish anthologies. Of the rest some of the highlights are; *The Spinoza of Market Street* set in early twentieth century Warsaw and which creates an excellent narrative from the adventure of intellectual conquest and scholarship; *The Destruction of Kreshev* with its fascinating detail of eighteenth century Polish peasant and Jewish life including the story of a follower of the 'False Messiah' Sabbatai Zevi; the terrific story *Yentl the Yeshiva Boy* that Barbara Streisand turned into a film; the humane and moving *The Letter Writer* set amongst ageing Jewish refugees in New York while the Dybbuk-and-Demon I.B. Singer is shown in stories like *Taibele and her Demon,* although he also gently satirises occult phenomena in *The Psychic Journey.*

A less obvious but fascinating moment of Jewish history is retailed in *The Manuscript,* a chilling account of the German-Soviet invasion of Poland in 1939 where Polish Yiddish writers fled from Warsaw to Bialystock in Soviet territory for uneasy meetings with their Soviet counterparts. *Three Encounters* beautifully combines the three major elements in Singer's stories, the Jews, marginal people of various sorts and, above all, great storytelling.

Finally, because quite a number of his stories deal with older people, *Old Love* an amazing, spare mediation on old age and the older person's vision of life, clearly written when Singer was at the height of his powers.

Singer has been compared with the famous painter of the Russian-Jewish shtetl Marc Chagall and his vivid portrait-painting seems to have never wavered in over fifty years of writing about the Jewish worlds of Europe and North America. R K

'When Dr. Fischelson tired of observing the sky, his glance dropped to Market Street below. He could see a long strip extending from Yanash's market to Iron Street with the gas lamps lining it merged into a string of fiery dots.

Smoke was issuing from the chimneys on the black, tin roofs; the bakers were heating their ovens, and here and there sparks mingled with the black smoke. The street never looked so noisy and crowded as on a summer evening. Thieves, prostitutes, gamblers, and fences loafed in the square which looked from above like a pretzel covered with poppy seeds. The young men laughed coarsely and the girls shrieked. A peddler with a keg of lemonade on his back pierced the general din with his intermittent cries. A watermelon vendor shouted in a savage voice, and the long knife which he used for cutting the fruit dripped with the blood-like juice. Now and again the street became even more agitated. Fire engines, their heavy wheels clanging, sped by; they were drawn by sturdy black horses which had to be tightly curbed to prevent them from running wild. Next came an ambulance, its siren screaming. Then some thugs had a fight among themselves and the police had to be called. A passer-by was robbed and ran about shouting for help. Some wagons loaded with firewood sought to get through into the courtyards where the bakeries were located but the horses could not lift the wheels over the steep curbs and the drivers berated the animals and lashed them with their whips. Sparks rose from the clanging hoofs. It was now long after seven, which was the pre-scribed closing time for stores, but actually business had only begun. Cus-tomers were led in stealthily through back doors. The Russian policemen on the street, having been paid off, noticed nothing of this. Merchants continued to hawk their wares, each seeking to out shout the others.

"Gold, gold, gold," a woman who dealt in rotten oranges shrieked.

"Sugar, sugar, sugar," croaked a dealer of overripe plums.

"Heads, heads, heads," a boy who sold fishheads roared.' (p81-2 *The Spinoza of Market Street*)

'I left home at seventeen. I told my parents the truth: I didn't believe in the Gemara or that every law in the *Shulchan Aruch* had been given to Moses on Mount Sinai; I didn't want a marriage arranged by a matchmaker; I was no longer willing to wear a long gaberdine or grow earlocks. I went to Warsaw, where my parents had once lived, to seek an academic education and a profession. My older brother, Joshua, lived in War-saw and had become a writer, but he wasn't able to help me. At twenty I came back home with congested lungs, a chronic cough, no formal education, no profession, and no way that I could see of supporting myself in the city. During the time I was away, my father had been appointed rabbi of Old-Stikov in Eastern Galicia — a village of a few dozen crooked shacks, with straw-covered roofs, built around a swamp. At least, in the fall of 1924 that's how Old-Stikov appeared to me. It had rained all October; and those shacks lay reflected in the swamp as if it were a lake. Ruthenian peasants, stooped Jews in gaberdines, women and girls wearing shawls over their heads and men's boots waded in the mud. Clouds of mist swirled in the air. Crows soared overhead, cawing. The sky hung low, leaden heavy with storms. The smoke from chimneys didn't rise but drifted downward toward the soaked earth.' (*Three Encoun-ters* p 473)

Enemies: A Love Story [Sonim, di geshichte fun a liebe] [Yiddish USA]

I. B Singer's extraordinary 1972 novel, written at the height of the great Yiddish writer's fame, centres on four Holocaust survivors. For those accustomed to the pious images of survivors presented by the likes of Spielberg's film *Schindler's List*, however, *Enemies: A Love Story* will come as a shock. For rather than sanctify the lives of his main characters, he unflinchingly portrays their cruelty, absurdity, and mutual destructiveness. Most disconcertingly of all, the book's plot has the outward shape of a sex farce, with its central character running haplessly between three women.

With its brilliantly controlled black humour and searing insight into the psychological condition of survivors, *Enemies* cuts through the well-worn clichés of much Holocaust literature and film.

Enemies is the story of Herman Broder, a survivor who has fled to post-war New York and married his former servant Yadwiga, a Polish peasant who hid him in her hayloft during the war. Whilst living with Yadwiga, he continues an affair with Masha, a beautiful and damaged survivor of the camps. Meanwhile, he discovers that his wife Tamara, presumed killed by the Soviets, has arrived in New York. The novel charts the emotional and sexual chaos that ensues after Tamara's arrival.

The tension between the novel's title and subtitle — a 'love story' about 'enemies' — goes some way to indicate the instability of the emotional lives of survivors. Love, the book seems to suggest, can never be uncomplicated after the experience of the Holocaust, because the faith and trust that makes love possible has been shattered. Consequently, the affairs portrayed in the book are marked by resentment and deception (Herman and Yadwiga), obsession and destructiveness (Herman and Masha) or simply by utter weariness (Herman and Tamara).

The memory of the Holocaust haunts Herman and his women at every moment, colouring their perception of the world with horror and disgust. This perception is particularly marked in the novel's portrayal of post-Holocaust American Jewry. Singer shows us a Jewish America dedicated to trivial materialism, bent on forgetting the destruction of its European counterpart. Thus, when Herman takes Masha on a secret vacation at the Jewish holiday resort of Lake George, he is disgusted at the sight of the guests, many of them survivors, gathering in the casino and laughing at vaudeville jokes about rabbis and loose women. For Herman, such vulgarity 'shamed the agony of the Holocaust'. His disgust is equally self-directed, however, for example in his shame at his work as a ghost writer of 'uplifting' books and sermons on Judaism — a religion in which he can no longer believe — for a rabbi who is too busy investing in real estate to write them himself.

For some, Singer's apparent failure to show due reverence for the survivors of the Holocaust may come across as presumptuous and tacky. However, for this reader at least, Singer's blackly comic vision in this small masterpiece is intended not to trivialise the experience of the survivors, but to bring out their ineradicable humanity, in all its painful complexity. Perhaps this is, after all, the truest and most respectful relationship to the survivors of Nazism a writer can assume. J C

"'In a hundred years, the ghettos will be idealized and the impression created that they were inhabited only by saints. There could be no greater lie. First of all, how many saints are there in any generation? Second of all, most of the really pious Jews perished. And among those who managed to survive, the great drive was to live at any cost. In some of the ghettos, they even ran cabarets. You can imagine what cabarets! You had to step over dead bodies to get in.'" p130

SINGER
Isaac Bashevis

Gimpel the Fool [Gimpl tam un andere dertseylungen] [Yiddish]

An excellent and widely-available selection of stories by the great I.B.Singer. The twelve short stories are mainly set in Singer's favourite realm, early pre-industrial Poland. Many of them, such as *The Diary of One Not Born,* which is the diary of the adventures of a devil (!) and *By the Light of Memorial Candles* a ghost story told one night in a rickety old synagogue by the flickering light of candles for the dead, are about the supernatural themes that Singer loved.

In these stories and in pieces like *The Gentleman from Cracow* or *Joy,* a story with a Hasidic message of contempt for the material world and literal belief in the happy afterlife, or *The Mirror* where a pretty woman is dragged down to hell as a price for her 'sinful vanity', Singer is continuing in a modernized way the inheritance of the folktale and the moral homily in Yiddish literature. This literary tradition was the unavoidable background for all the Yiddish prose writers, powerful and close to the popular audience they addressed. A lot of Yiddish writing seems to be in one way or another a response to that ethnic, unselfconscious, 'pre-rational' material.

Writers like Singer were addressing and transforming the Jewish folk literature rather in the way Smetana or Bartók addressed the folk music of their areas of Central and Eastern Europe in the Czech Lands and Hungary. That something other than spell-bindingly retold folk tales was beginning to emerge in Yiddish literature is clear even by just looking at I.B.Singer, as in his story *The Old Man,* set in Poland during World War One. Instead of the wishful magic reality of the folktale or religious tale there is the unpredictable narrative of an old man and the harsh physical reality of his journey across the frontiers of warring powers.

The title story *Gimpel the Fool* is one of the most famous Singer ever wrote, deeply ironical and sympathetic at the same time, demonstrating that Singer would have been a great writer even without the rich sources of material he had to draw on from the Jewish experience in Poland. R K

'Zirel had an attic which she called her boudoir, and where hung a mirror as blue as water on the point of freezing. The mirror had a crack in the middle, and it was set in a golden frame which was decorated with snakes, knobs, roses, and adders. In front of the mirror lay a bearskin and close beside it was a chair with armrests of ivory and a cushioned seat. What could be more pleasant than to sit naked in this chair, and rest one's feet on the bearskin, and contemplate oneself? Zirel had much to gaze at. Her skin was white and satin, her breasts full as wineskins, her hair fell across her shoulders, and her legs were as slender as a hind's. She would sit for hours on end delighting in her beauty. The door fastened and bolted, she would imagine that it opened to admit either a prince or a hunter or a knight or a poet. For everything hidden must be revealed, each secret longs to be disclosed, each love yearns to be betrayed, everything sacred must be desecrated.' (p78-79 *The Mirror*)

Passions and Other Stories [Yiddish USA]

The biography of Isaac Bashevis Singer, one of the towering figures of modern Jewish literature, is filled with intimations of a theme that animates so much of his fiction: the struggle between the sacred and the profane.

Born in 1904 to an impoverished rabbinic family in a tiny Polish *shtetl**, he experienced childhood in a world of almost medieval Jewish orthodoxy, of which only traces survive today. In 1920 however, he left Warsaw's Rabbinical Seminary in order to follow his elder brother Israel Joshua (also a writer of Yiddish fiction) into a literary career. During these years, he lived amongst 'enlightened' Jews in the heady atmosphere of sexual freedom and unrestrained cultural expression that defined Warsaw's emerging 'Yiddish avant-garde'.

In 1935, he followed his brother to New York (thereby escaping the fate of his fellow Polish Jews), where he became a freelance writer for the *Jewish Daily Forward*, the Yiddish newspaper in which his fiction continued to be published until his death in 1991.

Throughout his novels and short stories, the uneasy co-presence of these two worlds — that of his father's unworldly piety, and his brother's urbane modernity — is repeatedly brought to life. *Passions,* a collection of twenty late stories, written between 1970 and 1975, gives voice to this ambivalence with remarkable power. These stories' apparent clarity of style and simplicity of narrative belie an enigmatic, complex and disturbing vision.

The central tension of Singer's life and work is most clearly drawn out in *Sam Palka and DavidVishkover*, in which a millionaire landlord named Sam Palka tells the story of his double life. Palka falls instantly in love with one of his tenants, a beautiful immigrant from a Polish *shtetl**, just as he is about to evict her. Instead of doing so, he embarks on a long affair with her in the guise of a struggling insurance salesman and fellow immigrant named David Vishkover. Pure, trusting and unworldly, Chana Basha continues to her death to believe Palka's story, whilst the latter furtively continues his millionaire life uptown.

The self-division of the central character into Palka and Vishkover slyly represents the competing impulses of modern Jewish life — assimilation into the secular world on the one hand

(Palka's 'real' identity), preservation of the traditional life of piety and hard work on the other (his lost, longed-for 'other' self).

Similar themes emerge in *Three Encounters*; the encounters of the title are between the narrator and Rivkele, the beautiful shoe-maker's daughter in the shtetl of Old-Stikov. In the first, the narrator implores Rivkele to escape a loveless marriage and monotonous life and move with him to Warsaw. The next two encounters in Warsaw (two years later) and New York (a further nine years later) see Rivkele visiting the narrator and charging him with responsibility for her misfortunes at the hands of devious and violent men. Once again, Singer expresses profound ambivalence about the loss of the spiritual and sexual integrity of the 'old' shtetl world.

Each of the stories in this superb volume explores in different ways the experience of the Jew suspended between the worlds of Jewish tradition and secular modernity, pulled towards both, at home in neither. In *Hanka* this sense of homelessness is explicitly tied to the Holocaust: the Hanka of the title is a survivor of Auschwitz whom the narrator (surely a version of Singer himself) meets in Buenos Aires. Hanka is unable to take pleasure in love or life because of her conviction that she 'belongs to an exterminated tribe and we are not material for sex'. As in much of his later fiction, it is above all the memory of the Holocaust which imbues the world with a sense of unredeemable pain and loss. J C

'The night light made her face feminine and her black eyes emitted golden sparks. We stopped in the middle of the dirt road and kissed with fervor, as if we had been waiting for each other for God knows how long. Her wide mouth bit into mine like the muzzle of a beast. The heat from her body baked my skin, not unlike the glowing roof a few hours earlier. I heard a blaring sound, mysterious and other-worldly, as though a heavenly heifer in a faraway constellation had awakened and begun a wailing not to be stilled until all life in the universe shall be redeemed.' (p93 *The Yearning Heiffer*)

SINGER
Isaac Bashevis

The Penitent [Yiddish USA]

This late book is Singer's testament against the sins of the liberal modern world. Its protagonist, New York businessman Joseph Shapiro, has a mid-life crisis which sets him on a radical new path in life — religious Orthodoxy. He gives up his (unfaithful)

wife, his mistress, his business and flees to Israel.

Singer uses the stance of serious religious commitment to great effect, providing an interesting vantage point on the texture and tenor of the contemporary society he was in many ways hostile to. Waiting in an airport gripped by his decision to transform his life into that of a strictly observant Jew he looks on at the rest of us; 'I watched the crowds. I observed the people coming and going. Some were going to Paris, some to New York, some to London and some to Athens. Their eyes displayed the same restlessness, the same sense of urgency and the same queries: Why am I running like this? What am I seeking? What do I expect to find there?'. Joseph Shapiro's wry detachment from the everyday stream of little tasks and duties, the stimulations and desires that push and drag us through our lives is also the point of view of the writer or artist. An artist creates from inside a special kind of time; slow, intensely focused, unfolding, enriching — the exact opposite of the degraded and fractured time of waiting for planes in airports...

The kind of ideal Jew Singer proposes to us in *The Penitent* is perhaps the opposite to that proposed by Bernard Malamud in *The Assistant* [also reviewed here]. His is the Jew of outer discipline and observance who thereby resists distraction and enriches his soul. No doubt there is something in both visions.
R K

'One of the men suggested that the rabbi sit down for the Eighteenth Benediction, but he wouldn't hear of it.

I saw how he slowly raised a trembling hand and smote his breast as he uttered: "We have sinned" and "We have transgressed". He, the saint, repented his uncommitted sins while millions of evil-doers boasted of murder and tens of thousands of lawyers — Jews among them — sought means of freeing every thief, robber, swindler and rapist. I was seized by a sense of self-shame. There were saints in New York but I had spent my time with whores, with sly exploiters, with manufactures who dallied with call girls. Now I had a prayer shawl and phylacteries that someone had lent me but I had forgotten how to wind the thongs so that they formed the letter *shin* of the word *shaddai* — God.

I prayed and saw to my amazement that this was far from comedy and sham. I thanked the Creator for directing me to this room among true Jews, who still sought a minyan while the outside world swarmed with hate and evil theories. Here, old age was no disgrace. Here, no one boasted of his sexual prowess or his ability to hold liquor. Here, the elderly were treated with respect and pious humility. No one here dyed his hair, claimed to be 'eighty years young', or used the other banalities heard among the worldly aged.' p42-3

East of Eden [Chaver Nachman] [Yiddish USA]

The Brothers Ashkenazi [Di brider Ashkenazi]

Yoshe Kalb [Yoshe Kalb]

The Family Carnovsky [Di mishpohe Karnovski]

I.J.Singer (1893-1944) was concerned for Yiddish to break out of its confines, to achieve a more modern style. His younger brother, Isaac Bashevis Singer, on whom he was a major influence, said that Israel Joshua refused to romanticise Jewish life and was one of the first Yiddish writers to explore sexuality. His writing was often sensual, even exploring male homosexuality to some extent, albeit in a somewhat hostile way.

He wanted to break away from what he the saw as the confines of a Yiddish literature concerned with the folksy or the didactic and saw the messianic strain in Judaism as a destructive force, a barren temptation and refused to provide any sort of 'ideological haven' in his books. There was no alternative for the Jews but to accept modernity even though they could never fully be integrated into it. Hence, much of his writing was rather fatalistic. His characters strove to break free from the symbols of Jewish religious tradition, but could not do so. In the end they were destined to share a collective fate (most gruesomely in the journey to the gas chambers, which he could not have predicted).

Enthused by Communism, in 1917 Singer chose to live in Bolshevik Russia, but by 1919 he had become disillusioned and returned to Poland. In the mid 1920s he was commissioned by the editor of an American Yiddish newspaper to write a series of reports on life in the Soviet Union. A collection of these — *The New Russia* — was published in 1927, and provided material for his novel, *Chaver Nachman* published in English in 1938 as *East of Eden*. This was, perhaps, a misplaced title because, as Anita Norich has suggested, there is no real banishment from an Eden. The characters simply come to realise that it is one more illusion. Nachman, a revolutionary socialist harassed by the Polish authorities, flees to the Soviet Union, where he believes that his socialist dreams have been realised. Conditions are hard, but he just about manages to enable his family to survive. Though he brushes aside these difficulties as temporary, when he seeks to defend a fellow worker, he is accused of counter-revolution, and eventually he is expelled from the country.

Singer's writing could be sparse, direct, vivid in its depiction of landscape, character and social life, generally against a background of profound historical change. In *Spring,* (1937) for example, he shows the impact of the first world war and the establishment of independent Poland on the life of a Jewish family who survive only by fleeing from the countryside to Warsaw. In *The Brothers Ashkenazi* (1934-5) probably his greatest novel, he chronicles the life of a family of Jewish textile magnates in the booming industrial centre of Lodz before the World War One, where the inexorable forces of capitalism and social transformation dominate. The central character, Max (formerly Simcha Meyer) is trying to 'pass' in the gentile world. Physically he does escape from the ghetto, but in reality he cannot escape from what he is. Nonetheless, he is impelled by a self-delusion, which allows him initial financial success, but which ultimately leads to his destruction, overwhelmed as he is by the outside forces of war, revolution and pogroms.

Singer's most successful work was *Yoshe Kalb* (1933) which was immediately translated into English and also dramatised for the Yiddish stage by Maurice Schwartz. Set against a background of Hasidic rigidity in the shtetl*, it is a story of forbidden love, guilt and spiritual expiation. Hence it is basically a religious work in judgement of the religious. That, perhaps, explains its success on the New York stage, where a generation of Jews were trying to come to terms with their own rejection of the old Jewish religious values in favour of the new American ones. Yoshe Kalb was to pay dearly for his rebelliousness. A split personality, he became the ultimate homeless wanderer, not now the Jew driven out by the non-Jewish world, but an outcast even amongst the Jews themselves.

The rise of Nazism was to provide the basis for Singer's last major work *The Family Carnovsky* (1943) where he deals with the futility and tragedy of the German Jews' attempts to assimilate. The psychological element of rejection of the self becomes more explicitly an exploration in Jewish self-hatred, which Singer could resolve only by resorting to a melodramatic ending.

Singer believed that Jews could recognise their situation, and that this was where the writer could help, but that they could do little to alter it. Hence they were threatened by an endless repetition of their fate, rather than destruction. The Holocaust could not so easily be assimilated to his views and, in the end Singer had come to accept that if his literary imagination could remain homeless, something more secure had to be found for the Jews themselves. B D

'Yet where did these barracks ['*The Barracks'* are where Nachman and numerous others live in Moscow.— ed.] stand? In that country to the East where the workers had flung the chains of slavery from off their limbs and had become the masters. The walls of the barracks were covered with slogans which spoke of proletarian unity, of the liberation of woman, of the joys of the collective life, of joyous labour and creativity. But there seemed to be no connection between these slogans and pictures and the people among whom he lived.

They were poor, unwashed, ill-clad, and wicked, frightfully wicked. They were divided in groups and categories: those that earned more and those that earned less, the higher ones and the lower ones. Workers envied their foremen, foremen envied their directors. Ordinary workers hated the pacesetters, weak workers looked with envy on stronger workers, unskilled and clumsy workers on skilled and lucky workers, small earners on big earners, the rank and file on the higher-ups. In the kitchens the women fought and wrangled about food, about their miserable pots and pans, about the superior quality of someone's meals, the inferior quality of another's. Thieving was a common thing in the barracks; there were fights over pieces of bread which disappeared in the midst of a meal. Women jostled one another, fought one another, around the big stove, for the right of putting on a pot. There was a constant squabbling about whose turn it was to bring in firewood. No-one wanted to lend a hand in cleaning up the barracks; everyone swept his little heap of dirt toward the middle of the barracks.

Children cried and begged for bread, and their mothers answered them with blows. Women had scenes with their husbands because they caught them making up to other men's wives. The night was a bedlam. Children cried, young husbands and wives whispered, some made love, others quarrelled. Everything could be heard, it was impossible to hide anything from the prying eyes of neighbours, neither one's joys nor one's sorrows. Men who went to work on night shifts were afraid to leave their wives with so many young fellows in the barracks. Older people were furious with younger ones because the latter sang and played in the nights. The healthy were irritated by the coughing and groaning of the sick. People tried to hide from one another; they were afraid to speak out, lest someone report their words. Envy, hatred, bitterness, evil, and suffering reigned in the big barracks, the walls of which were adorned with slogans. Worse than the filth, the darkness, and the hunger was the hatred between the human beings. There was continuous fighting and quarrelling.' (p389-9 *East of Eden*)

The Deeps of the Sea [English Britain]

Proofs & Three Parables

George Steiner has long seemed to his admirers like the perfect model of the assimilated intellectual Jew; a leader in his field (literary criticism), a polyglot and a thinker who both argues and embodies a European cultural perspective.

The glories of European cultural achievements at the turn of the century; modern science, the novel, orchestral music, printing, liberal democracy etc. seemed to augur for a great European civilisation. In reality of course that promise has been betrayed by enormous crimes against humanity carried out using some of these same achievements.

Particularly in his fiction — only a small part of his intellectual output — Steiner has tried to find ways of coming to terms with, or perhaps just exploring, some of the dark realities of this century in Europe.

Part of the later and more complete collection of Steiner's fiction *The Deeps of the Sea* is taken up by *The Portage of A.H. to San Cristobal,* the novella version of a play of the same name. The play version, also available as a book, is well worth seeking out. The 'A.H.' of the title is the noted Austrian Adolf Hitler. Steiner imagines him as hiding out for years in deepest South America and finally being tracked down and captured by Israeli commandos. The moment in the play when the actor impersonating A.H. appears out of the stage darkness — which becomes there and then 'the black night of history' — is one of the most potent theatrical events ever.

Return no More is another 'what-if?' story with the unlikely but interesting premise that a German officer returns in 1950 to the French village where he had served during the war and had ordered the execution of a young partisan. He returns, so he says, because 'the stench of forgetting is so strong in Germany that I came back here to breathe real air.' He then tries to marry the partisan's younger sister. Unsurprisingly some of the less forgiving villagers have a few drinks and eventually do him in. In this piece Steiner (most of whose Jewish school-friends in Paris were murdered by Germans) seems to suggest that the actual German unresponsiveness, the passive reaction to having committed the greatest crimes of a century of crimes is the result of the very enormity of those crimes. The easiest, the only 'reasonable' thing for them to do is to sit back and breathe in 'the stench of forgetting'.

Cake too is set in the aftermath of World War Two and attempts to reverse the amnesia that means, for example, we have many films about the military campaigns of that period but very few about the murder of civilians organised by the Germans and their collaborators all over Europe. In this story of a young American in France some of the foetid air of occupied Europe is let out of the sealed casket where it's been kept for fifty years.

Some of the foetid air of dear old Blighty (England) is released in *Sweet Mars* which carries out a Jewish outsider's psychoanalysis on the rather schoolboyish psychology of the upper-middle class Englishmen that Steiner has mixed with. It is a sombre and clever story about what he calls the (English) 'voluptuaries of remorse.'

The three 'war aftermath' stories were written in the early 1960s and are about the long-term impact of World War Two on a generation, *Proofs* a story from 1992 is about the impact of the collapse of Communism. Communism is a proper European-Jewish theme for Steiner to get his teeth into as its form of secular messianism attracted great numbers of Jews in both Eastern and Western Europe. As a piece of fiction it is more expertly written than the earlier stories, with delicious phrases such as (describing the East German frontier guards the day the Berlin Wall was breached) 'Border guards grinned vacantly and reached for cigarettes as do the bears in a bankrupt circus'. Steiner's clever take on Communism is to compare it to Christianity; both share the same somehow ever-deferred millennium...

He also remembers Stalin's twenty-five million victims, ultimately, in the Steiner view, the result of an idealistic over-estimation of the human spirit.

Steiner writes a kind of intelligent and readable philosophical fiction like that of Bertrand Russell, that seeks to investigate what the book jacket calls 'the nightmares of reason' in our century. Very worthwhile stuff! R K

[*The crippled German ex-soldier Falk recounts his youth — ed.*]

"'I grew up in a very loud bad dream," said Falk. "I cannot remember a time when we were not marching or shouting and when there were no flags in the street. When I think of my childhood all I can remember distinctly are the drums and the uniform I wore as a young pioneer. And the great red flags with the white circle and the black hooked cross in the middle. They were constantly draped across our window. It seems to me I always saw the sun through a red curtain. And I remember the torches. One night my father woke me suddenly and tore to the window. The whole street was full of men marching with torches like a great fiery worm. I must have yelled with fear or sleepiness and my father slapped me across the mouth. I don't remember much about him but he smelled of leather."

"School was worse. The drums beat louder and there were more flags. On the way home we played rabbit hunt and went after Jews. We made them run in the gutter carrying their books and if they dropped any we held them down and pissed in their faces. In the summer we were taught how to be men. They sat us on a log two by two. Every boy in turn would slap his partner as hard as he could. First one to duck was a coward. I passed out once but did not fall off the log. I never finished school. I suppose my final exam came in Lemberg when they told me to clean out a bunker with a flamethrower. I had my graduation in Warsaw, marching with the victory parade. Now the drums never stopped. They were always pounding at us: in Norway; outside Utrecht, where I got my first wound; in Salonika, where we hanged the partisans on meat hooks; and at Kharkov, where this happened." Falk's hand trailed absently along his leg.' (*Return No More* p168-9)

TAMMUZ
Benjamin

The Orchard [Hapardes] [Hebrew]

This novel by the versatile writer, sculptor and art critic Tammuz, who emigrated with his parents from Russia to Palestine at a young age and started publishing stories in the early 1950s, is probably the most famous of his prose works. It recounts, in nineteen short chapters, the development and fate of an orchard near Jaffa, through the eyes of the narrator, a Jewish agronomist expert in the care of citrus trees. Crucially, the orchard is owned by two step brothers, one born of a Muslim mother (Obadiah) one of a Jewish mother (Daniel) but both with the same Jewish father.

Although the orchard is treated as a real place in the tale — there is experimentation in planting techniques, a swarm of deadly locusts blows over one year from the East with the *hamsim* wind, wars in Europe have effects on fruit sales, and so forth — it is also a symbol through which cycles of 'resurrection and destruction' in the land of Israel are explored, from the time of the Ottoman Empire to the war with Egypt in 1956. Specifically it shows the changing relation between Arab and Jew, presented as integrated and untroubled in the early years and murderous as the century proceeds.

According to the original Turkish owner of the orchard, a generation prior to Daniel and Obadiah, Arab and Jew had no fear of each other, lived in peace side by side, the country was polyglot, and Arab and Jew ate each other's food. But external events (property purchase, Arab massacres of Jews in the riots of 1929 and 1936) drive a wedge between Jew and Arab until the situation is such that Daniel's (or is it Obadiah's?...) son is born obsessed by weapons, with a secret arsenal of guns stashed away by the time he is ten, quick on revenge, and with no time for education or talk, since 'whoever wants life had better not talk of peace'.

With its solemn biblical cadences and tight focus on essential elements, this novel has an awesome tone to it (and Daniel and Obadiah hark back to the Biblical Isaac and Ishmael, sons of Abraham and [Jewish] Sarah, Abraham and the Egyptian woman Hagar respectively). This tone is reinforced by the mysterious character Luna, a woman dreamed of by Daniel before he even set foot in the orchard who is described as spell-bindingly beautiful, and who appears never to age... She is a magical presence in the orchard, appearing at several places at once between the trees and magnetising desires both adulterous and incestuous, fatally bringing Muslim and Jew into conflict.

Tammuz, who was briefly an advocate of 'Canaanism' in the 1950s, a short-lived movement which believed that the Jew of Israel should identify not with Europe — the Diaspora was seen as an irrelevance — but with the Levant, understood as a geographical, political, linguistic and cultural unit, clearly views this conflict as tragic (see also his sober story, *The Swimming Contest*, also about Arab-Jewish relations, in the *Oxford Book of Hebrew Short Stories* anthology, reviewed here).

Benjamin Tammuz's *The Orchard* has the compact power of tragic drama, neatly reworking the classic tragic structure of enemy brothers — Obadiah inscrutable and resentful, Daniel eaten up by guilt and attempting to assuage it by showering gifts on his brother — to show just how deadly conflict can be when it inserts itself within 'family' bonds (Arab and Jew as brothers).

Not only does Tammuz show how far hatred can go, but, again in keeping with the pure tragic line of this novel, what a catalogue of ills ensues when 'natural' bonds of solidarity are dissolved: bonds which should be sublimated erupt violently (some of the grimmest wounds are inflicted via Luna, the 'object' through which, silently, both brothers express their possession of the land), and the orchard, 'too thick and too dark' becomes the scene of incest and violation. As fundamental social limits are broken down (through murder and incest), so another tragic theme emerges, the threat of dissolution of differences: by the end of the novel one cannot know for certain whether Luna is indeed Jew or Arab, hence whether her son, the Israeli patriot, is one or the other....

This is a tense tale, written at a time when the sense of threat and of imminent conflagration was strong (the book was first published in 1971). But is also has a visionary aura to it, full of ambiguity and contradiction (the orchard reaches its peak yield at Daniel's death, just as it reaches its first full yield during the Arab attacks on Jews in 1929), making it a challenging read. S B

'But Daniel, whose neck muscles were strong — stronger, it appeared, than one would have guessed by appearances — pulled himself backwards a step or two, swung up his right leg, and kicked Obadiah in the chest, knocking him to the ground. Before Obadiah had time to recover and get up, Daniel tore the tie from around his neck and threw it away. Now the two brothers were tightly locked together, each trying to raise the other up in the air and throw him heavily back down onto the ground. They resembled two men in a primitive dance, wild and savage, a dance in appearance only, but in truth the last embrace before death.' p54-5

WEST
Nathanael

The Day Of The Locust [English USA]

Nathanael West was born Nathan Weinstein in New York City on October 17, 1903. His parents were Russian immigrants though his mother, Anna Wallenstein Weinstein, came from a rather wealthy family. West's father, Max, was a building contractor. Though West showed little writing aptitude as a youngster, fiction seemed to be in his blood as he was accepted at Tufts University by falsifying his high school transcript since he never graduated from high school. Failing at Tufts, he was admitted to Brown University on the strength of a transcript of another Nathan Weinstein. While at Brown, West not only did not participate in Jewish activities, but as one college friend wrote, West 'writhed under the accidental curse of his religion.' He was the classic case of the un-Jewish Jew whose perspective is that of the outsider looking in sardonically and yet sympathetically...

'Though the silence hovers endlessly the noise becomes undone; for the masses see with violence, the locusts grin with pain.' Arthur Rimbaud, the great Freench poet and rebel, once said that the poet should be a *voyant*, a seer, one who has within himself the capacity to transcend the pedestrian, whose voice reaches farther than the voice we hear today. Charles Baudelaire was a *voyant*, and paid for it with the phlegmatic accusations that his poetry was obscene. Nathanael West empathised with Baudelaire, and so too did he share with him the spoils of the *voyant*; misunderstanding, scorn, antipathy, and the vexation of the publishing industry.

West wrote only four novels: *The Dream Life of Balso Snell* (1931) was privately published (only 500 copies) and was hardly reviewed; *Miss Lonelyhearts* (1933) received mixed reviews, though most were favourable, but with *Liveright* the publisher, declared bankruptcy weeks later; *A Cool Million* (1934) was published by a small firm and almost immediately became neglected; *The Day of the Locust* (1939), published by Random House, sold less than 1500 copies. One year after *The Day of the Locust* was published, West was killed in an automobile accident. It would appear that with only four novels, none of which gaining any 'success', there would be little to say about the work of Nathanael West; but West was a *voyant*, and the work of *voyants* is not measured quantitatively...

Baudelaire wrote little and Rimbaud even less... Of his two best novels, *Miss Lonelyhearts* and *The Day of the Locust*, the latter may be one of the finest and most representative novels of twentieth century ennui. In it, West has synthesized the malaise of twentieth century man and woman into one hundred and twenty pages of poignancy, perception, and poetry. Though present, the influences of both Baudelaire and Kafka do not obscure West's own style, but, to the contrary, enrich it.

The Day of the Locust takes place in California, the paradise that searchers always seek before they die. The searchers are Homer Simpson, a trusting mid-western rube who moves to California only to be cheated by its 'warmth', and Tod Hackett, a Yale art graduate who attempts to satisfy the artistic and emotional needs of the searchers of the world. In Los Angeles they meet Faye Greener, the nubile embodiment of pretension and deceit, Tod's defeat and Homer's death; Harry Greener the aged embodiment of the artist who fails; and Abe Kusich the bookie dwarf who sells lies and dreams — these characters are all a part of West's wasteland, and they are personalities representative of twentieth century American neuroticism.

West weaves into his characters a preoccupation with decay, perversion, and violence: the logical consequence to the boredom inherent in the character of many twentieth century men and women. Predating the Absurdists, West cogently dramatizes the slow, lingering death of civilization, culminating in the last and most vivid scene of the novel, the riot at the theater.

It is in the riot, a juxtaposition of what has been called the 'cheated', or the lower middle class whose emotional needs demand satisfaction and the 'performers', or the cheaters who are attempting to satisfy the emotional needs of others, that Tod reflects on in his painting *The Burning of Los Angeles*.

This vision is West's epiphany, that which Joyce referred to as a revelation, and which Revelation itself states in 9:3-9: 'And out of the smoke there came forth locusts upon the earth.' The locusts, the demonic collective unity cheated by the 'artificiality of oranges,' by the mundanity of comfort and the boredom that is leisure. This was West's prophecy: the locusts have arrived, the Apocalypse is at hand, there will be death by fire. *The Day of the Locust* should be read, for the anguish on his lips is the pain within our soul, the terror within our vision. M A

'As he stood on his good leg, clinging desperately to the iron rail, he could see all the rough charcoal strokes with which he had blocked it out on the big canvas. Across the top, parallel with the frame, he had drawn the burning city, a great bonfire of architectural styles, ranging from Egyptian to Cape Cod colonial. Through the center winding from left to right, was a long hilly street and down it, spilling into the middle foreground, came the mob carrying baseball bats and torches. For the faces of its members, he was using the innumerable sketches he had made of the people who come to California to die; the cultists of all sorts, economic as well as religious, the wave, the airplane, funeral and preview watchers — all those poor devils who can only be stirred by the promise of miracles and then only to violence. A super 'Dr. Know-All-Pierce-All' had made the necessary promise and they were marching behind his banner in a great united front of screwballs and screwboxes to purify the land. No longer bored, they sang and danced joyously in the red light of the flames.'

Mr Mani [Mar Mani] [Hebrew]

A.B Yehoshua has created a masterpiece here on several levels.
The format alone is exciting and innovative as the author pursues
the lives of the Mani family over five generations. They are a
Sephardi* Jewish family, and their origins are revealed leading
backwards from the opening section in modern-day Israel, to Crete
during the Second World War, returning to Jerusalem during the
British mandate*, immediately after World War One. Earlier the
link in the Mani chain is found in Basel, and the final chapter, or
novella, representing the earliest scenario, takes place in Ottoman
times.

First, we have the presentation of protagonists — brief but
pointed background to the drama. Then follows the development
through a 'mono-dialogue', i.e. only one side is reported. This
system, although artificial of course, allows Yehoshua to explore
both the nature of dialogue, using language and jargon pertinent
to each specific generation, and the psychological nuance of
awareness or concealment that comes through this extended
'conversation'.

The reader becomes a participant in each of these dialogues,
as he needs to recreate the missing speaker, and certainly plays a
far more active role than he would in a traditional novel. Yehoshua
explores not only the Sephardi background of the Mani families
but also the environment of those who relate to them.

The development of each of these scenarios is what makes
them essentially Jewish, with the emphasis on the family and its
various ramifications, including loyalty, conflict and remorse.
Since the book is dedicated to Yehoshua's father; 'a man of
Jerusalem and a lover of its past', we can understand that this
work is a written in homage to a very dear person and place.

Spinning a web of history and personal interconnections,
Yehoshua subtly reveals facts, feelings and understanding. He
examines the points in everyday life when pivotal events occur,
when something changes forever in both perception and actuality,
leading to an entirely different and unexpected outcome. There is
Hagar, child of a kibbutz, living in Tel Aviv, who meets and
connects with her boyfriend's father, Mr Mani. Egon Bruner,
fairly disinterested German soldier on duty in Crete during the
German occupation, whose encounter with the Mani family

awakens all his sensibilities and alters the course of many lives. The middle section involves Lieutenant Horowitz, military advocate serving with the British forces during the early years of the mandate and Jewish himself. His professional interaction with the mysterious spy/infiltrator/secret agent Yosef Mani rouses inner emotions relating to his own Jewishness, and to the role of occupying power. This section was published independently in A.B Yehoshua's collection of short stories *The Continuing Silence of the Poet*, and must be seen as a response to Israeli occupation of the territories won in the Six Day War.

The fourth 'telling' recounts the confrontation of Ashkenazi and Sephardi Jew, set in Poland at the end of the nineteenth century, but concerns events at the Third Zionist Congress in Basel in 1899. Here Dr Mani encourages brother and sister, Ephraim and Linka Shapiro from Poland to travel on with him to Palestine. Once in Jerusalem another series of associations and relationships impact on all their lives with profound effect. The final section further explores the interconnected relationships between father and child, surrogate parents, and unrequited, unresolved love. It is set in the exotic multicultural cities of the Ottoman Empire, Athens, Constantinople and Jerusalem. Rather than tying up all the loose ends in a simple fashion, this 'telling' confirms the environment of intrigue and mystery, of intuition and premonition. The lingering sensation is the desire to read the entire book again. T L

'Indeed, sir. You know what we military advocates generally have to deal with: desertions, brawls, petty thefts, drunkenness, insubordination — in a word thirty- and sixty-day sentences and one guinea fines. And here was a real investigation, something to get to the bottom of, where possibly lurked a man's death. I was so beside myself that I left the club directly and went straight to the divisional guardhouse by the Jaffa Gate, under the assumption that that's where this Mani was being held. Of course, I had no idea at the time what his name was, but I was determined not to be elbowed aside, and soon I found myself standing out in the cold night across from the place called David's Tower which is a sort of minia- ture version of the tower of London, with my mind racing ahead. Just then I noticed a Jew dressed in black, hanging back by a little lane that ran into the empty square — and I knew directly that he was connected to the spy and had come to see what was being done with him; which meant that word had already reached the concerned parties in Jerusalem, who had sent a first scout to re- connoitre; and a most clandestine-looking, eternal-looking, metaphysical-look- ing scout he was... only later did I discover that he was not the least bit different from his scoutmasters...' p159-160

Midnight convoy and other stories [Sheyyara shel hazot] [Hebrew]

Yizhar is a key figure in the 'first wave' of Israeli fiction writers, born in Israel and first published there. A writer, member of the Knesset (Israeli parliament), farmer and teacher, his stories are fed by involvement with the land of Israel in both the agricultural and political senses, and he shows an ongoing fascination with the Israeli landscape. His stories are memorable above all for their distinctive, modernist style which departs from the more realist leanings of his contemporaries such as Moshe Shamir (see the anthology *Israeli Stories* and *The Oxford Book of Hebrew Short Stories*, reviewed here).

This collection of two short stories and the prize-winning novella *Midnight convoy*, is invaluable for showing Yizhar's development, from the slightly awkward staging of ideological debate in *Ephraim goes back to alfalfa* (1938) to the jubilantly anarchic tale of a violin-playing prophet in *Habakuk* (1960).

While the 1938 story is principally concerned with individual aspirations in their conflict with collective goals, this theme is shot through with startling reflections on the ambiguous quality of routine; that it gives tranquillity and reassurance while at the same time bringing despair at the unbending aspects of repetition: 'nothing has been forgotten, and the same wounds are still bleeding'. There are also striking descriptions of nature tamed by human forces yet still resistant, on the verge of breaking loose again, the complex lines of irrigation channels 'on whose swelling ripples danced dismembered, turbid suns'.

Midnight Convoy (1950) expands on the themes of the group and the individual, human and natural worlds. While only in the last twenty pages does anything actually happen in the strict sense of the word, the tale manages to be gripping, capturing the strange sense of solidarity between individual soldiers — people for whom one would risk one's life — and yet also the distance and unfamiliarity; the sense of elation at being a member of the group in the silence and darkness at the same time as experiencing a violent unravelling of the self, where 'unhealed scars open in an instant' and 'that same disquietude quivered in the air'.

Both tales depict with unusual sensitivity those rarely described perceptions and states of being which make up the most intimate fabric of daily lives: the transformation of the sense of space, distance and threat as we get to know a route or a place, the diverse qualities of silence, waking at night to an anxiety without cause, growing close to someone at a distance without knowing how the threads were woven...

The other story here, *Habakuk* (1960), is energetic and playful, full of asides to the reader and digressions swept aside they stray too far ('indeed it is time his story were told after all this delay'). The story mixes biblical and prophetic styles with the gleeful vision of a group of children who daily swoop down on an old man they have named Habakuk. They go to him in his basement and hear him play the violin and read the stars. But the story, which employs the most virtuoso narrative techniques of the whole collection, also has a current of melancholy running through it. This is partly conveyed through the shades of anxiety emerging in the playful questions about how to tell the story — where to begin, how to proceed, how to tell — and partly through the theme of the child now grown up who recalls his past. He is still haunted by a presence which he drifted away from but which at the same time he has not left. *Habakuk* is a moving and lyrical story, full of wonderment and eagerness, but which is also 'listening to... things unsaid, things that were and might have been were it not that.' S B

'Then silence was heard, spreading out and flowing over the warm fields to the farthest limits of the cultivated land, rising and falling in accordance with the contours, reaching out to pour itself like a soundless wind over the desolation of rolling expanses, until it became so broad and unfathomable that, without knowing when, and without any obvious connection with anything in particular, you suddenly began to feel like a lamb left behind, tiny and far off and lonely, or like a tamarisk tree in the wilderness.' p116

ZANGWILL
Israel

King of Schnorrers [English Britain]

Israel Zangwill was a prominent Anglo-Jewish writer of the early years of this century, enjoying great popularity with some of his comic stories of 'Whitechapel Ghetto' (East London) life. He is still remembered for this book and for his *Children of the Ghetto*, which is interesting, if a little florid for today's taste.

King of the Schnorrers though is pure delight and also gives an interesting picture of London's Jewish community in the Eighteenth century. The protagonist and Schnorrer-King is a magnificent Sephardi 'gentleman beggar' (beggar is *Schnorrer* in

Yiddish) Manasseh Bueno Barzollai Azevedo da Costa. The book is made up of a series of delicious running jokes, the main one being how a beggar, a Schnorrer, manages to completely dominate, even humiliate all his social betters and charitable benefactors. One sees how *schnorring* is not quite the same thing as begging — it implies not so much pleading for pity but the joyous, intelligent extraction of money or goods from the person who is 'schnorred'.

Manasseh Bueno Barzollai Azevedo da Costa successfully conducts his schnorring through the constant application of his gigantic chutzpah, helped to an extent by the lordly Sephardi* manner he directs at Ashkenazi* Jews.

In fact a running joke of *The King of Schnorrers* is the Sephardi community and their rather grand leaders. Zangwill shows us a kind of Jewish community rather different from the more democratic (and disunited) Ashkenazi one of immigrants from Germany, Poland and Russia that began to outnumber the Sephardis at the time Zangwill describes.

As every Schnorrer knows there is an awful lot of psychology in *schnorring* and Zangwill uses the opportunity of this book to display his grasp of human nature in an enjoyable and amusing way, so that *The King of Schnorrers* has a value that transcends the fast-receding time in which it was written. It is a worthy piece of the humorous Anglo-Jewish tradition of Bernard Kops, Peter Sellers, Chaim Bermant, Alexei Sayle etc etc. R K

"'Den de Synagogue allows me a little extra for announcing de dead.'"

In those primitive times, when a Jewish newspaper was undreamt of, the day's obituary was published by a peripatetic *Schnorrer* :

"Who's dead to-day?"

"So-and-so ben So-and-so — funeral on such a day — mourning service at such an hour," the *Schnorrer* would reply, and the enquirer would piously put something into the "byx" as it was called. The collection was handed over to the Holy Society — in other words, the Burial Society.' p68

A Shtetl and other Yiddish novellas [Yiddish Poland Russia Lithuania]

This is a collection of less obvious longer pieces from Yiddish writers mainly of the later or middle period of that literature's lifespan. What they have in common is the influence of the various political ideologies that swept the East-European Jewish world from the turn of the century. Marxist Socialism, Bundism*, Communism and Zionism all impacted on this world, not to mention the various nationalisms and fascisms amongst the non-Jewish population of the region.

I.M. Weissenberg's *A Shtetl* commemorates a small town in Poland riven and stirred by emerging (and rival) Socialist movements of the day; the Social Democratic Party of Poland and Lithuania — amongst its leaders the famous (and Jewish) revolutionary Rosa Luxembourg — which stood for joint Slav and Jewish political action while the Jewish Socialist Bund advocated Jewish proletarian solidarity and action (and promoted the Yiddish language). The period of this story is during the honeymoon of socialism when there was enormous participation in and excitement about socialist ideas amongst the working poor. As part of this, *A Shtetl*, no doubt somewhat propagandistically, shows the only religious figures as sweatshop bosses. In any case it is a well-told story showing what was no doubt felt to be an exciting process; the rapid dissolution of the old certainties of belief in Jewish towns.

In *At the Depot* Dovid Bergelson, a Soviet Yiddish author writes about the small-time traders, in this case grain-dealers, based at a railhead in the Ukraine and who were a mainstay of Jewish economic life. However, it's a very jaundiced view, narrated from the perspective of the embittered and unsympathetic Benish Rubinstein, envious of anyone doing better in love and money-making than himself. There's a message here about the awfulness of the mercantile petty-bourgeoisie that fitted well to the Soviet tune but nevertheless this is a real work of literature, unpredictable and original and not mere agit-prop*. In fact Bergelson was one of the most sophisticated of all the Yiddish writers.

Behind a Mask is by Solomon Ansky, famous for writing a play *The Dybbuk* * later made, in Poland, into the famous (and still enjoyable) Yiddish film of the same name. It's apparently quite autobiographical, recounting a fairly amazing story of a young, sceptical Jew taking a job as tutor to a pious family and joining other young men in a kind of underground Haskalah* group in an old-fashioned Shtetl. It's a pretty hair-raising business when he is found out as an unbeliever but it transmits very well the excitement then of leaving the world of Talmudic learning for the enormous promise of secular science and literature. Part of the great impact of rationalist ideas on Jewish communities in Eastern Europe was that they had lived in mental isolation for many centuries, so that a conflict was suddenly unleashed there that had already been raging outside the 'ghetto' for five hundred years.

Somewhat different from the other novellas here is Mendele Moykher Sforim's *Of Bygone Days,* important in any case for being the only autobiographical writing ever published by this major early Yiddish author. It's an intense and beautiful pastoral piece; a fine revelation of our connection to the natural order, a relief from all the claustrophobia and conflict in the usual tidings from the shtetl... Apart from the understanding of our place in nature there is at the same time a brilliant meditation on the 'flavour' of Jewish life; its existential condition; 'The bitterness in our life...is its most important ingredient'. Although perhaps now in Western countries it doesn't feel that way any more, understanding the experience of older generations, particularly of anti-Semitism, brings on that sense of 'Jewish woe' that Mendele Moykher Sforim was talking about...

There is also wonderful ethnographic detail here of the kind of small Lithuanian town that Mendele Moykher Sforim came from, where, in a typical Jewish house, roosting chickens and Slav peasants having a drink would apparently sometimes share the main room... R K

'Even though the life of the Jewish people seems repulsive from the outside, it is pleasant enough within. There is a mighty spirit, a divine spirit, blowing through it constantly, like a storm wind, purifying it of dirt and rot.' (*Of Bygone Days* Mendele Mocher Sforim)

'Narrow roads start their winding way in forsaken little towns of the countryside. Then cutting through sleepy villages, they creep up silent green hills, drop to the valleys, and join far off on a distant rise to bow before the red stone railway station.

The tall, two-storied building has been a regional landmark for years. Petrified and inert, it dominates the countryside like a spell-bound sentry, cast by some prankster into everlasting, melancholy sleep. Whoever that sullen magician may have been, he has long since returned to dust, and his bones have grown black in the damp ground. But the station has yet to be released from its trance: somnolently it stands guard over the incoming roads, over the near and distant hills and valleys, and over the pretty village, scattered at the bottom of a long valley, that has spent years clambering up the slopes of two adjacent mountains without ever reaching the top. The old station shares in the silence of the village and countryside; secretly, though, as it stares into the blue, unknown distance, it yearns for a proud and forceful hero to come storming the sleepy hamlets and recall to life everything languishing and dead. But the horizon is imperturbable and glum, and so deeply bored by the sleepy countryside that it too begins to doze. Occasionally its toothless old mouth opens in a weary yawn, and out spits a long rushing passenger train. The train comes from far away and is eager to impart its good tidings to the station and the surrounding countryside. But after hearing the first mournful echo of its expansive merry whistle, it realises that nothing will ever pierce this region's deep, eternal gloom. The train slows down to a dispirited crawl, and comes to a stop with a long heavy sigh of steam. The sigh hangs suspended in the air like a verdict: "Useless, useless, and doomed.'" (p84-5 *At the Depot* by David Bergelson)

'The tiny Jewish town was isolated from the rest of the world. Only rare echoes came straying here from the cities or even the large towns. No one needed the little shtetl, and it needed no one. It got along all on its own. With potatoes from its own fields, flour from its own windmill, and meat from its own sheep. As for clothing, Leybe the Tailor was a genius at his trade, and he sewed for both women and men. True, the material was brought in from the city, but this was done by Yankel, who was practically the only storekeeper in town; once a year, he would travel to the state capital to buy various goods. But Yankel was a quiet man. You didn't have to hawk your wares in the shtetl. And he was so quiet about his trip that it almost seemed like a secret. Every year, he would vanish for two days with no sign of life, and when he came back, only a few people, not all, would find out where he'd been. The curious ones would pounce upon him:

"Yankel, what's happening in the world?"

But Yankel had nothing to say. To his way of thinking, there was nothing to tell — everything was trivial! Once though, when they really cornered him and he felt he had to tell them something, he smirked, stroked his black beard, and replied:

"It's like, well, say — a hundred shtetls rolled into one. Altogether, it's a hundred times bigger than our little town, so how can you be surprised at the hubbub!"

And that was the only news that the townsfolk, Jews of course, ever received from the big world, once in a blue moon.' (p481 *Acquiring a Graveyard* by Avrom Reyzen)

A Treasury of Yiddish Stories [Yiddish Various Countries]

This is the 630 page heavyweight compendium of fiction in Yiddish, divided into eight sections, all pretty essential for getting an orientation and an overview of Yiddish writing and the world it arose from. The other anthologies of Yiddish literature can only seek to correct the weaker points of this solid introduction — the absence of women authors, the avoidance of the more avant-garde writers and the absence of writers from the minor centres of Yiddish like South Africa, Argentina and Britain.

The eight sections include a brilliant seventy-page *Introduction* to the whole history and fate of Yiddish literature; *The Fathers* which includes representative stories of the three founders of modern Yiddish fiction — Mendele Mokher Sforim, Sholem Aleichem and I.L.Peretz; the longest (and strongest) section is *Portrait of a World* which contains classic stories of Jewish life in Eastern Europe before World War One by Sholem Aleichem, I.L.Peretz, David Pinski, Mordecai Spector, I.M.Weissenberg, Sholem Asch, Zalman Schneour, Lamed Shapiro, I.B.Singer and his brother I.J.Singer, Jonah Rosenfeld and Joseph Opatoshu. Other far shorter sections cover something about the life of Jewish emigrants in the United States (*New Worlds*), the decline of religious belief and practice (*Breakup*), *Jewish Children,* and *Folk Tales* which includes too some authentically acid Yiddish sayings; 'Your health comes first — you can always hang yourself later'; 'One chops the wood, the other does the grunting' and 'Sleep faster, we need the pillows'. There is also a useful set of one-page biographies of all the twenty-three authors present.

Looking at some of the more notable or typical stories in this large collection, Mendele Mocher Sforim's *The Calf* is a heartfelt complaint against the misery of a poor Yeshiva* student, 'Almighty God, is it really your will that a human being be cooped up like a goose from childhood on, never to see the world, and to stuff his mind with such nonsense as mine is full of?'. Sholem Aleichem's *The Pair* is about the (brief) life of a goose, fattened up for Passover — a startling story as it's cleverly told from the goose's point of view. In fact there are a lot of animals in both Sholem Aleichem and Mendele Mocher Sforim's stories; in a rural familiarity with animalkind and a sympathy for their fates — hard like that of the poor Jews, not always eating well, having to work long hours, being cold and so on. Another side of Sholem Aleichem, that shows the breadth of this prolific writer is *A Page from the Song of Songs*, a lyrical and charming story of first love. I.L.Peretz's most famous story *Bontshe the Silent,* is here and it is a rich and puzzling piece where Peretz's own split between modernising socialism and respect for traditional Jewish culture is evident. Is suffering Bontshe just a pious idiot or a true and noble *mensch**? Decide for yourself. Another curious character is Berel the porter in David Pinski's *And Then He Wept* who lives with his benighted family in a soggy basement in the most horrible conditions possible but is always laughing uproariously; when yet another baby is born and there is yet another mouth to feed he comes up with; 'Children are a delight, a joy'.

Sholem Asch's *Kola Street* is populated with burly tough-guy 'teamsters' who, when anti-Semitic incidents brewed up in their Polish town, 'armed with shafts from carts and iron bars wrested from shutters...would go out into the streets and teach the hooligans a lesson.' And in fact Asch loved to write about these 'other Jews' 'unversed in Talmud, better versed in the everyday world of wheat and apples.'

Another Yiddish master, Abraham Reisen, is represented by four stories in this book including *The Recluse,* a rich and many-layered story, quite Chekhovian (which is to say very, very, very good). Another complex writer is I.M.Weissenberg with the amazing Expressionist-influenced piece *Mazel Tov* — 'The windows of the room in which the rabbi lies flame up and a thin cold rain drops from the dull sky.' — and the shocking and unrestrained *Father and the Boys.*

Zalman Schneour provides more meaty stuff still; *Revenge* is set in a village after a *pogrom** when all that remains of the Jewish houses are some red chimneys sticking up into the air... *The Girl* is another story in his earthy and powerful style, dwelling on grotesque poverty and misery. Lamed Shapiro's *White Challah* is also a pogrom story, set in Russia, being the horrendous tale of an ignorant peasant who commits violence against Jews. It attempts to explain the widespread and politically-manipulated nature of anti-Semitism in a dramatic and potent piece of writing.

I.J.Singer, elder brother and major inspiration for the now world-famous I.B.Singer contributes an ironical but nevertheless wonderful little story about the Hasidim*, focusing on the movement's anti-intellectualism; 'It's better to sleep two days than to entertain one thought.'

The book also contains truly notable stories by Lamed Shapiro, Dovid Bergelson, Joseph Opatoshu, Chaim Grade and I.B.Singer, all writers who were at the end of the Yiddish literary tradition, a tradition this book represents very well. Reading *A Treasury of Yiddish Stories* one can only marvel at a literature created in such hostile conditions and crushed from all sides; by the cultural assimilationists who felt Jews were better off using the languages of the populations they lived amongst, the religious traditionalists who frowned on any secular literature, the Zionists whose preferred language for the Jews was a revived, modernised Hebrew, the German murderers of the Yiddish-speaking masses of Eastern Europe, the Soviet political and cultural dictators who first encouraged, then restricted, then destroyed Yiddish culture in the Soviet Union… However the fact is that much of the very little we have left of the former European Jewish Heartland in Poland and Russia is to be found in these writers and this literature — check it out! R K

'…it was not a third of our people who were murdered, but rather that a third was cut out of the flesh and soul of every Jew who survived.' (p602 Chaim Grade's *My Quarrel with Hersh Rasseyner*)

'Jewish heads — men's heads, women's heads — peeped out of the doorways of the little shops like mice out of their holes.' (p459 Lamed Shapiro's *Eating Days*)

'It was a night after the High Holy days, a rainy night, a night in autumn, such a night one can come upon only in small Polish towns, when the darkness is so intense that the downpour seems to consist of the blackest ink.' (p414 Joseph Opatoshu's *May the Temple Be Restored*)

[*The elderly Polish Jewish shoemaker Abba has emigrated to America to live with his sons*]

'Eventually he recovered enough to take a few steps outdoors, in front of the house, but his senses remained disordered. He would walk into clothes closets, lock himself into the bathroom and forget how to come out; the doorbell and the radio frightened him, and he suffered constant anxiety because of the cars that raced past the house. One day Gimpel brought him to a synagogue ten miles away, but even here he was bewildered. The sexton was clean-shaven, the candelabra held electric lights, there was no courtyard, no faucet for washing one's hands, no stove to stand around. The cantor, instead of singing like a cantor should, babbled and croaked. The congregation wore tiny prayer shawls, like scarves around their necks. Abba was sure he had been hauled to a church to be converted…' (p542 I.B. Singer's *The Little Shoemakers*)

Ashes out of Hope. Fiction by Soviet-Yiddish Writers [Yiddish Soviet Union]

On the general subject of Soviet-Yiddish writers, that's to say those Yiddish writers who lived in and were published in the Soviet Union, one can't put it better than the editors of this anthology; 'In the entire thwarted and scarred history of modern Yiddish literature there is no chapter more tragic than that of the Soviet Yiddish writers. Elsewhere in Europe scores of Yiddish writers were destroyed by avowed enemies; here, in the Soviet Union, a generation of gifted Yiddish novelists and poets came to its end in the prison cells or labour camps of the very state to which they had pledged themselves, sometimes with naïve enthusiasm, sometimes with wry foreboding.' In fact one of the main reasons why writing in Yiddish today is the very faintest of faint sparks is that in the last 'homeland' of Yiddish, Russia, where Yiddish culture was neither exterminated nor entirely assimilated, its fate was to fall into the hands of a psychotic maniac, Stalin, who at first allowed it an ideologically-controlled life then destroyed it overnight in 1952, in a fit of paranoid and anti-Semitic madness.

This little collection, however, gives us some glimpses of the most important writers at work before this disaster struck. The best story is probably Dovid Bergelson's *The Hole Through Which Life Slips,* which manages to be distant both from Soviet Socialist Realism (the state-approved fantasy of the workers' paradise) and folkloric Yiddishism.

A 'bourgeois' is living in the Ukrainian capital, Kiev, as the Bolsheviks arrive to take the city over. He finds himself enveloped by a nameless, draining psychological paralysis as the change of regime occurs — the event itself presented as if entirely off-stage to his own life. On one reading the story is as an allusion to a hopeful 'new dawn' but on another it is a prescient reflection of profound and destructive social disturbance. The atmosphere of *The Hole Through Which Life Slips* is reminiscent of Edmundo Desnoes' *Memories of Underdevelopment,* a famous Cuban novel — later a film — that profiled a middle-class Cuban's 'moral crisis' about the new hostile/promising world coming into being...

Bergelson writes in an impressionistic style that demonstrates how literary modernism was breaking through into Yiddish letters at this period. Another piece by Bergelson here is entitled *Civil War*, and Civil War was of course the great topic for many Russian writers of the 1920s; Isaac Babel (*Red Cavalry*) and Mikhail Bulgakov (*The White Guard*) for example. This piece is even more impressionistic than *The Hole Through Which Life Slips*, conjuring up the transience and instability of this period (roughly 1918-1921) with its images of railroad stations, woodcutter encampments, of families and regiments dispersed to the four winds and everywhere multiple and fleeting political, military (and sexual) alliances.

A more traditional piece of Yiddish writing is Moshe Kulbak's *Zelmenyaner* but more interesting is Der Nister's *Under A Fence*. Der Nister (meaning 'the Hidden One') was the pen-name of Pinhas Kahanovich, an adherent of the important Russian school of Symbolist writers. Unsurprisingly he ran into plenty of trouble with Soviet censors and the party-line literary critics who, incidentally, often applied the term 'politically correct' to literature, a term which has worked its way, via the (famously Stalinist) Communist Party of the USA in the 1930s to the American New Left of the 1960s into Academia, Feminism and the wider world. *Under A Fence* is approximately the same story as Heinrich Mann's *Professor Unrat*, made into the film *The Blue Angel* with Marlene Dietrich. In this version a respected, conventional Professor falls in love with a circus performer, the bareback rider Lili. The story subtly re-creates the mysteries of physical attraction and, like Professor Unrat, opens up the problem of shame as the middle-aged scholar leaves the proper path for the ways of desire, with terrible social consequences...

The story, published in the fatal year 1929 — Stalin was now fully in control in Russia — outraged the Soviet critics and in fact it strongly hints at the dissolution of cultural tradition and intellectual freedom; it is perhaps a coded account of the death of independent scholarship in the USSR. The 'cultural values' of the circus seem to triumph in the end and there is even a hallucinatory trial scene... R K

'And the trial didn't last long, only as long as a circus number should last, but the whole time the circus building was full of laughter that resounded up to the roof at the accused when they defended themselves, at the judges when they questioned them, and at me, the chief judge. And I don't know how so much insult and abuse came out of me. But I suppose that I was influenced by the clowns and the circus air in general and the huge audience that I was performing for, and I plunged into the hubbub, and I mocked more than any of them, and when I told the scholars off, I was wittier than anyone. And finally the sentence was pronounced: dirt and garbage that had to be burned. And assistant clowns came in dressed like executioners and axemen, and set up a bonfire, and they brought in straw effigies of the people sentenced, laid them on the woodpile and skilfully lit the fire, and the flame shot up, and the straw effigies burned. It was Lili who lit the fire, and she invited the audience to come down and light their cigarettes at the flame, and the crowd laughed again; and for some time after, whenever they thought of the number, they laughed out loud, and they had a fine time at the circus that day.' (p213 Der Nister *Under A Fence*)

ANTHOLOGY

Echad, an anthology of Latin American Jewish writings [Latin America Spanish, Portuguese, Yiddish, English]

(Kalechofsky, R &R eds.)

Tropical Synagogues [Latin America Spanish, Portuguese, Yiddish, English]

(Stavans, I ed.)

The vast majority of Jewish writing available in English comes from either English-speaking Jews, from the state of Israel or is translated from various European languages, including Yiddish. The *Babel Guide to Jewish Fiction* reflects this and so can't truly reflect the diversity and global spread of Jewish settlement. These two anthologies exist however to remind us of how many Jews settled in the southern part of the New World, that there were converted Jews who sailed with Columbus and that there was a group of observant Jews on the next expedition to the Americas.

The first anthology, *Echad,* is an earlier and more unconventional book than *Tropical Synagogues*, mixing stories with poetry and essays. In particular one can read about an early Zionist enterprise of the 1870s that settled Russian Jews in the rural Argentinian provinces of Santa Fe and Entre Ríos. Out of these colonies came a prominent literary figure in the Argentine, Alberto Gerchunoff, who wrote (in Spanish) *Los gauchos judíos* (translated as *The Jewish Gauchos:* see the *Babel Guide* database), a touching piece of optimism and idealism about the bright future of these 'other Zionists' in the land of Argentina.

Both these anthologies point to what seems to have been an often uncomfortable situation for Jews in Latin America. On the one hand there is the 'sore thumb' phenomena of small, often mainly Sephardi* rather than Ashkenazi* dominated communities in countries which have been too socially explosive and mono-culturally Catholic to easily accept a group so separate economically and philosophically from its surroundings. Victor Perera, a Guatemalan Jew settled in New York, gives a good example of this in the piece *Growing up Jewish in Guatemala* quoted below.

On the other hand there is the tradition of deep assimilation that the Brazilian Clarice Lispector, present in both anthologies with the same marvellous story, *Love,* represents. It's a Latino Jewish tradition that goes back to the Marranos* in Spain, forced by Christian intolerance between the Devil and the Deep Blue Sea, either to lose Spain where their homes, lives and traditions were or to lose themselves by abandoning the beliefs and the community of believers that made them distinctive. The tradition of profound intolerance by Christianity of other creeds, that Jews have borne a long and martyred witness to, hardly says much for this supposed religion of compassion.

Another noted Latin American Jewish writer represented in *Echad* is Isaac Goldemberg, a Peruvian who emigrated to the US and produced a famous novel *The Fragmented Life of Don Jacobo Lerner* (see *Babel Guide* database), an interesting and episodic work, a pastiche of narrative with quotations from articles about Jewish history in Latin America.

The *Tropical Synagogues* anthology also has a useful introduction — indicating amongst other things the relative sizes of Latin America's major Jewish populations; in Argentina 250,000, Brazil 125,000 and Mexico 50,000 — and a bibliography of Latin American Jewish writers. Major pieces in this anthology not already mentioned in discussing the *Echad* anthology (with which it overlaps in many cases), are Moacyr Scliar's *Inside my dirty head the holocaust* a clever and honest illustration of the immediate post-Holocaust period amongst Brazilian Jews, not themselves directly affected but left with a subsequent guilt and unease according to Scliar. Brazil's Jews could at least share the honour of their country's participation in World War Two against the Axis powers. Not so Argentina which saw widespread anti-Semitic campaigns during this century and whose leader in the 1940s, General Peron, pursued a profitable neutrality during World War Two and then lent himself and his country's good name to the work of saving German war criminals from justice by issuing blank Argentinian passports for their use.

Isidoro Blaisten, well-known as an Argentinian writer is represented with a genial and funny story *Uncle Facundo* about the kind of long-lost relative everyone alternately dreams of and has nightmares about. It's a Surrealistic story in the real sense of the term which, as in this case, points to the reality that lies below the surface of social behaviour — *'Sous les pavés il y a la plage'* (underneath the tarmac — the beach!) as the free spirits of Paris 1968 put it.

Rather different is the allusive, elusive and elegiac *Passion* by another Argentinian, Gerado Mario Goloboff, who captures the overheated, tense atmosphere of Peron's Argentina when nationalism, sometimes combined with anti-Semitism, was in the air. There is also a suggestion of the (later) terrible era of military rule and the 'disappearances' and Goloboff's story brings us very close to its particular reality and milieu, as does the much happier piece by Nora Glickmann, *The Last Emigrant*. This introduces us to a peaceful world of (Ashkenazi) Jewish bakers and farmers in Mexico. Also from Mexico another Ashkenazi, Margo Glantz contributes an extract from her book *The Family Tree* which has been published recently in the UK and the USA. It's the story of Russian Jews in Mexico and makes a fascinating contrast to all the similar narratives we have of these immigrants in North America.

Tropical Synagogues is rounded off with three brief pieces by Jorge Luis Borges on Jewish themes. Altogether it is an excellent introduction to Jewish existence in that other, perhaps more human if less humane, America. R K

[the Russian Jewish settlement of Rajil celebrates Argentina's National Day — ed.]

'The dawn found Rajil bedecked like a ship: the doorways were covered with flags and banners of all colours. The Argentine colours were there, too, though the colonists did not realise it. A mild sun shone bright but not too warm as it lit up the flat countryside and bathed the yellowed shrubs and the white walls of the huts with its new warmth. The Commissary sent his little band, and they swept into the music of the National Anthem as soon as they arrived at the colony. The hearts of the Jews filled with joy at the sound and, though they were still confused about what this date meant, the thought of this patriotic festival they were celebrating in their new homeland filled their spirits with a new happiness.

The service in the synagogue was attended by all the men and women... After the reading from the Sacred Book, the Mayor spoke. "I remember", he said, "that in the city of Kishinev, after that most terrible of po-groms, we closed our synagogues. We did not want to have to bless the Czar. Here, in our new country, nobody forces us to bless anyone. That's why we bless the Republic! That's why we bless the President!" Nobody knew who the President was, but that didn't seem to matter.' (p32 Alberto Gerchunoff *The Jewish Gauchos* [*Echad*])

[*Mar Israel Abramowitz is a Polish Jewish refugee in Guatemala — ed.*]

'Mar Abramowitz did not attend services in our temple. With a dozen or so other Ashkenazi refugees from Eastern Europe he worshipped in a tiny down-town loft which was said, by those who had never been in it, to smell of rancid butter and pickled herring. Only on the High Holidays were the Poles and Litvaks* allowed to defile our synagogue, and they had to sit toward the rear, next to the women.

Although I did not learn Hebrew for another two years, I was very early inculcated with the gospel of Sephardi caste. If all the other Jews were Chosen, we were the Elect. We were sole heirs to a remote but glorious Golden Age whose legacy we could batten on, without any effort on our part, until the Day of Judgement. At the end of the Golden Age we had nobly suffered the Inquisition, which resulted in our Expulsion from Spain and resettlement in a place called the Diaspora. One day we would all reunite in the Promised Land, Eretz Israel, and begin an even more glorious second Golden Age, with God's blessing.' (p78 Victor Perera *Growing Up Jewish in Guatemala* [in *Echad*])

'the Jew has been a polyglot through the ages, a self-made rationalist, a persis-tent fighter for his right to exist as an extraordinary citizen.' (Jorge Luis Borges quoted p19 *Introduction* in *Tropical Synagogues*)

'It was just a few blocks away, we walked. Lanuse's bar exhaled its beery and smoky breath that followed us as far as the corner. The Viners and the Shames would set up their wicker chairs next to the entrances of their respective stores to be able to kibitz with each other. The women seemed older than the men; they rocked slowly and chatted in Yiddish mixed with Spanish. Then we would pass Litner's bakery where a furry, dirty dog stretched out and blocked the sidewalk, undoubtedly paralysed by the aroma of freshly baked loaves. Or perhaps by age. Anyway, Mama would buy a few pastries there and Mrs. Litner would keep her posted on the rheumatism that was swelling her knees as well as on her mother who lay dying in the room in back. Mama always listened quietly: things seemed to worsen at a comfortable rate, and there would be months and months to enjoy the same pastries and same conversation.' (p90-1 Nora Glickman *The Last Emigrant* [*Tropical Synagogues*])

'Uncle Facundo approved whole-heartedly, saying it was healthy and part of life and that in life things had to be killed off by living them to the hilt, that beauty and sex should go hand in hand, and that people's real problem — when there were no wars to worry about — was that they were all bored out of their minds. That's why — he would say — neighbours stand at the door all day long living the life of others, that gossip was a form of frustrated romanticism, and that people gobbled up crime and pornography because they needed them, because they supplanted life, because real life was a whirlwind.' (p55-6 *Uncle Facondo* Isidore Blaisten [*Tropical Synagogues*])

ANTHOLOGY
Forman, Frieda et al (ed.s)
Found Treasures: Stories by Yiddish Women Authors
[Yiddish Various Countries]

Found Treasures' introduction points out that Yiddish fiction by women writers has been pretty much left out of the anthologies and novels translated into English, so that our image of Yiddish literature is as a men-only reserve... This substantial anthology aims to compensate.

In fact, right from the start of the book, in the powerful and moving *My Mother's Dream* by Sarah Hamer-Jacklyn, you realise that some uniquely female points of view have definitely been left out, in this case the plight of a woman with a dangerous pregnancy, prevented from getting medical aid by the harsh and prudish piousness of her husband and mother-in-law. It's a particular side of the general tensions and conflicts among traditionalist Jews that much of Yiddish literature discusses.

Many of these stories are by Americans rather than the Poles or Russians who also contributed heavily to Yiddish letters, and the heartfelt, effective story *Through the Eyes of Childhood* by Malka Lee tells of struggling in and then leaving the warm but limiting world of the early twentieth century Shtetl, capturing very well the sadness of leaving everything and everybody behind for America. This is a surprisingly uncommon theme in American writing in general; partly perhaps because the pain of emigration, the whole strange distortion that jumping from one culture to another involves, is something of a taboo in an upbeat society like the U.S.

Through the Eyes of Childhood counts amongst the many straightforwardly autobiographical pieces here but there are also more convincingly literary works like Yente Serdatzky's *Unchanged*, an abbreviated, tight-lipped rendition of the crises and disillusionment in love and politics of a young radical woman in the first third of this century.

Celia Dropkin's *A Dancer* is a beautiful, wistful paean to the lost dreams of youth, a strong piece with unusual physicality.

Yiddish was the chosen vehicle, almost the 'sacred language' (in contrast to Hebrew which they saw as elitist, the Rabbis' tongue) of the Jewish Socialist Bund* (Federation) an influential movement in Russia (until the Bolsheviks suppressed it) and in Poland. As this book's introduction points out, it encouraged a programmatic kind of literature meant to light up the masses as much as anything else. *Zlatke* by Miriam Raskin is somewhat in this vein but with very interesting detail in its story of a young woman, a Bundist revolutionary factory worker in Bialystock (Poland). Later in the book is the same author's *At a Picnic*, looking back at the militant days from the drowsy comfort of a more prosperous New York existence.

Between the glorious epoch of the Jewish Left before World War One and the present liberal, conservative or apathetic age is the horror of the early 1940s and in *The Road of No Return* Rachel Korn unpicks one tiny corner of the Holocaust and you shudder all the same. Another story that comes out of that period is *Edgia's Revenge* by Chava Rosenfarb, an interesting late author in Yiddish, interviewed (25:1997) in the excellent (English-language) *Pakn Treger* magazine (National Yiddish Book Centre, Amherst, Massachusets). Rosenfarb's novella explores the haunted psychology of a concentration camp survivor living in Canada. Her survival was at the price of a degree of collaboration with the Germans running the camp. It's also a story that reveals in quite a skilful way the anxiety of the immigrant experience; the sense of inferiority about having a 'funny accent' and so on. Anxieties transmitted in subtle ways to the following generation...

Finally there are two interesting contributions from Yiddish writers about Israel, particularly the little suite of five tales by Rikudah Potash which deal with Mizrachi ('Oriental') Jews from places like Yemen, Bokhara (in Central Asia), Salonika (Greece) and Iraq. Just as this anthology shows us, despite its variable literary level, another side of the Yiddish-speaking Jews' experience, this Yiddish woman writer tells us about a side of the Jewish world little heard-of by Western Jews. R K

'Zlatke made progress: she could now be trusted to sew a pair of sleeves, to hem a dress with fine little stitches. These were skilled workers in the workshop, great artists who could make a coat or a dress of the most complicated fashion. Sewing was music in their hands and Zlatke watched them in wonder. Her trusting smile won their affection and they gladly taught her. ''Just don't hurry, just don't rush," they advised.

Eight in the evening exactly, the workers began winking to one another: time to put down the work and go home. It was a tense moment; someone from the owner's family was always there just then, checking which of the workers would be the first to rise from the table.

Stories from the past were recounted in great secrecy. "There were times when we worked till twelve, till one o'clock at night, and on Thursday, or before a holiday, we would stay all night. What goings on, then! The more daring young apprentices were not passive. More than once a stone flew through the workshop window during the night. They would snatch the owner and pour oil on his face. The rebels were apprehended, sent to Siberia. No-one knows what became of them."

Zlatke listened to their stories breathlessly. These unknown heroes became her own. To be sure, their methods of terrorism were not hers; in her organization, terrorism was forbidden. But those first ones forged the path and now others had to carry on.' (p110-111 *Zlatke* by Miriam Raskin)

'Welcome to New York

We all left the island and got into a comfortable warm train, headed for New York.

I looked out from the well-lit train carrying us through the night. Inside, there was great joy amongst the young immigrants who were travelling through the new land. They hoped to transform their lives of sorrow in Europe into more joyful, creative days. Nurses dressed in white from the Red Cross came in to distribute bread, white as snow, from white paper bags.

White bread, so many slices of fresh, white bread for all of us. My eyes lit up with hunger. Was this a dream? I reached out my hand and the friendly face of the nurse looked at me, as she handed me the white velvety bread with yellow cheese.

Fresh white bread — my first thought was not to taste it, but to bring it to my aunt in New York as a gift. I opened my basket, hid the bread inside and closed the basket. Then I spread myself comfortably across the plush seat and looked out into the night, as small, solitary lights danced in the darkness…

Suddenly, I was engulfed in a shower of illumination. It was the city of a million lights: New York! Brilliant stones were scattered and took root in the night's darkness. All the passengers rose spontaneously and sang "Hatikvah", as they greeted the "golden land" with song.' (p172-3 *Through the Eyes of Childhood* by Malka Lee)

Israeli Stories [Hebrew]

Blocker, Joel (ed.)

Modern Hebrew Stories [Sipurim 'ivriyim moderniyim] [Hebrew]

Spicehandler, Ezra (ed.)

These two anthologies, which together provide samples of Israeli writing from the 1940s, 1950s and 1960s, contain short stories from the older, immigrant generation S.Y.Agnon from Galicia (Poland), Haim Hazaz from the Ukraine, Aharon Megged from Poland, Benjamin Tammuz from Russia, Yehuda Amichai from Germany as well as writing from *Sabra* (Israeli-born) authors such as Moshe Shamir, Yoram Kaniuk or S.Yizhar and up to younger writers such as Aharon Appelfeld and A.B. Yehoshua, who are now quite well known outside of Israel for their prose fiction.

The stylistic range of these slim volumes — nine short stories in *Israeli Stories*, eight in *Modern Hebrew Stories* — reflects something of the complexity of the cultures from within which these writers write. For example, Yoram Kaniuk's *The Parched Earth* (*Israeli Stories*) presents a view, through the eyes of an excited child for whom 'days were arranged like sliced bread, for meat, for cucumbers, for apples', of the complex linguistic and ethnic worlds of Tel Aviv in the British Mandate (c.1918-1948) period (his father's poetic Hebrew, Aunt Shlomit's robust Russian, Yemenite Jewish women, British policemen, the nearby Arab village where he eats sesame seeds...). This ethnic richness is mirrored in the joyous, almost preciously worked lyricism of the prose.

Stylistically more tense, and disjointed to the point of incoherence is Yehuda Amichai's story, *Battle for the Hill* (*Israeli Stories*), set during the 1956 Sinai campaign. This presents a startling blend of order and disorder, as flashing thoughts are bound in with comments on the immediate surroundings or on military tactics and it also makes use of superimposed times and places or surreal images to bring the situation to life ('Her eyes are as hard as metal screws. Once she wanted to rivet herself to the world with those eyes, but she didn't succeed'). Amichai — one of Israel's best known poets — addresses war from a different angle in *The Times My Father Died* (*Modern Hebrew Stories*), through the watchful eyes of a young son growing into an adult. The narrator tries to come to terms with the changes and 'deaths' which he perceives in his father: his father's 'deaths' through Nazi persecution, his father's bewilderment — so common to that generation of Central European Jews — at having fought on the side of the Germans in World War One, while having a son who signs up with the British in World War Two; and the more personal 'deaths' — retreats, numbness, dead times — which the son learns to see in the father.

Amichai's stories, like Yizhar's *The Prisoner* and Benjamin Tammuz's *A Roll of Canvas* (both in *Israeli Stories*) rewrite the traditional war story to show an oblique and nuanced relation to war, to militant forms of commitment (Tammuz's almost shockingly gentle story of the encounter between a committed book-loving pacifist and a brash young Irgun* member) and to patriotism, generating some singular and complex styles: neither heroising, nor cynical but a tense and disturbing combination of involvement and alienation which is perhaps a prototype of the Israeli relation to Israel. *The Prisoner*, for example, set in the late summer of 1948, concerns the loss or disturbance of values brought about by life as a soldier. Into a simple story of the capture and interrogation of an Arab shepherd, Yizhar manages to weave both a sharp questioning of militarism and broader reflections on ethics and compromise, in a prose which takes off into internal monologue and surprising focused detail, plucking the moment (of decision, action, resistance) out of the present to turn it over for its full ethical and aesthetic value.

Alongside the experimentation of Kaniuk, Amichai or Yizhar, there is the solemn, simple tone of Megged's *The Name* (*Israeli Stories*), a story about what it is for a Jew to carry a name, and the burden and hope invested in that name. A younger Israeli-born generation desires to choose a 'new' (Hebrew) name for their child over 'a Ghetto name, ugly, horrible'; whereas the grandfather — representative of an older generation — wants the name to be that of a young grandson murdered by the Nazis, hoping to commemorate this slaughtered twelve year old through the passing down of his name. In its delicate depiction of these two experiential worlds, which despite 'belonging' to the same family are separated by an unbridgeable distance, *The Name* is a moving story and one which resonates in many different areas: family alienation, generational rifts, the terrible task of mourning such a death. Some of the usual richness of Megged's prose is foregone in this story, but shines out again in *In the Attic* (*Modern Hebrew Stories*), a story which explores a young boy's apprehension of the sacred, of profanation and of the forbidden, through a simple tale of climbing into an abandoned loft above a synagogue one boiling Sabbath noon while all the village sleeps.

More ideologically motivated is Haim Hazaz's *The Sermon* (*Israeli Stories*), a tale of an ill-educated but passionate kibbutznik brandishing the power of the spoken word to his colleagues on the subject of the history of the Jews and the emergence of Zionism, a thought-provoking (and provoking *tout court*) argument laced with statements such as 'when a man can no longer be a Jew, he becomes a Zionist', or the history of the Jews as a history of 'begging for mercy'... If the committee meeting of a kibbutz is something of a pretext for a discourse on history and destiny in this tale, tensions at the Israel-Jordan border are also a mere backdrop in Moshe Shamir's *Next of Kin* (*Israeli Stories*), a suspenseful action story, narrated for tension and atmosphere, whose real focus is love and betrayal.

The *Modern Hebrew Stories* anthology contains also what are now better known, more recent authors, Yehoshua and Appelfeld, as well as, in both anthologies, some predictably magnificent Agnon (see reviews of these authors in the *Babel Guide*).

The *Modern Hebrew Stories* anthology also contains Yizhar's breathtaking story, *The Runaway*, a simple tale of cultivating a plot of land and of a horse bolting, but gripping for its extraordinary blend of sharp-focus description ('...a whole wide stretch of soil, a bit crumbly to the touch, perhaps like the good feel of a handful of warm soft-shelled nuts, which, when you lick them slightly, give off a tantalizing clayish smell like the coming of the first rain...'), of suggestive psychological or metaphysical states ('folks that have horses in their farmyard... go through life differently, have a different smell, and a different look in their eyes. Haven't you noticed that?'), and then the multiple narrative points of view, sometimes directly addressing the reader, inviting questions and responding to them, sometimes unobtrusive, always dynamically working with the narrative.

Overall, the Joel Blocker's anthology (*Israeli Stories*) is more involved with recognisably political issues in the broad sense — Jewish history, Jewish memory, war, the world of Jerusalem —

although the inventiveness and critical edge of these writers certainly dispel any idea that Israeli literature is bound by narrowly patriotic, heroic or nostalgic discourses (as might well be expected of a new, embattled State relying on military prowess and Zionist conviction). A bolder selection is found in *Modern Hebrew Stories* which, at the later date of 1971 after the Six Day War, perhaps felt more confident to present stories where the material of contemporary Israel is allowed to take on surreal and fantastical shape and to travel on some stylistically more experimental journeys (often achieved by focusing the narrative through the eyes of a young boy — five out of the eight stories use this device)). *Modern Hebrew Stories* has the added advantage of being a dual-language text (with some vocabulary and good notes at the back), one of the few such texts available.

These anthologies illuminate the immensely rich resources which these writers draw upon — diverse geographical, religious, political and linguistic backgrounds — and display the accomplishment with which they condense these materials into the stringent form of the European short story (simplicity of line, economy of expression and so forth). Quite apart from considerations of content, the English language reader can feel the interweaving of styles and idioms in these tales: Haim Hazaz's folktale of a shtetl good-for-nothing, *Hidden Puddle*, is peppered with colloquialisms and snatches of Ukrainian, Nissim Aloni's story *Shmeel* about a young boy in the Sephardi slums of Tel Aviv introduces Ladino (Judaeo-Spanish) syntax (both of these in *Modern Hebrew Stories*), the Hebrew of these writers yields to spoken styles working in a range of registers, and throughout one can feel the infusion of biblical cadences and quotations. S B

'The voices soared, passed out of the classroom, flitted over the bare hills to the left, congregated at sea, raced towards distant lands, circled in the skies of reverie, played football on the sandy lot...' (Yoram Kaniuk *The Parched Earth* [*Israeli Stories*] p125)

'Further on, open to the sun and the dogs, sprawled the tents of the Bedouin. A flat horizon stretched out like white-hot tin. In the East two clusters of eucalyptus trees rustled in intimate conversation, their bases strewn as if with baubles. From the North and the West the isolated houses were suffused in idle sleep, bowed under weary branches. A seething silence'. (AharonMegged *The Name* [*Israeli Stories*] p126)

'She didn't want to cry but the tears came. Her whole body shared them, her hands and her legs, her hair and her thighs, until her torso became heavy and only her face remained dry... Her blood cried like an infant. She had to calm it. Her body was like a cradle for her blood, but the more she rocked it the harder it cried...' (Yehuda Amichai *Battle for the Hill* [*Israeli Stories*] p220)

'Ah, do you know what it means to run!... How all of a sudden you are in the open. All of a sudden you're in it. Wide open, and everything is permitted. Wide open and you're in it. All of you inside the possible, like... what shall I say... like someone plunging into the sea and he's in it, surrounded and swallowed up by it. All of him becomes what the sea is... And it's all the same to the sea — your caring or your not caring doesn't affect it the least bit; it remains changeless, not even scratched, not even the faintest smile. But *you* care. Oh, yes, to you everything matters. Your heartbeats are now absolutely different'. (S. Yizhar *The Runaway* [*Modern Hebrew Stories*] p108)

Other worthwhile anthologies [Hebrew]

Since the preferred genre of Hebrew writing — after poetry — is undoubtedly the short story or novella, a few more anthologies of English translations will be mentioned here. A collection which focuses on stories and poetry from the late 1960s and 1970s is *New Writing in Israel*, edited by Spicehandler and Arnson (Tel Aviv: Sabra Books, 1976). Another full collection, including some more unusual voices such as Avraham Raz and Dan Ben-Amotz, as well as the better known writers such as Nathan Shaham and Yitzhak Ben-Ner is *New Israeli Writers*, edited by Dalia Rabikovitz (Funk & Wagnalls: NY 1969). If you want depth rather than breadth — none of the above contain material from before the 1940s — then a good anthology is *A whole loaf. Stories from Israel* edited by Sholom Kahn (Karni Publishers: Tel Aviv 1957), which contains some interesting material from the 1930s, such as a tale by Moshe Smilansky (S. Yizhar's uncle), while focusing principally on the period around the War of Independence into the early 1950s. For range — apart from the *Oxford Book of Hebrew Short Stories*, reviewed here separately — a good choice is *Great Hebrew Short Stories* edited by Alan Lelchuk and Gershon Shaked (Signet: NY 1983), which includes novellas by Gnessin and by Brenner — both 'founding fathers' of modern Hebrew literature — as well as a quirky selection of later material, such as the lesser known Yehoshua Kenaz (*Musical Moment*) and David Fogel (*Facing the sea*). Lastly, *Meetings with the angel* edited by Benjamin Tammuz & Leon Yudkin (Andre Deutsch: London 1973), if only for the inimitable piece by Yaacov Shabtai: *A Private And Very Awesome Leopard*... S B

Jewish Voices, German Words [German West Germany East Germany Austria]

This collection of nineteen short stories, novel extracts, the odd essay and several poems is by young Jewish writers writing in German, in Austria and the two Germanys, and who grew up in these countries after 1945. The idea of being Jewish in post-Holocaust Germany or Austria already starts from such a bleak premise — you're living amidst a nation of Fred Wests who've put your brothers, sisters and aunties under the Fatherland's great patio in the sky — that anything is possible.

In fact quite a variety of situations are explored and different conclusions reached, often no more or less sour about their uncomfortable homeland than are *Goyish* German writers. The book's editor — also Jewish and (partly) raised in Germany — does an excellent job posing the kind of issues that many Germans would prefer to be overlooked. As she says in her introduction while 'for most young German writers, the past appears to have been deleted... for their Jewish counterparts it is an indelible part of their consciousness of the present'. Until younger Germans wake up to the fact that Germany can only clear its name by trying, for a suggestion, to do a tenth of the good in the next one hundred years as the evil that was done in those infamous twelve years of the Third Reich, then Jews in dealing with Germans are, as Peter Jungk says in his contribution, 'obliged to forget, forget each day anew, what took place there, forty years ago', to forget on behalf of the Germans and Austrians, to spare *their* feelings.

In the actual collection a particularly interesting piece is by East German Chaim Noll who grew up as the son of faithful Party parents but writes laconically, 'The country to which our part of Berlin belonged called itself the GDR (German Democratic Republic). That name stood for three claims: Germany, democracy, and republic, none of which would bear close examination. One saw them everywhere, in block letters: on bridges, on roofs, in store windows among baby carriages and cabbages. Usually associated with promises of a brilliant future.'

Thomas Feibel in a beautiful, hilarious piece *Gefilte Fish and Pepsi: A Childhood in Enemy Territory* also plays it for laughs, in a long Jewish literary (and oral) tradition; 'We were neurotics in the marinade of Jewishness.' Another contributor, Katja Behrens, like a lot of young Jews from Western countries, is attracted to visit Israel in a search for roots — implicitly the roots that otherwise might have been sought in the Yiddish Heartland between Berlin and Moscow that was destroyed by the Germans under their famous Austrian leader and then further (culturally) filleted by Stalinism. Behrens' Israeli tale is poignant, funny and horribly true-sounding as she gets chased around Jerusalem by a sexually frustrated Ultra-Orthodox old man.

The identity crush, often very complex for non-religious Ashkenazi Jews because of secularism and the Holocaust, is also addressed in two pieces by Barbara Honigmann where she talks of the curious 'lost' state of a creative, clever woman trapped between identities (German/East German and Jewish/World Citizen).

This confusion over identity is to some extent the condition of all Europeans, especially since the end of World War Two, but especially of the continent's Jewish citizens, 'super-Europeans', with a long tradition of presence in all European countries — amidst expulsions and exterminations — and with a common European culture. All in all the authors in this book are appropriate witnesses to the way Germany and Austria have (not) dealt with their recent past.

The book also includes many other thoughtful and well-written pieces and is a beautifully produced and translated book, a tribute to its small American publisher, Catbird Press. R K

'In the longer run the German nation will not be forgiven for Auschwitz, or for the calculated attack on humanity this word has come to symbolise. How Germany comes to terms with this is its own problem. When a people makes such a spectacle of itself, its name becomes emblematic of something revolting; for centuries that was the case with the Huns, Tartars, and Mongols.' (p54 Chaim Noll *A Country, A Child*)

'Could any people be more uprooted than the Germans?... they have lost the ground under their feet and cannot recover it with the gravitational pull of money. Abroad one gets to look at them under a magnifying glass. A German tourist enters a restaurant in Holland with his family and does not dare to say "Guten Tag", because he would not want to be identified with the Germans who invaded Holland; even so, he feels guilty. This man is the civilised façade of the same man who goes to his club with fellow Germans and sings soldiers' songs... The Germans are a schizophrenic people. The hatred they feel for their own identity comes from the lost war, forced democratisation, and the incomprehensible crimes of the Second World War... Nothing in this country's consciousness has done as much harm as the notion of collective guilt. The fascists' crimes were unloaded on the entire people, and the executioners, the fellow-travellers, the merely indifferent, and the resistance fighters were all tarred with the same brush... If Herr Krupp's chauffeur is as guilty as Herr Krupp, both may feel free to continue going about their business — or neither. Thus the Germans blocked themselves from calling their criminals by name, from distinguishing between them and the fellow-travellers, the indifferent, and the resistance fighters, and building their future on the right people.... Not guilt but shame would have been appropriate. Guilt is a religious emotion and obscures one's understanding. But a person who feels shame about something contemplates that thing and tries to get to the bottom of it, even if that means pursuing his father's crimes... Then he can purge them and live without guilt. The child who promises to be better only because of a guilty conscience is already paving the way for the next misdeed.' (p35-6 Benjamin Korn *Shock and Aftershock*)

'If you ask me whether I have a *Heimat* (Homeland), and where it is, I reply in classic Jewish style: evasively. I think I have a *Heimat*, but I can't localize it. It's the odour of gefilte fish and potato pancakes, the taste of borscht and pickled herring, the melody of the Hatikva and the sound of the Internationale, but only when it's sung in Yiddish by old members of the Bund in Tel Aviv on the first of May. It's the Marx brothers' night in Casablanca, and Ernst Lubitsch's to be or not to be. It's Karl Kraus's Torch and the autobiography of Theodor Lessing. It's a spot on the Aussenalster in Hamburg, a little stairway in the old harbour of Jaffa, and the Leidseplein in Amsterdam. Isn't that enough?' (p101 Henryk M. Broder *Heimat? No, Thanks!*)

ANTHOLOGY
Perova, Natasha & Tait, Arch (ed.s)

Jews and Strangers. Glas New Russian Writing 6 [Rus-sian]

Glas (from 'glasnost') is the name of a book/magazine (in Britain it's sold as a magazine, in the US as a book) that has, since the outbreak of Glasnost, been bringing English-speakers the best of contemporary Russian writing. They combine the publication of Russian authors suppressed and marginalised by the Soviets with contemporary authors.

They do a wonderful, wonderful job and *Glas* is one of the best literary productions available in English and — of course — its distribution is limited, so keep trying if your bookshop has never heard of it.

This particular volume focuses particularly on Russian

Jewish writers and features a mixture of *belles lettres*, poems and stories from and about Russian Jews. There's a fine short piece by Osip Mandelstam, *Mikhoels,* written in his typically dreamy and suggestive style about a famous actor, Mikhoels, of the (then) recently-formed Jewish National Theatre; 'And yesterday, on this very stage, there were slender dancing girls in English-style jockey suits, there were patriarchs, drinking tea in the clouds, like old men sitting on a balcony in a Gomel shtetl.'

Osip Mandelstam is now fairly well-known outside Russia but less so the excellent Soviet Jewish writer Vassili Grossman who like, Isaac Babel, wrote about the Civil War period. Like Babel this writer was eventually silenced by the Soviet authorities. His story here *The Commissar*, is a charming, very clever story set in his hometown, the Jewish centre of Berdichev, during the Civil War. It's particularly interesting about women in those highly revolutionary times. The Commissar of the title is a female Red Army officer who, rather to her amazement and disgust, is about to have a baby.

Bringing Glas' glimpse of Russian Jewish life up to date is Larissa Miller whose autobiographical piece *Home Address* sadly details the everyday Soviet anti-Semitism she experienced at school, at college and as a young writer in the 1950s and 60s.

Also worth special mention is a photo-essay on Moscow Jews and there are also other good pieces here by writers, some not identified as Jewish, but with Jewish characters. *Glas* is worth tracking down; it's a great window on the soul of contemporary Russia, evidently a place where Jews are still very active in literature. R K

'The Yakti bubbled like a cauldron all day long. Peasants were trading birch-logs white as chalk. Women rustled strings of onions, and old Jewish ladies presided over downy piles of geese, tied together by their feet. Buyers blew into the down between their legs and pinched the yellow fat beneath the soft warm skin. Girls in colourful skirts, with sunburnt legs, carried tall red pots brimming with wild strawberries. They looked nervously at the buyers, as if getting ready to run away. Carts carried butter for sale, golden sweating pats wrapped in plump dock-leaves. A blind beggar with the white beard of a wizard was uttering tragic prayers of lamentation, holding out his hands, but his grief touched nobody's heart — they passed him by indifferently. One woman, taking the smallest onion from her string, threw it into the old man's tin bowl. He felt the onion and, interrupting his prayer, angrily scolded: "May your own children give you as little when you are old" — and again sang out his keening prayer, as old as the people of Israel.

People were buying and selling, probing, tasting, and raising their eyes towards heaven as if waiting for someone to advise them from the gentle blue sky above whether to buy the pike, or better take the carp. And all the time they shouted and swore, cursed each other and laughed.' (p9 *The Commissar* by Vassili Grossman)

'Part of my homeland was school No. 585, and my schoolmates, whom I missed when, in 1952, we moved to another district. And my old literature teacher, Yevlavia Stanislavovna.

Part of my homeland were the crowded and noisy streets of Kuznetsky Most and Petrovka, so tipically Muscovite, where as a teenager I would stroll for hours.

Part of my homeland were the woods off the Severyanin and Yauza suburban stations, and the camp-fires on the river Pra in Meschora country, and the tiny town of Plyos perched on the tall bank of the Volga. Also part of my homeland was the deserted shore of the White Sea, and on its beach the lonely log on which somebody had carved "Paradise". And northern forests with mosquitoes and cloudberries. And Sokolniki park in Moskow, where I went for long ambles with the blue-eyed boy who was my first love. And the leafy alley in that park which bore the wondrous name of Maytime Cutting.

It has all been ground to dust. Ground by the destruction machine, which was set into motion before I was born and which has not stopped to this day.

I do not mean the Moscow of "gardens, cobblestones and churchbells" described by Marina Tsvetayeva's daughter Ariadna Efron. That Moscow disappeared long before my time. But now they have pulled down my childhood home and the lilac garden where I used to take my elder boy for walks. The place where they once stood is now a busy thoroughfare dominated by a cast-iron monument. Surely this Bolshaya Polianka could never become part of someone's beloved childwood memory! Or could it? So many districts, neibourhoods and streets have ceased to exist.

Can I feel at home in a city which I once loved yet which has died before my very eyes? Can I feel at home hearing raucous voices on all sides shouting "Get back to Israel, Jews! Kikes! You have ruined Russia!" Feeling today, just as I did back in 1953, that pogroms could begin at any moment? It is difficult to tell if many people are really out for our blood or if it is only a noisy small mob of scum. But for how long can you tempt fate? Ever since I can remember I have feared for my dear ones. First for my grandfather, with his typically Jewish face and accent. Now for my children, with their Jewish surname. As a child I was ashamed of my relatives' Jewish names. And today at poetry recitals, I find myself counting the number of Jewish participants and wondering if there are too many of them. Goodness, what paltry, ignoble thoughts! But am I really to blame for these thoughts?' (p141-2 *Home Address*

Larissa Miller)

'The strength and glory of Jewishness in the visual arts is that it developed and brought through the centuries a sense of form and movement which has all the features of a style that is unchanging, thousands of years old. I'm not speaking of the cut of clothes, which change and thus do not have value. I'm not even thinking of the artistically-justified ghetto or the shtetl lifestyle. I'm speaking of the visual impression of the ghetto and it's enormous artistic force, which always survives the ghetto's destruction and will finally flourish when the ghetto is destroyed.' (p137 from *Mikhoels* by Osip Mandelstam)

ANTHOLOGY
Domb, Risa (ed.)

New Women's Writing from Israel [Hebrew]

There are anthologies and anthologies, and with a title like this one could grow suspicious. Is the inclusion of pieces here heavily ideologically motivated or on the basis of genuine literary quality? In fact Dr. Risa Domb, a leading British academic in the field of Modern Hebrew literature has produced a real anthology reflecting, as she says in her useful introduction, a recent explosion in women writing in Israel. This, apparently, followed the early and middle periods of writing in Modern Hebrew which were dominated by (broadly) Zionist themes of pioneering and conflict, themes that women writers found it hard to attach themselves to.

The overall sense reading these thirteen stories is of receiving glimpses, often quite intimate ones, of this foreign and not-foreign (to a cosmopolitan European) society. Leah Aini's *Until the Entire Guard has Passed* is a case in point; a charming vignette of a neighbourhood scene in sunny Tel Aviv and the daily life of a young couple is suddenly intruded on by the black fear of a memory made in the shadow of the camps. This story reflects the twin streams of utopian hope (Zionism) and actual despair (the flight from persecution and extermination) that fed into the creation of the Israeli state.

Another story, Shulamit Lapid's *Male and Female* has a similar uneasy shift in it; a jolly Jewish party with company and good grub, but underneath the fun, are the built-up frustrations of family life. More unease, but of a more interesting kind, is in the gender, ethnic and social gulf in the relationship of a Palestinian Arab workman employed as a builder by a middle-class Israeli Jewish woman in Savyon Liebrecht's *A Room on the*

Roof. This precise and excellent story is unafraid to really engage with its subject and cover dangerous territory.

If we are to some extent familiar with the dangerous ground of Palestinian/Jewish relations there are more universal dangers and difficulties in Israeli women's lives too of course, as in Mira Magen's well-written *Will Somebody please shut the Gate,* a harsh slice-of-life as a young girl's mother literally goes raving mad.

In the penultimate story, a writer born in 1954, Nava Semel, takes on her share of what will be the long job of understanding and coming to terms with the German mass murder of European Jews. Her piece *A Hat of Glass* about the last year of the camps is both moving and interesting.

This work of attempting, at a distance, to cast these events in an artistic framework is a necessary and very hard task for the Jewish inheritors of this legacy. Unfortunately though, history has to be digested and assimilated because, without the past, the present lacks meaning; it has no real access to its culture, its tradition and, therefore, self-understanding. Not to mention that that in ignorance and 'innocence' history can horribly repeat itself. A very hard process for Jews, this assimilation of the unthinkable, unbelievable, disgusting and terrifying Shoah or Holocaust, but how much harder for the Germans and Austrians (and Swiss war profiteers?) — and when are *they* going to get started on it? R K

[A middle-class Israeli woman has hired Palestinians for some building work on her house. — Ed.]

'Examining them from below, she saw how their faces grew sweaty with the effort, and their hands got dusty and were scratched by the rough blocks. By the time she had put the baby to bed and come out again, she saw they had unloaded the rest of the blocks on the lawn and disappeared with the truck, though she hadn't heard the sound of the motor. The next day after turning the matter over during sleepless hours she decided she must demonstrate her authority over them, and she was ready and waiting for them in her window, cradling her baby in her rounded arms, anger breathing force into her movements. From the window she shouted at them as they approached: "Why did you leave work in the middle of yesterday? And today..." She looked at her watch with a clumsy movement, stretching her neck over the baby lying at her breast. "Today you come at nine! You said you'd start working at six! This way you won't finish in ten months!"

"Lady," said the one with the gilded eyes, insulted. "Today was police roadblocked. Not possible we leave early before four morning lady."

Something in her recoiled at the sight of the beaten dog's eyes he raised up towards her in her window, at his broken voice. But tensing her strength to suppress the tremor that awoke within her and threatened to soften her anger, she shouted:"And yesterday what happened? Was also road-blocked?" Maliciously she imitated his grammatical error."You went away and left half the blocks down there on the grass."

For the first time she saw the movement that was later to become routine: the jaws clamping down on each other as though chewing something very hard, digging a channel along the line of his teeth. Later she was to learn: that's how they suppress anger, hatred. They clench their teeth to overcome the wild rage that surged up, that only rarely breaks out and flashes in their pupils." (p156 *A Room on the roof* by Savyon Liebrecht)

ANTHOLOGY
Abramson, Glenda (ed.)
The Oxford Book of Hebrew Short Stories [Hebrew]

This recent anthology of short stories translated from the Hebrew does for short stories in Hebrew what has patiently been done for countless national literatures over the years, namely, give a sense of the influences at work in later periods by including examples of work from earlier ones, an approach adopted less frequently in earlier anthologies of Hebrew stories which tended to want to give a taste of the present. A concise *Introduction* sketches the history of the emergence of a modern secular Hebrew literature from its roots in an exclusively religious (and male) domain, and useful biographical notes head each story.

The result is a fascinating range of writing, especially precious for the amount of space — at least a quarter of the book — devoted to stories published in the late 1980s and early 1990s which give a flavour of really contemporary Israeli writing.

Of the earlier works, Mendele Mokher Sforim — who contributed to both Hebrew and Yiddish literature — has here his sprightly, mocking tale *Burned Out* which upbraids a Jew's destitute brethren (the 'Beggarsburghers'!), admonishing them for their backwardness and declaiming homilies on self-improvement, while Berdyczewski's tale *Without Hope* is a strikingly frank and corrosive rejection of traditional ways of life in a small town in Russia, 'all those books, beliefs, ideas, which were my stumbling-blocks'. In contrast to these negative portrayals, Uri Nissan Gnessin, in *Uproar*, relishes the mild anarchy of Jewish life in a small town, with its range of simpletons, oddball apprentices, carters, awkward young men and not very authoritative rabbis. This is a slapstick tale, rich in action and with invective ranging from 'The blagues of Egybt take im' to 'You unclean shaushage'. Very differently indulgent is Joseph Hayyim Brenner's *Travel Notes*, a carefully told, suspenseful tale which plays artfully on false leads and preconceptions, about four men being secretly taken across a dangerous border by a perhaps not trustworthy baker who doubles up as 'leader'.

Following in the footsteps of Mendele Mokher Sforim's allegorical style is Haim Hazaz's story from the 1930s, *Rahamim*, revolving around the opposition between Oriental and Ashkenazi* Jew. The Easterner is a talkative, laughing Kurdish Jew who, with his simple faith and simple pleasure in life, has a more bountiful existence than the more fortunate but constantly beset, wearied and bothered Ashkenazi Menashke Bezprozvani. While tending to sentimentality, this tale is certainly interesting sociologically.

While S. Yizhar's radiant *Habakuk* (reviewed here in his collection *Midnight Convoy*) recalls Brenner's use of detail and changing focus, Benjamin Tammuz's *The Swimming Contest* is a clipped, stern tale of youthful friendship between a Jewish and an Arab boy which ends, later on, in deadly combat. Another story focused on adolescence is Amalia Kahana-Carmon's absorbing *Bridal Veil*, about a young girl's chance meeting with an older UN soldier, the anxious and exciting universe opening up for her: '...what the grown-up girls are privileged to. Canadian girls. Blissful girls. Mysterious, haughty and deserving'; a close and unusual angle on a familiar theme.

Other examples of stories from the 1960s and 1970s, apart from ones by better known authors such as Yehuda Amichai, Aharon Appelfeld, Amos Oz, A.B. Yehoshua and David Shahar (see their major works reviewed here), include a rather down-beat Yaacov Shabtai in *The Visit*, Yehoshua Kenaz's *The three-legged chicken*, a moving account of a boy trying to understand the death of his grandfather through all sorts of displacement activities (including tense night-time manoeuvres with a woodworm...), and Yitzhak Ben-Ner's nostalgic tale *Cinema*.

The fullest and most unusual section is the selection of stories from the 1980s and 1990s, where women writers are well represented, and where a rich stylistic range is evident: Yehudit Hendel's *A Story with No Address* uses a prose gutted of embellishments and peopled with quirky and grotesque figures (a girl relentlessly upbraiding an unknown adult; the ghost of a dog; indifferent morgue attendants...), to explore in fantastical ways the themes of death and being haunted, as well as the cold bureaucratic intrusions around death (identifying the body, certificates, registers, Town Halls...). Another woman writer, Yehudit Katzir, entertains us with the remarkable *Schlafstunde*, the title referring to the siesta time when a boy and girl cousin undertake sexual explorations in the attic, and an uncle intrudes...

This story is narrated in flashback in cascades of childhood images (Hitler as a big gorilla by the pool, the Hungarian circus, child-snatchers...), descriptions of concrete sensual objects, details of secretive rituals (burying 'treasure, swearing oaths), in a confusion or profusion of narrative voices (the 'I' of the boy and the girl at times indistinguishable), and uses stylistic differences to distinguish between present and past. This is very accomplished writing, as is, in a different way, Yitzhak Orpaz's *Talitha Kumi*, a funny, shrewd tale of a middle-aged man doing his old friend a favour by meeting up with the latter's teenage daughter — for business reasons. Orpaz brilliantly gets inside the head of this at once distracted and calculating property salesman, whose perceptions of the world depend on the momentary state of his feelings, whose anticipatory eagerness and dreams about the unknown Dana spark associations with a past which he has lived but hardly dwelt in or on, never quite realising that he is living a life of constant evasion.

The most contemporary Israeli women writers represented here — Orly Castel-Bloom with *High Tide,* Ruth Almog with *Dora's Secret* and Savyon Liebrecht with *Morning in the Park with Nannies* tend to use a flattened, prosaic style, much like that of neutral speech, relying on oddity — or, in the case of Savyon Liebrecht, on horrified fascination — for their effect on the reader.

Overall, this is a magnificent selection, although unfortunately it lacks full bibliographical details, and emphasises at once the very contemporary yet gives a thorough survey of writing from the early decades of the century. A must for anyone interested in Hebrew fiction. S B

'A strange hush hung over the streets, a suppressed sort of quiet, humming, it seemed, deep in the throat, like the stifled silence of a besieged city. Whoever has not experienced the silence of those border towns cannot imagine what it is like...would not know or understand. The very air was charged with suspicion...hush!...no one passes...Who goes there?' (Yossef Hayyim Brenner *Travel Notes* p.70)

'Well, I have been meaning to tell the story of Habakuk for a long time, and always kept putting it off for one reason or another. But today I'll begin without more ado.

The beginning of Habakuk is rather well known, and it's very simple too. Like this —

Ah, but it seems I must stop here, even before I've begun, and give warning to any of you boys who cannot bear sad stories, for I'm not at all certain this story won't be sad. Its beginning is bound to be a little bit sad, and so is its end — inescapably so — and only in the middle, maybe, it'll be a bit different and not just sad. Anyone who has reservations about sadness, therefore, well, he's been warned here and now, so let him leave off before we've begun and go in search of something that'll make him happy, and more power to him.' (S. Yizhar *Habakuk* p.102)

'And the backlash swept over her. Like a forgotten melody. The burst of freshness of a power that draws one back, and anguish, akin to regrets, over that which is massacred here at your feet each time anew and gets trampled, you know not what it is. They recapture that which is extinct and by now is nothing but tenderness, all the tenderness. Yet in it are preserved all its lost flavour, fully retained, and its true colours — with a punch that is like a fist-blow to the jaw. In the great wide world only this time, only for me, only in my case — won't I, please — some day find you again?' (Amalia Kahana-Carmon *Bridal Veil* p203)

'And at the same time — from unknown depths inside me — there rose a voice, the voice said: I, I, I, I. And although the voice came from inside me, it wasn't my voice. And the voice was quiet, solemn, redeeming and very dangerous, and it stiffened my hand on the chilly metal of the big tap, which had become rounder and more slippery... . Out of the twilight silence the voice spoke to me and I looked around me, tried to rise to my feet and could not, like at night in my bed when the dark, loathsome thing came at me from all the corners of the room.' (Yehoshua Kenaz, *The Three-Legged Chicken* p278)

'He asked if it made a difference that she was wearing a white dress. Anyway somebody has to identify the body, he said.

The clerk said there was a dog.

Now the doctor stared at the clerk. He said he didn't know if they'd take a dog's identification.

In fact, why not? said the clerk.

Yes, said the doctor, But anyway, the dog won't be able to take care of the funeral arrangements.

The dog leapt up wildly as if he had been shot. He jumped on the doctor.

Oh no, said the doctor.' (Yehudit Hendel *A story with no address* p365)

'Once, when summer vacation stretched over the whole summer and tasted of sand and smelled of grapes and a redhead sun daubed freckles on your face and, after Sukkot, *[Jewish harvest festival — ed.]* the wind whistled into a gang of clouds and we galloped home through the ravine in a thunderstorm and the rain stabbed your tongue with mint and pine and the neighbourhood dogs set up a racket, barking like uncles coughing at the intermission in a winter concert, and suddenly spring attacked with cats shrieking and the lemon trees blossoming...' (Yehudit Katzir *Schlafstunde* p341)

ANTHOLOGY
Ben-Shaul, Moshe et al (ed.s)
PEN ISRAEL 1997: A Collection of Recent Writing in Israel [Arabic, English, Hebrew, Romanian, Russian & Yiddish]

PEN ISRAEL 1997 is the most recent of a series of paperback translations of stories and poems from Israeli writers published regularly every two years since 1991. One of the advantages of this collection is that it recognises the existence of writers in Israel using languages other than Hebrew. Because of this we receive an unusually varied picture of the country, one of whose chief advantages in any case is its cultural mix — however much the Zionist idea has been to create a united Israeli nation from Jewish diversity.

One of the first pieces in the book, *Untitled Story*, was in fact translated from the Yiddish of Yossl Birstein, and is a short and amusing vignette of Jewish literary life, but set in Australia rather than Israel. Amela Einat's *Now or Never* could almost be set in Manchester or Manhattan; a woman in her forties is warned by her doctor that her 'biological clock' is not just ticking but that the alarm has gone off. This drives her into an extended speculation about what it would be like to have a child, on the great loves she has and hasn't had. It's a very good piece, putting us directly inside the heard of a lonely woman for whom everything emotional somehow seems to go wrong.

There is a more exotic and unfamiliar atmosphere in Eli Amir's *Farewell Baghdad*. Amir left Iraq aged twelve and this amusing story is about an elite Iraqi Jewish family and their complex relations with various royals and corrupt government officials.

Elisha Porat who was born on, and still lives in, a kibbutz contributes a beautiful autobiographical piece about the joy of reading and writing which transmits a kind of pioneer enthusiasm about the possibilities of life, about the fundamental things.

Other excellent stories are by Zygmunt Frankel, written in

English, by Bracha Klopstein, written in Yiddish and by Corinna (who was born in Romania) who, in *Pink Pages* tells of a hypothetical? impossible? desirable? friendship between a Jewish and an Arab family in Israel.

As the Babel Guide deals only with fiction it would not be appropriate to do more than signal an appreciation of some of the poetry included in *PEN ISRAEL 1997*, particularly that of Dror Elimlech, Yehudit Kafri and Rony Somekh.

The PEN series, if you can track it down, is a convincing and enjoyable update on Israel's wealth of writing. R K

[*May 1945 on a kibbutz, a little boy reads the (Hebrew) newspaper for an old Yiddish-speaking couple*]

'I no longer remember what was written in the newspaper I read then.

Except for the last day. The old man was very exited and urged me to hurry up and read. Not on the big bed, as usual, but standing up. The moment I came in at the door. And this time the old lady was there too, waiting for me begin. I read aloud: "War over. Hitler dead." The banner headlines were in huge black letters. They took up half the page. I didn't have to read any more. The two old people seized each other in a trembling embrace and burst into tears. They did not see me putting the newspaper down softly on the threshold and slipping quietly from the room.

Outside on the lawn my friends were playing with a ball. Their wild cries rose to the sky.' (p93 *Kamatz Alef* Elisha Porat)

ANTHOLOGY
Litvinoff, E (ed.)

The Penguin Book of Jewish Short Stories [Various Languages International]

Compiled in 1979, this remains today an essential collection of pieces by the century's great Jewish writers. The editor, Emmanuel Litvinoff, is himself a considerable writer and his story here — *Fanya* — beautifully captures its time and place, the world of 1920s Whitechapel (in the East End of London), Britain's largest Jewish population centre for many years. In controlled and vivid lines Litvinoff evokes both the garment business located 'Up West' where one aspired to gravitate to, as well as the 'industrial grime of half a century' of the East End where you probably had to live in reality. These settings form the background to a classic theme — the proud young beauty seduced and abandoned by an older man.

Moving much further East than Whitechapel, into the old

Jewish heartland of Poland, we get to the setting of Isaac Bashevis Singer's *A Friend of Kafka*, one of Singer's modern-world stories which may come as a surprise to those more familiar with the 'demons and dybbuks*' Singer, who typically retails magical goings-on in olde-worlde Shtetls*. Here instead he portrays the frenetic, hard-up world of Yiddish writers and actors in 1930s Warsaw. Singer is in full, fascinating flow with some curious anecdotes about one of the century's most famous Jewish writers, Franz Kakfa.

One of the most noted writers in modern Hebrew, the Nobel-winning S.Y.Agnon is here with two of his most accessible stories (although once you've 'got access' to Agnon you may want to read more). *First Kiss* is as mysterious, unexplainable and unsettling as a first time should be while *Friendship* is classic Agnon; letters are torn up in inexplicable rages, everyone has lost something but they're not sure what and these losses coincide with seemingly casual allusions to the time 'before the world went topsy-turvy' (as the Germans wrecked Jewish lives). Perhaps it's also the other side of Israel; not the Israel of idealistic Zionist pioneers and Jews back in their Holy Land but the land of refugees, of loss and exile...

Isaac Babel the great Russian Jewish writer is here with his unique and breathless style of storytelling; Babel on war and revolution manages what Ernest Hemingway strove for but achieved only in his dreams... Over both his pieces here, *Story of My Dovecot* and *The Journey,* looms the Russian Revolution and the Russian Civil War that followed it, within whose violence and dislocation Jews suffered on a scale unparalleled except by the Holocaust.

Another, but more contemporary great writer, Aharon Appelfeld, is represented by his story *Badenheim 1939* set amongst Austrian Jews on the precipice before the Holocaust. This is expanded in his novel of the same name reviewed separately in the *Babel Guide*.

Getting out of Europe, Saul Bellow's *The Old System* is the engaging but entirely unsentimental saga of a family of larger-than-life Jewish immigrants. Bellow is pretty acerbic on the materialism of New World Jews; 'America. Extraordinary times. If you wanted the young women to bless Sabbath candles, you had to start their rabbi at $20,000, and add a house and a Jaguar.' Bellow ranges wide in this story, from the relations between up-

and-coming Jews with the old East coast moneyed Wasps (White Anglo-Saxon Protestants) to the pollution of the Hudson river valley. Finally though the power of the story is in the blinding passionateness of his Jewish milieu.

Another world-famous American Jewish writer is Philip Roth with the hilarious *The Conversion of the Jews,* where twelve-year-old Oscar Freedman takes on the Jewish world in his quest for freedom of thought. Essentially it's the same theme as in his notorious book *Portnoy's Complaint,* with a young Jewish male going head on with the sceptical, intellectually and sexually liberating 1960s, except that there's no sex in this story, apart from a reference to the Virgin Birth of Jesus Christ.

Muriel Spark better known as a Catholic writer, although partly Jewish by descent, explores her Jewish side in the marvellously funny *The Gentile Jewesses,* which is all about being part-Jewish and how that works.

South Africa is represented with one of Dan Jacobson's most telling African-set stories *The Zulu and the Zeide,* funny and touching but with a tragic quality too that subtly creeps up on the reader.

There are also important stories here by the Israeli Amos Oz, American Bernard Malamud and Yiddish writers I.L.Peretz, Sholom Aleichem, Lamed Shapiro and Abraham Reisen all of whom are covered in other reviews in this *Babel Guide.* R K

'All the men in our family were trusting by nature, and quick to ill-considered actions. We were unlucky in everything we undertook. My grandfather had been a rabbi somewhere in the Belaya Tserkov region. He had been thrown out for blasphemy, and for another forty years he lived noisily and sparsely, teaching foreign languages. In his eightieth year he started going off his head. My Uncle Leo, my father's brother, had studied at the Talmudic Academy in Volozhin. In 1892 he ran away to avoid doing military service, eloping with the daughter of someone serving in the commissariat in the Kiev military district. Uncle Leo took this woman to California, to Los Angeles, and there he abandoned her, and died in a house of ill-fame among Negroes and Malays. After his death the American police sent us a heritage from Los Angeles, a large trunk bound with brown hoops. In this trunk there were dumbells, locks of women's hair, uncle's *talith*,* horsewhips with gilt handles, scented tea in boxes trimmed with imitation pearls.' (p94 Isaac Babel *The Story of My Dovecot*)

(an old Zionist pioneer looks at the 'youth of today' in contemporary Israel — ed.)

'He sees the boys and girls, grandchildren of the Maccabees, heirs of the guardians and defenders and dreamers, and here they are wrecking the public

telephones or singing dirty songs in the streets at night.' (p287 Amos Oz
Setting the World to Rights)

ANTHOLOGY
Rosenfeld, Max (ed.)

Pushcarts And Dreamers [Yiddish USA]

This recently reprinted anthology originally appeared in 1967
when, at the end of his introduction, Max Rosenfeld made the
point; 'Without a background of American Yiddish literature,
contemporary writing about American Jews is disconnected from
a vital part of its own past. Without this background, a distorted
picture results — a record of Jewish experience with a gap that
will hurt the self-understanding of American Jews.'

His introduction as a whole in fact makes fascinating and
informative reading, precisely for the reason that it itself
documents the state of Jewish-American confidence and self-
assertiveness of thirty years ago. For example Max Rosenfeld
quotes (and italicises!) the sociologist C. Bezalel Sherman when
he says: 'A Yiddish literature of great scope was created, *the most
important non-English literature ever to arise in the United States.*'

It is indeed precisely the scope of this writing that *Pushcarts
and Dreamers* so strikingly illustrates. A short biographical note
about each of the writers precedes the short stories, or excerpts
of longer works, which are selected to represent their writing.
Altogether twenty-four pieces by the ten authors are collected,
and while the question of the survival of 'Yiddishkeit', or Old
World values, or religious observance in the New World are perhaps
inevitably the themes most frequently touched on, they not
infrequently prove really to be secondary to other questions. In
Abraham Reisin's *The Trial*, for example, the narrator's reflections
on the curtailment of his personal freedom of association by the
Union at the time of the tailors' strikes, while ostensibly
contrasting the ways of his native Russia with modern 'free'
America, in fact he creates a telling critique of the social
implications for the 'little man' of the struggle between labour
and capital. Deceptively simple, as are most of the stories, in the
telling, there is an accumulative complexity and wry detachment
which permeates from the original Yiddish into the English
translation.

Far from producing a nostalgic portrait of the old ways, the
stories again and again reveal themselves as sharp, modern and

236

penetrating, and while the commonest setting by far is the urban, big city scene, the immediate locale is usually more intimate: the synagogue, the tailors' cutting room, the backyard in the Bronx. The most unusual setting, however, is to be found in Isaac Raboi's piece *Mister Goldenbarg Settles in the West* (from his novella *Mister Goldenbarg*) where we see Goldenbarg building himself a homestead in the Dakotas, and the language takes on some of the weight of Biblical narrative.

In contrast to this Zalman Libin's *My First Theft* is playful, even whimsical, while Moishe Nadir treats us to comic paradox and absurdity, and Joseph Opatoshu to a harder, seamier world, where a synagogue depends upon a circle of poker players to raise the money to hire a cantor for the High Holy Days, and a well-to-do factory owner refuses his unemployed cousin a job unless he changes his name so he should not shame him.

Pushcarts and Dreamers works well as an introduction to writers who are less well known than they deserve, and most readers who are not particularly familiar with Yiddish writing are likely to discover at least one new writer they will want to read more fully. T H

'Some years ago I worked for a short time in a cigar factory that did not hire Jewish "hands." Although the factory was practically "one of our own" — it belonged to one of our brothers in Israel, a German Jew — nevertheless, the foreman, Mr McCarthy, an Irish gentleman, would always send a Jewish worker, if such would ever come looking for a job, "to Jerusalem." And at the same time he would also remind him — the Jewish worker — to "take his whiskers with him."

Devil take that dear Mr McCarthy, that's the kind of fanatical Zionist he was!

How did it happen, then, that he hired me? I can't give you the real answer to that question. Most likely he took me for a Spaniard, because I do somewhat resemble one of Torquemadas lantsleit, *[fellow-countryman — ed.]* and then again, I came in asking for work on "Spanish cigars"... Among the cigar-makers around me I recognise two other "unofficial" Jews who have smuggled themselves into this place... Often, Mr McCarthy begins to spew out jokes about Jews, silly jokes, stale jokes, unfunny wisecracks full of venomous idiocy. Both of them laugh now, too, the red-headed young man even harder than usual... The laughter of the other one, the stout one, at times like this sounds a little unnatural — "Excuse me, I'm laughing, but I don't really like it..."

Poor little souls, in their laughter they try to hide from themselves!...'
(*Little Souls* Leon Kobrin)

'So they talked about this in the town and the Jew Goldenbarg soon acquired a good name and they began to foresee much wealth and a good home.

Later, when he finished building the house, which consisted of a large square room and a small kitchen with a brick oven, and when he had dug the well and lined it with stones, and all his neighbors came and admired his work, Mister Goldenbarg sent for his wife.

The first day that Mister Goldenbarg's wife came west, he conducted her over the plains and hills and valleys of their new home...

...When she grew thirsty after all the walking, he took her over to the well and pulled up a pail of water for her. She drank the cool water and rested and drank again and her heart was delighted...

...That same evening all their neighbors from the nearby countryside came to visit. She sensed that there were no Jews among them, that she was the only Jewish woman here...Anxiety tapped lightly at her heart. (*Mr. Goldenbarg Settles in the West* Isaac Raboi)

'And that's where my troubles began. I wasn't worried about not being able to work as many hours as before the strike. You want me to work only nine hours, OK. Let all the cloak-makers have work — maybe it's not such a bad idea. But why should it bother you if I am friendly with the boss? Or if I come in to work a bit before anybody else and *shmuess* [*chat* – ed.] with him a bit? Or stay after work half an hour and listen to his complaints. Sometimes he's right, you know. When he starts complaining about the Union, my heart breaks.

You take a king and deprive him of his crown, his powers, his army. You tell him: "Keep your gold and your treasures, we won't touch it. But don't interfere in the government!" Exactly as it is happening now with the Persian Shah and the Portuguese King and Turkish Sultan, like the papers write.

I tried to console him...' (*The Trial* Abraham Reisin)

ANTHOLOGY
Solotaroff, Ted & Rapoport, Nessa (ed.s)

The Schocken Book of Contemporary Jewish Fiction (formerly 'Writing our way home') [English & Yiddish USA]

This is an anthology of North American Jewish writing, principally from the 1980s and 1990s, with a few pieces from the 1970s. Its writers come from a post- (or even post- post-) immigrant generation, whose understanding of being Jewish does not pass predominantly through remnants of European language and culture (*Yiddishkeit*), and whose world is resolutely modern, multi-cultural and liberal — why not, after all, arrange a second (symbolic!) circumcision if the first one was a trauma now standing in the way of re-experiencing the original birth trauma in your primal scream therapy, as Max Apple describes in *The Eighth Day*?

The range of themes reflects the changing social and cultural influences in the United States and the changing identifications and occupations of Jewry there: the 'Modern Orthodox' movement is represented alongside stories about intermarriage, single parenthood, fighting in the Israeli army, Beverly Hills non-Jews imitating Jewish mannerisms (in Michael Chabon's *S Angel*), shadows of the Holocaust (alongside I.B.Singer's *A Party on Miami Beach* and Lore Segal's *The Reverse Bug*, there is Deirdre Levinson's suggestive *April 19th, 1985*, set on the commemoration day of the Warsaw Ghetto uprising, about the difficulty of conveying this past to the younger generation, bred on 'meretricious pop-culture humanism', where if you 'ask him what he wants to be when he grows up, he says rich'...); a young Jewish woman writing copy for the Salvation Army (in Robin Roger's *The Pagan Phallus*) and a good range of intense family dramas: mourning, rivalry (the loveless mother-daughter struggles ensuing upon the father walking out in Marsha Lee Berkman's aptly entitled *Deeds of Love and Rage*), even a sensible thirteen-year-old boy wanting his father to sue his mother for exclusive custody of him (in Adam Schwartz's *Where is it written?*).

From the modern Orthodox movement there is Cynthia Ozick's haunting reworking of the reading about sin-offering from the Book of Numbers which is read on *Yom Kippur**, in *Bloodshed*, which pits the curious Bleilip, who thinks himself enlightened, against the pained and passionate Hasidic rabbi in their small and secluded community; and Allegra Goodman's nicely observed piece on the fastidious orthodoxy of Cecil, a scholar of George Bernard Shaw who is on a sabbatical at Oxford University, and the clash of English and American cultures which he encounters; the school where he sends his young daughter threatens to send her home for wearing dungarees, 'non-*tsniustic*' clothes [*Tsniut* in Hebrew means modesty, the code of practice which men and particularly women should follow], whereas Cecil himself is shocked that someone should be wheeling a pushchair to synagogue on the Sabbath, which goes against the Sabbath commandment that no work is to be done on that day. Goodman interestingly does not italicise the Hebrew words she uses in her texts, suggesting again the way in which the sacred language and Orthodoxy are both integrated into and disruptive of — in reading one is forced to go back over the word — the modern secular world.

A beautiful piece by Nessa Rapoport, more to do with tradition than with Orthodoxy, but again about the fraught relation of Judaism to the modern world, is entitled *The Woman who lost her Names*, and shows the seemingly small and inconsequential ways in which whole swathes of the past are wiped out through thoughtless 'adapting'. The teacher at school suggests that Sarah should be called Sally to 'help her integrate and make the adjustment easier', while her future husband, an Israeli, publishes poetry under an assumed name. However, when it is Sarah's turn to choose a name for her baby girl, she wants a new poetic name — the 'dawn star' — not realising that she is in this way repeating the effacement (of the mother's name passed down to the daughter) which she herself suffered from. The drama of this is heightened by the fact that her husband wants to follow the traditional line, and the tale reflects this attachment in its biblical cadences and poetic lilt, and in the decision which the couple take between life in the United States and Israel, parallel to the decision about a new naming or a traditional one.

A complicated story, where the old and the new jangle together and each new move in the present sends reverberations back down the past, is Lynne Sharon Schwartz's *The Melting Pot*. In a prose which is light and tender, the thoughts, memories and nightmares of Rita are scooped from her confused and paralysed present (she has dreams of suddenly being immobilised). Rita is the daughter of a Mexican called Carmen and a second generation Russian Jewish immigrant and lives on the West Coast. Her partner is an Indian called Sanjay who is twenty-two years her senior, has lived thirty years in the United States and is convinced that the moment will come when Rita will at last want to marry him, 'he wants her to turn around and live facing front'. The prospect of marriage provokes Rita to try to narrate her very mixed background (apart from her Mexican, presumably Catholic, mother and Jewish father, there is also an anarchist Jewish grandparent as well as a traditionalist one), and she finds herself lapsing into silences 'during which she tried to extricate herself from her history' and becomes increasingly confused and speechless. This is a poised and sensitive tale of differing cultures, ancestries and ages brought together; first and second generation immigrants, Indian and Jewish, with all the richness and difficulty, excitement and sense of fragmentation which such intricate interweaving — and diverging — lines can bring.

A more light-hearted but still profound piece on the awkwardness of identity is Adam Schwartz's *Where is it written?*. This is a funny role-reversal tale of a fastidious, houseproud and kitchen-friendly thirteen-year-old infuriated by his wayward mother who can't cook, can't iron, and whose patients (she is a therapist), wander into the kitchen, taste his stews and add paprika, while afterwards the mother protests 'Where is it written that I can't be both friend and therapist?'. Apart from being a satire on the American tendency to sue anything that moves — the boy wants to get his father to sue for custody — the story is also a sensitive presentation of the boy's growing awareness that in some areas people will never change, even if they say they want to, and that however much one may want them to be ideal they most probably are not.

An important voice amongst Jewish-American writers today is Grace Paley. Her story here *Zagrowsky Tells* is one of her cheeky, energetic and life-enhancing tales of family tensions meshing with racial tensions, of old worlds with new. As often in her short stories, the 'bite' (the tension provoked by the birth of a Jewish baby who turns out also to be black) is conveyed between the lines, while the language, close to natural patterns of thought and speech, carries the reader forward with its vivacity and directness.

Altogether, this anthology offers a broad range of subjects and styles, showing how a predominantly assimilated and middle-class Jewry takes on literary tradition, Jewish tradition and United States multi-culturalism; how Modern Orthodoxy confronts the two words of its name, how both new interest and disinterest in Israel expresses itself and how old tales and old words turn up in and transform new places. The range is so broad as to be eclectic, even though each story focuses on recognisably Jewish themes (from foreskin to foreign policy). *The Schocken Book of Contemporary Jewish Fiction* gives a real insight into the literary trends of contemporary North American Jewish writing, which is inventive, often playful and suitably diverse. S B

'It is not the cautious who die, but the overcautious. The married men are trying to strike an exact balance between their responsibility as soldiers, their fervent desire to stay alive, and their only hope — which is to go into battle with the smooth, courageous, trancelike movements that will keep them out of trouble. Soldiers who do not know how (like dancers or mountain climbers) to let their bodies think for them are very liable to be killed. There is a flow to hard combat; it is not (as it has often been depicted) entirely chance or entirely skill. A thousand signals and signs speak to you, much as in music. And what a sad moment it is when you must, for one reason or another, ignore them.' (Mark Helprin *North Light — A Recollection in the Present Tense* p111)

'She would bring out the thin, serrated knife I wasn't allowed to hold. And she would tell me about the tall mango trees she used to climb, how many different kinds there were, how laden with fruit free for the taking — greenies and tarts and spice and buxom — and how she used to puncture them and suck the juice out.

She would slice it very carefully, giving herself the smaller sections, and we would eat the fruit right to the skin. Nothing remained but the peel ridged with teeth marks and the yellow pit I didn't like to touch. Around mangoes my mother abandoned decorum; she would put the large, oval pit in her mouth and get all sticky while I watched.' (Eppie Zore'a *Orchards* p362-3)

'Ninety-first Street glows pink under the high crime street lights. Cars are bumper to bumper alongside the curbs. Heavy brownstone staircases crowd down onto the quiet sidewalk. The buildings, small (a bay window, a fancy balustrade), the garbage cans few, the trees scraggly. And all is soft and pink in the pellucid pink of the sodium arc. You could touch it and it wouldn't be rough. It is unreal and very intimate. Mr. Isaacson takes my arm. Behind us we hear a stammering farewell. We turn to acknowledge Mr. Sobel's third goodnight. "A gute nacht". And Mr. Sobel plunges off down the street in a stuttering motion, for every step taken, three starts.' (Allen Hoffman *Building Blocks* p125-6)

ANTHOLOGY

Neugroschel, Joachim (ed. & tr.)

The Shtetl: A creative anthology of Jewish Life in Eastern Europe

Joachim Neugroschel is an active and brilliant translator of Yiddish (and several other) literatures. He has assembled here a mighty paperback book that roams widely across the literature of Eastern European Jews. Amongst the several compendium-type books of this type it can certainly hold its ground and contains a distinctly different selection of Yiddish pieces to the *Treasury of Yiddish Stories* edited by Howe and Greenberg, which would be its main rival.

Neugroschel's *The Shtetl* kicks off with some of the 'pre-history' of modern Yiddish fiction with some tales of the Baal Shem Tov, the miracle-working founder of the Hasidic* movement of religious enthusiasts. The stories are both fascinating and sometimes almost embarrassing in their credulousness about the super-powers of this 'miracle Rabbi'. In a similar vein are some folk stories about the Prophet Elijah, who is believed to roam the world working miracles and various kindnesses amongst the Jews. At the Passover festival a seat is still left for him at the table in case he should want to put in an appearance.

While the first section of this anthology is called *Religious Roots* the second part moves onto *The Jewish Enlightenment*, the period when Jewish intellectuals and reformers, based initially in Germany, tried to bring a modern, rationalist philosophy to what they saw as their brothers still sunk in superstition and ignorance. There is a lot of writing in Yiddish associated with the values of this movement or commenting on its effects, particularly the enormous conflicts that blew up between rationalists and the pious within Jewish settlements and sometimes families. Examples here are I.L.Peretz's *A Woman's Fury,* a terrifically powerful and angry story about the treatment of women in the traditional shtetl system. Mendele Moykher Sforim, like Peretz a giant of early Yiddish fiction contributes *Travels of Benjamin the Third*, the story of a Jewish *Candide*, an innocent abroad on his way to the land of Israel, and, as one would expect, Mendele Moykher Sforim is fairly sardonic about the ignorance and general savagery of the world which the bold but naïve Benjamin travels through on his way to the Holy Land.

Neugroschel calls his third section *Tradition and Modernism* and the fourth *War, Revolution and Destruction* and it is here that one finds the rare and fascinating stories by less obvious writers that really justify the existence of this book. Amongst others there is *The Dog* by Avrom Reyzen, a sombre but original story of protest about a marginal and ostracised character in a Jewish community in Russia. Also around the subject of social isolation is Dovid Bergelson's *The Convert* with its 'mixed' couple of a Jewish girl married to a Christian living on the fringes of a Jewish village — but the isolation here seems to be as much that of the village Jews as of the couple.

Also talking about a kind of Jew that doesn't figure in too much Jewish fiction is Fishel Bimko's *The Draft* where Jewish village lads of the hard-drinking, hard-talking and punching variety are contrasted with the softer sons who beg their fathers to pay for someone else to take their place in the Tsar's army. Although sardonic and played for laughs — 'By early autumn, you can smell the Draft Board in the air' — lurking beneath the gaiety is the horrible reality of youngsters being forced into the harsh and hostile life of conscript soldiers for years on end. A situation that was perhaps worse for a Jewish youth who would be separated from his usual food, religious practices etc and instead united with all the sadistic tricks of Russian anti-Semitism.

The collection ends with an interesting Russian Civil War story, *Monday*. Moshe Kulbak's strange little novella is laconic but quite pointed in its picture of the constant disruption of middle-class life by succeeding waves of armies and revolutionaries; 'And machine-guns cautiously pecked, pecked, banged, and stitched in a familiar way, like sewing machines.' Clearly influenced by Expressionism, *Monday* creates a suggestive picture of the decay of the way of life of Russian Jews after World War One. The final piece is a late story *Meyer Landschaft* by the Soviet Yiddish writer Der Nister set in German-occupied Poland circa 1942, exploring the suffering of a father forced to confront the knowledge that his family will shortly be destroyed. Der Nister's approach to this awful subject is oblique but intimate, appropriate and effective.

Neugroschel adds brief but interesting introductions to the four sections of his book which add to the value of an undoubtedly valuable anthology. R K

"'All my days," writes Benjamin the Third... "All my days did I dwell in Moochville, I mean, I spent my whole life in Moochville until my great voyage. I was born there, I was raised there, and there I married *the wife of my bosom,* my missus, that pious spouse, Zelda — *long may she live!"*

Moochville is a tiny, jerkwater shtetl, far from the highway, and so cut off from the rest of the world that if ever anyone happens to come driving in, the townsfolk open their doors and windows to gawk and gape at the new-comer. Neighbours, peering through open windows, ask one another: "Ha! Now just who could that be? Now just where did he pop up from out of a clear blue sky? What's he after anyway? Doesn't he have something up his sleeve? It just doesn't look kosher. You don't just up and come like that. There's more here than meets the eye, we'll have to get to the bottom of this..."' (*The Travels of Benjamin the Third* by Mendele Moykher-Sforim p181)

ANTHOLOGY
Lyndon, Sonja & Paskin, Sylvia (ed.s)
The Slow Mirror and other stories. New Fiction by Jewish writers. [English Britain USA South Africa]

Published in 1996, this anthology tries to track the themes and obsessions of Jewish writers from Britain, the USA and South Africa, focusing on younger authors and new pieces rather the standard, time-tested voices.

While some of the stories err towards the soft-centred and politically-correct there is also much excellent writing amongst the twenty-six pieces that make up the book. Jonathan Wilson's *Dead Ringer* for instance, which creates a real sense of a character and his life, with an acerbity and realism that makes a refreshing contrast to the 'celebratory' aspect of some of the other stories. Also excellent is Tamar Yellin's *Kafka in Brontëland*, a classic kind of Jewish story, haunted by shadows of the past, the occasional uneasiness of assimilation and regrets for the loss of cultural distinctiveness and warmth; possibly the typical condition of many British Jews today.

Another story that approaches this theme of a lost but perhaps-recoverable past and does it in an oblique but highly artistic way is the collection's title story, *The Slow Mirror* by American Richard Zimler who lives in Oporto, Portugal and explores the Sephardic* Jewish past. A more usual motif for this 'excavating the past' is to be found in *Christmas in Berlin* by Elaine Feinstein which reconstructs the lives of Jews evading deportation in 1940s Berlin.

Another theme pursued by several writers in this anthology is (Jewish) family life, seemingly forever teetering between intimacy and neurosis. It's that world we all know from Philip Roth, Arnold Wesker or plain old direct experience... *Life with the letter 'F' Missing* by Londoner Rachel Castell Farhi probes the claustrophobic side of the family universe while the brief and wonderful *Strudelbakers 1951* by Zvi Zagendorf — who came to England as a child from Vienna in 1939 — is warm and funny with lots of waspish Jewish dialogue; 'When he married her they said she couldn't boil water'. Zagendorf wonderfully captures all the family discord and exaggerations in a story as good as warm Strudel.

Lentils in Paradise doesn't seem terrifically Jewish on the face of it; it's mostly set in a Turkish *Hamam*, or bathhouse, but perhaps by introducing us to a very *other* kind of world it speaks of the Wanderlust of many contemporary young Jews...

Sylvia Paskin, one of the book's editors contributes a fine story *Afterlife*, and she and her co-editor are to be congratulated on putting together a diverse and interesting collection. R K

'Make of me what you will, but give me a life: dress me in lamé or coat me in tweed, see me in stilettos or sandals or brogues... give me a waist that is thick or thin, a deep voice or a light trill, make me plain or ugly, the possibilities are endless. But make me wholesome, make me whole. Give me a long line of ancestors whose graves I can visit in verdant graveyards with whispering trees and creaking gates, set against a Constable landscape and a scudding sky. Write me into the book of life, shroud me in sheets of English prose. This is my living, dying, lying wish. Amen.' (p119 Sonja Lyndon *The Egg Baby*)

'The good mood was gone, replaced by some whirlwind of cruel memory which I knew nothing about but which was strong enough to invade any moment when I thought my mother and I might be happy. Her face turned thunderous with anger and I noticed her hands quiver. The familiar nausea of fear which always seemed to happen at mealtimes to put me off my food, crept up my gullet and into my mouth, filling me up. I wanted to escape, to be down there with the market people whose noise and shouts I could hear like a faraway echo of all that was commonplace, all that was normal, all that was to be despised as being part of the *goyim**, so it was wrong to desire it. Instead, I was trapped behind the kitchen table...and my mother, manic, in front of me.....'I think I'd better take one of my pills," she said quietly, "and then we can go out.'" (p30 *Life with the Letter "F" Missing* by Rachel Castell Farhi)

ANTHOLOGY
Cheyette, Brian (ed.)

Contemporary Jewish Writing in Britain and Ireland [English Britain & Irish Republic]

This large and well-produced anthology presents a wide range of Jewish writers — some at the heart of British culture, others outside the mainstream — who in some way write about Jewish identity in Britain and Ireland.

This kind of literature is often thought not to exist in its own right and gets included under the umbrella of a general British literature, thereby making invisible the specifically Jewish aspect of a writer.

Surprisingly it's the first work of its kind where the multiple voice of contemporary British- and Irish-Jewish writing is given full expression. The anthology collects some of the most influential writers in Britain and Ireland — such as Anita Brookner, Ruth

Prawer Jhabvala, and Harold Pinter — and explores their hitherto unfamiliar Jewishness. Altogether a very varied range of writers are brought together, including the emigrés and exiles Ruth Fainlight, Dan Jacobson, Gabriel Josipovici, Elena Lappin, and George Steiner, the British-born writers like Elaine Feinstein, Emanuel Litvinoff, Howard Jacobson, Bernice Rubens and Clive Sinclair and post-modern and feminist authors like Eva Figes, Ronit Lentin, Simon Louvish, Jonathan Treitel, Michelene Wandor, and Jonathan Wilson.

These writers are all often reviewed but hardly ever as *Jewish* writers — their Jewishness seems almost to be something of an embarrassment for British literary critics. They are sometimes defined as 'European' or 'modernist', as 'outsiders' or 'hybrid', but never as 'Jewish'.

The editor sees his aim here as not to impose a Jewish identity on his selection of authors but, instead, to show that Jewishness is one of various possible identities and voices available to them.

In a long and often provocative introduction Cheyette traces the history of British-Jewish writing from its origins to the present day. Although *Contemporary Jewish Writing in Britain and Ireland* focuses only on contemporary fiction (from the 1960s onwards), the introduction also usefully deals with poetry and drama. Here Cheyette shows the extent to which many traditions of Jewish writing in Britain have a Victorian pedigree. Even the left-wing 'Proletarian novel' and poetry date back to the 1920s. Coupled with this historical continuity however is a growing sense of discontinuity. Cheyette's introduction, and the bias of the collection, is towards what he calls a *diasporic* mode of writing. He argues that each writer anticipates the end of a narrow English national identity and attempts to replace it with a broader, more pluralistic, diasporic vision. Cheyette shows how the old Englishness has become superseded in recent years and that Jewish writers, along with their postcolonial counterparts, have been in the vanguard of either transcending or transfiguring this narrow national culture.

The fiction in this collection is always readable although some writers are more accessible and user-friendly than others. Intellectual heavy-weights such as Harold Pinter, George Steiner and Gabriel Josipovici contrast markedly with easier-going writers such as Bernice Rubens, Elaine Feinstein and Ruth Prawer Jhabvala.

However the book is clearly aimed at a general readership and the introduction is, thankfully, short on academic jargon. In fact *Contemporary Jewish Writing in Britain and Ireland* is one of those books that as soon as it appears we realise we've actually needed it for years! R K & B C

'It seems to be doing me some good, forcing myself to remember actual words that Camilla spoke. Her presence has been getting unhealthily generalized and diffused of late, particularly when I'm not walking the cliffs or following the course of rambles that we used to take together deep into Valency Valley. There has been a touch of Heathcliffe about me recently, I fear, that is if someone who is called Barney Fugleman and what's more looks as if he is called Barney Fugleman can approximate to such a gentle, such a Christian, such an English, such an essentially Cornish spinster's fantasy. But then why not? Might it not be possible to show, without going so far as to claim Jewish parentage for her Liverpudlian gypsy foundling, that it was precisely someone such as me, swarthy and saturnine and inhospitable and liable to vent my spleen on other people's pets, that the poor girl dreamed about, my fur coat and Bally shoes notwithstanding, in the back room of that draughty rectory? It's not out of the question. I've stirred the imagination of more than one lonely bookish vicar's daughter in my time. Either way, it's a surprise to me how morbid I've become. I listen to voices in the wind for God's sake! I trudge moors. I haunt country graveyards. Dogs I have always wanted to kick and I might myself, at any time, have hung up Isabella Linton's — the more the worms writhe, and all that — but now, I swear, and this is absolutely uncharacteristic of me, if I knew what an ash tree looked like or where one was to be found I could very easily fall to dashing my head against it.' p145-6 from Howard Jacobson's *Peeping Tom*

'Mr Lumbik glanced towards Otto's photo by the sleeping-couch. The wonderful forehead, he thought, was mainly created by the absence of any hair on the head. He remembered Otto Wolf as a small, bald, shrinking man, very tired, very sick, very old, in an expensive German dressing-gown which had grown too big for him. Mr Lumbik had always thought what a pity it was that a fine woman like Sonia couldn't have married something better. Though, of course, Otto Wolf had been a very wealthy factory-owner in Berlin, and it wasn't fair to judge him as he had been in his last years — only a poor refugee who couldn't speak English, had no work and lodged in Mrs Gottlob's house.' (p6 from Ruth Prawer Jhabvala's *A Birthday in London*)

GLOSSARY OF HEBREW, YIDDISH ETC. WORDS USED IN THIS BOOK

Agit-prop short for 'Agitation and propaganda'; Material produced to convince the masses about the Communist message by party cultural workers etc. in the USSR in the 1920s and then by other Communist parties elsewhere

Aliya 'ascension' Emigrating to Israel

Ashkenazi, Ashkenazic Jews are the Jews of France, Germany, and Eastern Europe, originally Yiddish-speaking. *Ashkenaz* is from the Hebrew for Germany. Thought of as refering to Jews whose traditions developed in Christian Europe.

Blintzes Jewish crepes. A blintz is a thin, flat pancake rolled around a filling

Borscht soup made with beetroots, dark red and with the taste of the Russian earth

Bund, Bundism the Jewish Socialist Bund (Federation or Union) was an important socialist organization of Jews in Russia and Poland

Dybbuk a Dybbuk, in Jewish folklore is a wandering spirit that possesses living people with dire results

Goyim, Goy Gentile, not Jewish

Haskalah the Jewish Enlightenment. Arose in Germany in the mid-eighteenth century. Main figure was Moses Mendelssohn who translated the Pentateuch into German for Jewish use. A reform movement that spread into Eastern Europe and Russia, bringing modern ideas and education.

Hatikvah literally 'hope', a song expressing Jewish yearning for the land of Israel, for freedom and independence. Adopted by the Zionist movement at the end of the nineteenth century and subsequently the State of Israel as its national anthem

Hassidim, Hasids, Hasidic also *Chasid* 'pietism', a movement of religious enthusiasm, led by *tzaddiks* or 'wise men', very important in Poland and the Ukraine. Founded by the Baal Shem Tov

Heder or *cheder* an elementary Hebrew school for the young

Irgun an armed Zionist group resisting British and Arabs in Palestine

Litvak Lithuanian Jew

Luftmensch a man with no clear means of support who uses his wits to get by

Maccabees name adopted by Judah Maccabee, involved in a revolt against the Seleucid rulers of Palestine in the second century B.C.E. and refers to members of his dynasty.

Mandate British Mandate period from 1918 to 1948 in Palestine, formerly a province of the Ottoman Empire the country was administered by the British by decree of the League of Nations, later the United Nations

Marranos Jews forcibly converted to Christianity in Spain in the fifteenth and sixteenth centuries. Many of these continued to practice Judaism in secret. Their descendants can be found today in Brazil, Mexico, the southwestern United States, and Majorca, as well as in mainland Spain and Portugal

Maskilim follower of the *Haskalah*, the Jewish Enlightenment

Melamed teacher in a *heder*

mensch a *mensch* is a person who is felt to be genuinely human, to have a soul...

Pogrom A collective attack on Jewish homes, businesses, institutions. Pogroms were widespread and encouraged by the Russian Tsarist government and right-wing political and religious forces in the nineteenth century, stimulating massive Jewish emigration

Minyan the minimum number of ten Jewish males assembled for communal prayers

New Christian see *Marrano*

Sabra a native-born Israeli

Schlemiel born loser, simpleton

Sephardic Jews are historically the Jews of Spain, Portugal, North Africa and the Middle East. Small communities exist in other countries too. Thought of as refering to Jews whose traditions developed in the Moslem world. *Sepharad* is from the Hebrew word for Spain. Historically many used the *Ladino*, Judeo-Spanish language. *Shamosim* pl. of *Shammes* A Synagogue sexton or official

Shoah desolation or ruin, term preferred by some for The Holocaust

Shtetl literally 'small town'

Spieler a great and convincing talker, used ironically.

Talith ritual garment

Trayfe food forbidden to pious Jews: pork, shellfish etc.

Tzaddiks see *Hasid*

Yeshiva school for higher religious studies, trains Rabbis

Yom Kippur The day of repentance. The holiest and most solemn day of the Jewish year, its central theme is atonement and reconciliation. *Yom Kippur* comes to an end with the blowing of the *shofar*, the ram's horn, which marks the conclusion of the fast

Editors

Ray Keenoy BA founded the *Babel Guides* series and runs Boulevard Books, a publishing house specialising in contemporary world fiction

Dr Saskia Brown taught French Literature at Warwick University and has a special interest in Franco-Jewish thought. She currently lives in Paris

Contributors

Dr Mark Axelrod is a novelist and screenwriter and teaches Comparative Literature at Chapman University in Southern California

Marion Baraitser is a playwright and editor

Dr Brian Cheyette is Reader in English & Judaic Studies at Queen Mary & Westfield College, London and recently edited *Contemporary Jewish Writing in Britain and Ireland* (Peter Halban 1998)

Dr Fiorenza Conte edited the *Babel Guide to Italian Fiction* and writes for Italian television

Marina Coriolano-Lykourezos BA is editor of the forthcoming *Babel Guide to Modern Greek Literature in Translation*

Dr Clara Corona teaches Italian literature in Treviso, Italy

Richard Crownshaw lectures in English and American Literature at Goldsmiths College, London and is researching *Representations of the Holocaust in American Culture.*

Dr Patrick Curry reviews for the *Times Literary Supplement* and the *New Statesman*. His most recent book is *Defending Middle-Earth* (Floris 1997)

Barry Davis BA lectures in History at Thames Valley University and teaches Yiddish at the Spiro Institute, London

Alex Gordon MA works at the Spiro Institute, London lecturing on Film and the Arts and is currently contributing to a book on Yiddish film

Tony Hammond MA, a Literature specialist, is Director of Education at the Spiro Institute, London

Dr Theo Hermans is Professor of Dutch at University College London and is editing the *Babel Guide to Dutch & Flemish Fiction in English Translation*

Tamara Levine MA, born in Johannesburg, lectures at the Spiro Institute, London and researches in Modern Hebrew literature

Derwent May writes for *The Times* and wrote *Marcel Proust* in the *Oxford Modern Masters* series

Dr Mike Mitchell is a leading translator of Austrian fiction

Giovanni Pontiero translated major works of Clarice Lispector

Giose Rimanelli is an Italian-American novelist and Professor Emeritus of Comparative Literature at SUNY Buffalo, NY

Dr Gareth Stanton lectures in Media and Communications at Goldsmiths' College London & recently co-edited *Postcolonial Criticism* (Longman 1997)

Louise Sylvester is a Research Fellow at King's College London. She has published articles on feminism and Jewish identity.

Dr David Treece heads the *Centre for the Study of Brazilian Culture and Society* at Kings College, London. He is an active translator and co-edited the *Babel Guide to the Fiction of Portugal, Brazil and Africa in English Translation*

Database of Jewish fiction available in English

This database is a resource for anyone who wants to read Jewish writers in English. Its main goal is to let you know what's been translated. The reviews section of the guide generally emphasizes books that are currently in print and that you can find or order at your bookshop now but this section includes *most* of the contemporary (written after 1900) fiction translated from Yiddish and Hebrew, published in the UK, the USA and Israel. Some bibliographic information was supplied by the Institute for the Translation of Hebrew Literature, Tel Aviv. Books from other languages reviewed in the *Babel Guide* have also been added.

Please note that there may be discrepancies in the transliteration of Yiddish and Hebrew names and titles and that the *Babel Guide* is primarily a guide to reading in English.
Price and availability of books changes from day to day as publishers withdraw, re-price and reprint. This database is a handy guide but for the latest information on a particular book ask your bookseller or librarian. A few prices are included, but again please check with your bookseller.
For our readers' convenience all anthologies are listed together under 'Anthologies', in title order, rather than the editor's name.

Abbreviations:
HB = hard cover edition
PB = paperback edition
OP = out of print

Record details:
Author (surname)
Author (first name)
English title
Year this edition was published in the USA or Israel
Original language title
Year published in the original language
Translator's name
US (or Israeli) Publisher
Pages
Hardback or paperback
Price in $/Out of print
UK Publisher
Year this edition was published in the UK
Pages
Hardback or paperback
Price in £/Out of print

Kahana, T
Henry Schuman
1953
342
Abelard-Schuman
1953(1958)
342
Aleichem
Shalom
Around the table: family stories of
Sholom Aleichem
Shevrin, A
C. Scribner, New York
1991
84
Aleichem
Shalom
Best of Sholom Aleichem, The
Howe, I; Wisse, R
Walker, New York
1991
388
18.95
Aleichem
Shalom
Best of Sholom Aleichem, The
eds Howe, I; Wisse, R
J. Aronson
1989
274
Aleichem
Shalom
Best of Sholom Aleichem, the
Weidenfeld and Nicolson
1979
276
Aleichem
Shalom
Bloody hoax, The
Shevrin
Indiana UP
1991
373
Aleichem
Shalom
Childhood of honey and tears, A :
delightful stories to warm the heart
Hallmark
1975
60
Aleichem
Shalom
Early Passover, An
A friher Pesah
Zinberg, G
Clifton
1966
32
Aleichem
Shalom
Favourite Tales of Shalom Aleichem
Shevrin
Amereon
1992
23.95
Kuperard

1995
hb
14.99
Aleichem
Shalom
Holiday tales of Sholom Aleichem
Shevrin, A
Scribner
1979
145
Aleichem
Shalom
In the storm
Shevrin, A
New American Library
1984
220
Aleichem
Shalom
In the storm
Shevrin, A
G.P. Putnam's Sons
1984
220
Aleichem
Shalom
Inside Kasrilevke, three stories
Fun Kasrilevke
Goldstick, I
Schocken Books
1948
127
Aleichem
Shalom
Inside Kasrilevke, three stories
Goldstick, I
Schocken Books
1968(1948)
222
Robson Books: London
1973
222
Aleichem
Shalom
Marienbad
Marienbad
Shevrin, A
Weidenfeld and Nicolson
1982
222
Aleichem
Shalom
Marienbad
Marienbad
Shevrin, A
Perigee Books
1982
222
Aleichem
Shalom
More Favourite Tales of Shalom
Aleichem
Amereon
1992
25.95
Aleichem

Shalom
Nightingale, The, or, The saga of
Yosele Solovey the cantor
Shevrin, A
New American Library
1985
1vol
Aleichem
Shalom
Nightingale, The, or, The saga of
Yosele Solovey the cantor
Shevrin, A
Putnam
1985
240
Aleichem
Shalom
Old country tales
Leviant, C
Putnam
1979
319
Aleichem
Shalom
Old country, The
Butwin, J & F
Garden City Bks
1953
446
Deutsch
1958
h
319
Aleichem
Shalom
Old country, The
Butwin, Julius & Francis
Crown Books: NY
1946
Aleichem
Shalom
Old country, The: short stories
Butwin, J & F
Crown publishers: NY
1956
434
Vallentine Mitchell
1973
h
434
Aleichem
Shalom
Selected stories
Modern Lib.
1958
432
Aleichem
Shalom
Some laughter, some tears; tales
from the old world and the new
Leviant, C
Putnam
1968
254
Aleichem
Shalom

Stories and satires
Leviant, C
Yoseloff: NY
1959
381
Yoseloff: London
1960
381
Aleichem
Shalom
Stories and satires
Leviant, C
Collier Books: NY
1970
h
381
Collier-Macmillan: London
1970
381
Aleichem
Shalom
Tevye stories and others, The
Tevye der milkhika
Butwin, J & F
Pocket Books
1965
230
Aleichem
Shalom
Tevye the dairyman and The
railroad stories
Halkin, H
Schocken Books
1987
309
Schocken Books
13.99
Aleichem
Shalom
Tevye; oh, a miracle!
Fleet P.: NY
1971
19
Aleichem
Shalom
Tevye's daughters
Butwin, F
Crown
1949
319
Vallentine Mitchell
1973
302
Alir
D
Through the Prism of Life
Miba'ad li-frizmat ha-hayim
Lask,I M
s.n.: Ramat Gan (Israel)
1976
228
Almagor
Gila
Summer of Aviya, The
Halkin, H
Collins

1991
92
Almog
Ruth
Death in the rain: a novel
Mavet ba-geshem
Bilu, D
Red Crane Books: Santa Fe, NM
1993
pb
204
Alterman
Nathan
Little Tel Aviv
Tel Aviv haketana
Super, A. S.
Hakkibutz Hameuchad, Tel Aviv,
Israel
1981
100
Amichai
Yehuda
Not of this time, not of this place
Lo me-'akhshav, lo mi-kan
1963
Katz, Shlomo
Harper & Row
1968
344
Vallentine: London
1973
Amichai
Yehuda
World is a room, The and other
stories
Ba-ruah ha-nora'ah ha-zot.
(Selections)
Grumet, Elinor et al
Jewish Publication Society of
America: Philadelphia
1984
199
15.99
Amir
Eli
Scapegoat: a novel
Tarnegol kaparot
Bilu, D
Weidenfeld & Nicolson
1987
218
An-Ski
S
Dybbuk, The and other writings
Werman, G
Schocken Books: NY
1992
230
ANTHOLOGY
Maoz, Rivka (ed.)
Arab in 20th Century Hebrew
Fiction, The
Hebrew University: Jerusalem
1976
136
ANTHOLOGY

Howe, I & Greenberg, E (ed.s)
Ashes out of hope: fiction by Soviet-
Yiddish Writers. Joseph Schur. The
hole through which life slips (David
Bergelson) Civil War. Zelmenyaner
(Moshe Kulbak) Under a fence: a
revue (Der Nister);
Various
Schocken Books: NY
1977
hb
218
ANTHOLOGY
Boyarsky, A Sarna, L eds
Canadian Yiddish Writings
Harvest House (Canada)
1976
149
ANTHOLOGY
Cheyette, Brian (ed)
Contemporary Jewish Writing in
Britain and Ireland
Nebraska University Press (USA)
1998
pb
336
18.95
Peter Halban Books
1998
pb
336
10.99
ANTHOLOGY
Ofek, U (ed.)
Dog that flew, The and other
favourite stories from Israel
Funk & Wagnalls
1969
154
ANTHOLOGY
Kalechofsky, Robert & Roberta
(ed.s)
Echad, an anthology of Latin
American Jewish writings
Micah Publications: Marblehead,
MA.
1980
pb
282
ANTHOLOGY
Lelchuk, A & Shaked, G
Eight great Hebrew short novels
New American Library:NY
1983
392
ANTHOLOGY
Sherman, Joseph (ed.)
From a Land Far Off. South African
Yiddish Stories in English
Translation
Sherman, Joseph
Jewish Publications South Africa:
Cape Town (South Africa)
1987
hb
209

ANTHOLOGY
Michener, James A.
Firstfruits: a harvest of 25 years of
Israeli writing
Jewish Publication Society of
America: Philadelphia
1973
344

ANTHOLOGY
Michener, James A.
Firstfruits: a harvest of 25 years of
Israeli writing
Jewish Publication Society of
America: Fawcett: Greenwich,
Conn.
1974
344

ANTHOLOGY
Noy, D & Ben-Amos, D
Folktales of Israel
Baharav, G
University of Chicago Press
1963
221

ANTHOLOGY
Forman, F et al (ed.s)
Found Treasures. Stories by Yiddish
Women Writers
various
Second Story Press: Toronto
(Canada)
1994
pb
289
Second Story Press: Toronto
(Canada)
1994
pb
250
12.99

ANTHOLOGY
Schwartz, Howard (ed.)
Gates to the new city: a treasury of
modern Jewish tales
Avon: NY
1983
815
Kuperard
39.95

ANTHOLOGY
Teitelbaum, E (ed.)
Gems from Jewish literature
Pardes
1953
223

ANTHOLOGY
Penueli, S Ukhmani, A eds
Hebrew Short Stories. (Two
volumes)
Institute for the Translation of
Hebrew Literature: Tel Aviv
1965
335,380

ANTHOLOGY
Furstenberg, Rochelle (ed.)
Images of Jerusalem.

Hadassah: NY
1995
142

ANTHOLOGY
Maoz, Rivka (ed.)
In the Land of the Patriarch's Desire
Hebrew University: Jerusalem
1985
pb
274

ANTHOLOGY
Gluzman, Michael (ed.)
Israel: A Traveller's Literary
Companion
Whereabouts: San Francisco
1996
236

ANTHOLOGY
Halevy-Levin, I et al
Israel Argosy VII. Bialik, H;Ben
Shalom, B;Fichman,J et al
Halevy-Levin, I et al
WIZO: Jerusalem
1960
196

ANTHOLOGY
Blocker, J (ed)
Israeli stories: a selection of the best
contemporary Hebrew writing
Schocken
1962,1975
pb
256

ANTHOLOGY
Sobel, Samuel (ed.)
Jewish Sea Stories
David: Middle Village, NY
1985
337

ANTHOLOGY
Lappin, E. (ed.)
Jewish Voices, German Words
Winston, N
Catbird Press
Catbird Press
1995
hb
334
16.95

ANTHOLOGY
Married Woman, A and other short
stories from Israel
Star: New Delhi (India)
19951

ANTHOLOGY
Tammuz, B & Yudkin, L eds
Meetings with the angel: seven
stories from Israel
Pessah, C et al
Deutsch
1973
hb
252

ANTHOLOGY
Alter, Robert (ed.)
Modern Hebrew Literature (stories

by Mendele Mocher Sforim, Peretz,
Y. L. Feierberg, M. Z.. Ahad Ha-
Am. Bialik, H. N. Brenner, Y. H..
Barash, A.. Agnon, S. Y. Agunot.
Hazaz, H. sermon. Yizhar, S..
Amichai, Y.. Oz, A.. Yehoshua, A. B.)
Behrman House: NY
1975
398
Behrman House: NY
11.99

ANTHOLOGY
Spicehandler, Ezra (ed)
Modern Hebrew stories. (Dual
Language Book)
Sipurim 'ivriyim moderniyim
Bantam Books, Toronto, Canada
1971
341
Bantam Books
1971
341

ANTHOLOGY
Ravikovitch, Dalia (ed.)
New Israeli writers
Funk & Wagnalls
1969
319

ANTHOLOGY
Sonntag, Jacob (ed.)
New Writing from Israel
Transworld: London
1976
256

WIZO
Omer: an anthology of
contemporary Hebrew literature
WIZO: Jerusalem
1973

ANTHOLOGY
WIZO
Omer (4): an anthology of
contemporary Hebrew literature.
The Way Out (Brenner) The Whole
Life (Agnon)
various
WIZO: Jerusalem
1975
82

ANTHOLOGY
ANTHOLOGY
Abramson, Glenda (ed.)
Oxford Book of Hebrew Short
Stories
Oxford University Press: NY
1997
hb
409
35
Oxford University Press: Oxford
1997
409
17.99

ANTHOLOGY
Abramson, Glenda (ed.)
Oxford Book of Hebrew Short

713
14.99
ANTHOLOGY
ed Ayalti, H
Yiddish Proverbs
Goldstick, I
Schocken Books
1949
127
ANTHOLOGY
ed Leftwich, J
Yisroel, the first Jewish omnibus
Beechhurst Press
c.1952
723
ANTHOLOGY
Flantz, Richard (ed.)
Until daybreak : stories from the
kibbutz. selected and with an
introduction by Amos Oz ; edited by
Richard Flantz.
Hakibbutz Hameuchad Pub. House
; [S.l.] : Institute for the Translation
of Hebrew Literature
1984
pb
280
ANTHOLOGY
Spicehandler & Arnson (ed.s)
Writing in Israel
Sabra Books: NY
1976
Appelfeld
Aharon
Age of wonders, The
Tor ha-pela'ot
1981
Bilu, D
Kudos & Godine
1982
224
Appelfeld
Aharon
Age of wonders, The
Tor ha-pela'ot
1981
Bilu, Dalyu
D.R. Godine: Boston
1981
270
Weidenfeld & Nicolson
1987
207
Appelfeld
Aharon
Age of wonders, The
Tor ha-pela'ot
1981
Bilu, Dalya
Quartet Books
1993
216
Appelfeld
Aharon
Badenheim 1939
Badenhaim, 'ir nofesh

1979
Bilu, D
Godine: Boston
1980
Dent
1981
148
Appelfeld
Aharon
Badenheim 1939
Badenhaim, 'ir nofesh
1979
Bilu, D
G.K. Hall
1981
214
Appelfeld
Aharon
For every sin
Al kol ha-peshaim
Green, J M
Quartet
1995
pb
168
10
Appelfeld
Aharon
For every sin
Al kol ha-peshaim
Green, J M
Vintage Books
1989
168
Weidenfeld
1989
hb
168
10
Appelfeld
Aharon
Healer, The
Be-'et uve-'onah ahat
Green, J M
Grove Weidenfeld
1990
220
Weidenfeld & Nicolson
1990
184
Appelfeld
Aharon
Healer, The
Be-'et uve-'onah ahat.
Green, J M
Quartet
1992
220
Appelfeld
Aharon
Immortal Bartfuss, The
Bartfuss ben almavet
Green, J M
Perennial Library
1988
137

Weidenfeld & Nicolson
1988
hb
137
Appelfeld
Aharon
Immortal Bartfuss, The
Bartfuss ben almavet
Green, J M
Quartet
1995
pb
137
7
Appelfeld
Aharon
Iron Tracks, The
Mesilat barzel.
Green, JM
Schoken
1998
Appelfeld
Aharon
Katerina
Katerinah
1989
Green, J M
Random House
1992
212
Quartet
1992
pb
212
9
Appelfeld
Aharon
Retreat, The
Bilu, D
Penguin Books
1984
164
Appelfeld
Aharon
Retreat, The
Bilu, D
Schoken
1998
Quartet
1985
pb
125
Appelfeld
Aharon
Retreat, The
Bilu, D
NY, Dutton
1984
Quartet
1985
160
Appelfeld
Aharon
To the land of the cattails
Green, J M
S. Yarmouth, Mass, J. Curley

Macdonald
1952
h
494
Asch
Sholem
Nazarene, The
Der man fun Nazres
Samuel, M
Pocket Books
1958
684
Asch
Sholem
Passage in the night, A
Samuel, M
Putnam
1953
367
Macdonald
1954
h
388
Asch
Sholem
Salvation
Der Tehilim
Muir, W & E
Putnam
1951
351
Macdonald (Also Gollancz 1934)
1953
h
374
Asch
Sholem
Three cities
Moskve, Peterburg, Varshe
Muir, W & E
Bantam
1967
pb
821
Asch
Sholem
Three cities
Moskve, Peterburg, Varshe
Muir, Willa & Edwin
Putnam: NY,NY
1933
Asch, Sholem et al
Union for Shabbos, A
Rosenfeld, M
Sholem Aleichem Club P.
1967
221
Avidan
David
Cryptograms from a telestar: poems,
transmissions, documents
Tishdorot milavyan riggul
Now & Thirtieth Century Press:Tel
Aviv, Israel
1980
90

Avnery
Arieh
Sabra Commandos
Peshitot ha-tagmul: esrim shenot
tagemul yisreeli, meever leqawwe ha-
oyev
Olive Books: Tel Aviv
1972
173
Avnery
Arieh
War of Attrition, The
Peshitot ha-tagmul:peullot Zahal
bekhol he-hazitot meever leqawwe
ha-oyev
Olive Books: Tel Aviv
1972
192
Ayal
Ora
Ugbu
Harper & Row:NY
1979
31
Ayalti
Hanan J
No escape from Brooklyn
Vayter fun Bruklin
Sloan, J & MacLow, J
Twayne
1966
215
Babel
Isaak Emmanuilovic
Benia Krik; a film-novel
Hyperion
1973
95
Babel
Isaak Emmanuilovic
Benya Krik the Gangster and other
stories
various
Schocken Books
1985
Babel
Isaak Emmanuilovic
Benya Krik, the gangster
Yarmolinsky, A
Schocken Books
1969
128
Babel
Isaak Emmanuilovic
Collected Stories
Dnevnik 1920
Yale UP
1994
pb
400
Babel
Isaak Emmanuilovic
Collected Stories [includes Red
Cavalry, Tales of Odessa] (Ed.
Trilling, L.)
Konarmiya, Odesskie rasskazy etc.

various
New American Library: NY, NY
1974
pb
380
Babel
Isaak Emmanuilovic
Collected Stories [includes Red
Cavalry, Tales of Odessa] (Ed.
Trilling, L.)
Konarmiya, Odesskie rasskazy etc.
various
S.G.Philips
1974
hb
380
36.95
Babel
Isaac Babel 1920 Diary Carol J.
Avins (Editor)
Dnevnik 1920
Willetts, H. T.
pb
Babel
Isaak Emmanuilovic
Isaac Babel The Forgotten Prose.
(ed. Stroud, N)
Ardis: Ann Arbor
1978
143
Babel
Isaak Emmanuilovic
You must know everything; stories,
1915-1937
Hayward, M
Farrar, Straus & Giroux
1969
pb
283
Baram
Meir
Fateful mission, The
Ha-shelihut ha-goralit
Handel, E von
Feldheim (Israel)
1987
168
Baram
Meir
Fateful mission, The
Ha-shelihut ha-goralit
Handel, E van
Feldheim: Jerusalem
1987
168
Baram
Meir
Parnas, The
Ha-parnas mi-Colonia
Handel, E von
Feldheim (Israel)
1987
183
Baram
Meir

Bialik speaks
Mi-pi Bialik
El-Dror, A
Herzl P
1969
192
Bialik
Hayyim Nahman
Selected Poems (Heb, Eng)
Union of American Hebrew
Congregations: NY
1972
132
Biber
Yeho'ash
Adventures in the Galilee
Jewish Publication Society of
America: Philadelphia
1973
149
Biber
Yeho'ash
Treasure of the Turkish pasha, The
Otsar ha-pehah ha-turki
Hochman, B
Scribner
1968
128
Bin Gorion
Micha Josef
Miriam: a novel about life in two
townships
Miriam: roman mehayye shete
'ayyarot
Super, A. S.
Ha-kibutz Hameuchad: Tel Aviv
1983
288
Bin-Gorion
Micha Josef
Miriam: a novel about life in two
townships
Miriam: roman mehayye shete
'ayyarot
Super, A
Hakibbutz Hameuchad (Israel)
1983
288
Blinkin
Meir
Stories
Rosenfeld, M
State University of New York Press
1984
166
Blum
Eliezer
Revolt of the apprentices and other
stories
Oyfn veg tsum Perets Skver
Blum, E
Yoseloff
1969
232
Botwinik
Berl

Lead pencil: stories and sketches
Klukoff, P
Wayne State University Press
1984
163
Brandwein
Hayim
In the courtyards of Jerusalem
Be-hatsrot Yerushalayim
Halkin, H
Jewish Publn Society of America
1967
244
Brenner
Joseph H
Out of the depths
Min ha-metsar
1908-9
Patterson, David
Westview Press: Boulder, Colorado
1992
101
Westview Press: Oxford
1995
pb
101
9.5
Brenner
Joseph Hayyim
Breakdown and bereavement
Shekhol ve-khishalon
Halkin, H
Cornell University Press
1971
310
Cornell University Press
1971
311
Brookner
Anita
Family Romance, A
Cape: London
1993
hb
218
Brookner
Anita
Family Romance, A
Penguin
1994
hb
218
Bryks
Rachmil
Cat in the ghetto, A. Four novelettes
Engel, M
Bloch Pub. Co.
1961
160
Bryks
Rachmil
Kiddush Hashem
Berhamn House: NY
1977
113
Buber

Martin
For the sake of heaven
Gog u-Magog
Lewisohn, L
Greenwood Press
1970
316
Buber
Martin
For the sake of heaven
Gog u-Magog
Lewisohn, L
Meridian Books
1960
316
Burko
Helen
Bridge to love
Gesher ahava
Metcalf, F
Progress Books (Israel)
1987
308
Burla
Yehuda
In Darkness Striving
Naftule adam
Schachter, J
ITHL: Jerusalem
1968
135
Cahan
Abraham
Education of Abraham Cahan, The
Bleter fun mayn leben
Stein, L & Conan, A & Davidson, L
Jewish Publication Society of
America
1969
450
Cahan
Abraham
Rise of David Levinsky, The
1917
Carr (ed)
Maurice
Waiter there is a fly in my orange
juice
Shikmona Pub. Co., Jerusalem,
Israel
1975
272
Castel-Bloom
Orly
Dolly City
Dolly City
1992
Bilu, D
Loki Books: London c/o
www.lokibooks.u-net.com
1997
Loki Books: London
1997
pb
182
7.99

Sidgwick & Jackson: London
1978
Goldstick
Isadore
Inside Kasrilevke
Dos naye Kasrilevke
Schocken
1965
222
Goor
Batya
Literary murder: a critical case
Bilu, D
Harper Collins
1993
357
Goor
Batya
Murder on a kibbutz: a communal
case
Linah meshutefet
Bilu, Dalya
Harper Collins
1994
350
20
Goor
Batya
Saturday morning murder, The : a
psychoanalytic case
Retsah be-Shabat ba-boker
Bilu, Dalya
Aaron Asher Books: NY,NY
1992
294
Grab
Herman
Town Park, The & other stories
Stadtpark und andere Erzählungen
1934
Hoare, Q
Verso
1988
hb
250
10.90
Grade
Chaim
Rabbis and wives
Rabinowitz, H & Grade, I
A.A. Knopf
1982
307
Kuperard (dist.)
10.99
Grade
Chaim
Seven little lanes, The
Leviant, C
Bergen Belsen Memorial Press
1972
111
Grade
Chaim
Well, The
Der brunem

Wisse, R
Jewish Publn Society of America
1967
276
Gross
David C.
Love poems from the Hebrew
Doubleday
1976
83
Grossman
David
Book of intimate grammar, The
Sefer hadikduk haprimi
1988
Rosenberg, Betty
Farrar Straus Giroux
1994
343
Picador
1994
pb
343
6.99
Grossman
David
Book of intimate grammar, The
Sefer hadikduk haprimi
1988
Rosenberg, B
Farrar Straus Giroux
1994
343
Cape
1994
hb
343
14.99
Grossman
David
See under - love
'Ayen 'erekh: ahavah
Rosenberg, B
Washington Square Press
1989
1v
Grossman
David
See under - love
'Ayen 'erekh: ahavah
Rosenberg, B
Farrar Straus Giroux
1989
458
Grossman
David
See under - love
'Ayen 'erekh: ahavah
Rosenberg, B
Cape
1990
458
Grossman
David
See under - love
'Ayen 'erekh: ahavah

Rosenberg, B
Pan / Cape
1991
458
Grossman
David
Smile of the lamb, The
Rosenberg, B
Washington Square Press
1990
325
Grossman
David
Smile of the lamb, The
Hiyukh ha-gedi
Rosenberg, B
Farrar Straus Giroux
1990
325
Picador
1992
325
Grossman
David
Yellow wind, The
Zeman ha-tsahov
Watzman, H
Farrar Straus Giroux
1988
216
Grossman
David
Zigzag kid, The
Yesh yeladim zigzag
Rosenberg, Betty
Farrar Straus Giroux
1997
Cape
1994
hb
343
14.99
Grossman
David
Zigzag kid, The
Yesh yeladim zigzag
Rosenberg, Betty
Bloomsbury
1997
pb
309
GRUNBERG
Arnon
Blue Mondays
Blauwe maandagen
1994
Pomerans, Arnold & Erica
Farrar, Straus & Giroux: New York
1997
Secker & Warburg: London
Gur
Motta
Azeet, paratrooper dog
'Azit ha-kalbah ha tsanhanit
T. Nelson
1972

Oz
Amos
Elsewhere, perhaps
Makom aher
de Lange, N; Oz, A
Harcourt Brace Jovanovich
1973
Secker & Warburg
1974
309
Oz
Amos
Fima
Ha-matsav ha-shelishi
Harcourt Brace
1993
322
5.99
Oz
Amos
Fima
Ha-matsav ha-shelishi
Chatto
1993
hb
298
15.99
Oz
Amos
Fima
Ha-matsav ha-shelishi
Vintage: London
1995
pb
298
5.99
Oz
Amos
Hill of evil counsel, The: three stories
Givat ha-etsah ha-raah
de Lange, N; Oz, A
Flamingo
1985
210
Oz
Amos
Hill of evil counsel, The: three stories
Givat ha-etsah ha-raah
de Lange, N; Oz, A
Harcourt Brace Jovanovich
1978
210
Chatto & Windus
1978
210
Oz
Amos
Hill of evil counsel, The: three stories
Har ha-etsah ha-raah
de Lange, N; Oz, A
Fontana
1980
210

Oz
Amos
Hill of evil counsel, The: three stories
Har ha-etsah ha-raah
de Lange, N; Oz, A
Vintage
1993
pb
210
5.99
Oz
Amos
My Michael
Mikha'el sheli
Vintage Books
1992
287
Oz
Amos
My Michael
Mikha'el sheli
de Lange, N
Flamingo
1984
224
Oz
Amos
My Michael
Mikha'el sheli
de Lange, N; Oz, A
Knopf
1972
287
Chatto & Windus
1972
216
Oz
Amos
My Michael
Mikha'el sheli
Bantam
1976
247
Oz
Amos
My Michael
Mikha'el sheli
de Lange, N: Oz, A
Fontana
1975
224
Oz
Amos
My Michael
Mikha'el sheli
de Lange, N; Oz, A
Flamingo
1984
224
Oz
Amos
My Michael
Mikha'el sheli
de Lange, N: Oz, A
Vintage

1991
216
Oz
Amos
Panther in the Basement, A
Panter BaMartef
1995
Vintage: London
1997
122
Oz
Amos
Perfect peace, A
Menuhah nekhonah
Halkin, H
Schocken Books
1986
374
Oz
Amos
Perfect peace, A
Menuhah nekhonah
Halkin, H
Flamingo
1988
374
Oz
Amos
Perfect peace, A
Menuhah nekhonah
Halkin, H
Chatto & Windus
1985
374
Oz
Amos
Perfect peace, A
Menuhah nekhonah
Halkin, H
Vintage
1993
pb
374
5.99
Oz
Amos
Soumchi
Oz, A; Farmer, P
Chatto & Windus
1980
89
Oz
Amos
Soumchi
Oz, A; Farmer, P
Harper & Row
1980
89
Oz
Amos
To know a woman
La-daat ishah
de Lange, N; Oz, A
Harcourt Brace Jovanovich
1991
262

Oz
Amos
To know a woman
La-daat ishah
de Lange, N; Oz, A
Vintage
1992
264
Oz
Amos
To know a woman
La-daat ishah
de Lange, N; Oz, A
Chatto & Windus
1991
265
Oz
Amos
Touch the water, touch the wind
La-ga'at ba-mayim, la-ga'at ba-ruach
de Lange, N; Oz, A
Flamingo
1986
158
Oz
Amos
Touch the water, touch the wind
La-ga 'at ba-mayim, la-ga 'at ba-ruah
de Lange, N; Oz, A
Harcourt Brace Jovanovich
1974
179
Fontana
1976
158
Oz
Amos
Touch the water, touch the wind
La-ga 'at ba-mayim, la-ga 'at ba-ruah
de Lange, N; Oz, A
Harcourt Brace Jovanovich
1974
179
Chatto & Windus
1975
179
Oz
Amos
Touch the water, touch the wind
La-ga'at ba-mayim, la-ga'at ba-ruach
de Lange, N; Oz, A
Flamingo
1986
158
Oz
Amos
Touch the water, touch the wind
La-ga 'at ba-mayim, la-ga 'at ba-ruah
de Lange, N; Oz, A
Vintage
1992

158
Oz
Amos
Unto death
Ad mavet Ahavah meuheret
de Lange, N; Oz, A
Harcourt Brace Jovanovich
1978
166
Chatto & Windus
1976
168
Oz
Amos
Unto death
'Ad mavet. Ahavah meuheret
de Lange, N & Oz, A
Harcourt Brace Jovanovich
1975
166
Fontana
1977
125
Oz
Amos
Unto death
Ad mavet Ahavah meuheret
de Lange, N; Oz, A
Vintage
1992
175
Oz
Amos
Where the jackals howl, and other stories
de Lange, N; Simpson, P
Flamingo
1983
217
5.99
Oz
Amos
Where the jackals howl, and other stories
de Lange, N; Simpson, P
Chatto & Windus
1981
217
Oz
Amos
Where the jackals howl, and other stories
de Lange, N; Simpson, P
Chatto & Windus
1981
217
Oz
Amos
Where the jackals howl, and other stories
de Lange, N; Simpson, P
Vintage
1992
217
Ozick
Bloodshed and Three Novellas

1983
Ozick
Cannibal Galaxy, The
1983
Ozick
Pagan Rabbi and other stories, The
1983
Perec
Georges
W or the Memory of Childhood
W ou le souvenir d'enfance
1975
Bellos, D
Harvill
1988
pb
164
7.99
Peretz
Isaac L
Book of fire, The: stories by
I.L. Peretz
Leftwich, J
Yoseloff: NY
1962
448
Yoseloff: London
1961
448
Peretz
Isaac L
Stories and pictures
Frank, H
Books for Libraries Press
1971
455
Peretz
Isaac Loeb
Bontshe the silent
Rappoport, A
Books for Libraries Press
1971
259
Peretz
Isaac Loeb
Case against the wind, The and other stories
Hautzig, E
Macmillan
1975
96
Peretz
Isaac Loeb
I.L. Peretz Reader, The
Wisse, R
Schocken Books
1990
381
Peretz
Isaac Loeb
In this world and the next; selected writings
Spiegel, M
Yoseloff
1960
377

Peretz
Isaac Loeb
Selected stories of I.L.Peretz
Schocken Books
1974
159
Elek
1975
159
Peretz
Isaac Loeb
Seven good years, The and other stories of I.L.Peretz
Hautzig, E
Jewish Publication Society of America
1984
94
Peretz
Isaac Loeb
Three canopies, The
Feinerman, T
Shoulson Press
1948
128
Perl
Joseph
Revealer of Secrets
Megaleh temirin
Westview: Oxford
1997
hb
377
Perl
Joseph
Revealer of Secrets
Megaleh temirin
Westview: Oxford
1997
pb
377
Perlov
Yitzchok
Partizaner, The
Namerovsky, N
Award
1968
315
Perlov
Yitzchok
People of Exodus
Dos folk fun Exodus
1949
Shokam, J E
Yechiel: Tel Aviv
1960
Perutz
Leo
By night under the Stone Bridge
Nachts unter der steinernen Brücke
1975
Mosbacher, E
Harvill
1995
pb
198

6.99
Picard
Jacob
Marked one, The and twelve other stories
Lewisohn, L
Jewish Publication Society of America
1958
267
Pinkus
Oscar
House of ashes, The
Union College Press
1990
272
Pinsky
David
Temptations; a book of short stories
Goldberg, I
Books for Libraries Press
1971
325
Pinsky
David
Ten plays
Core Collection Books: Great Neck, NY
1977
209
Posy
Arnold
Messiah's chains
Leftwich, J
Bloch
1963
290
Prager
Emily
Eve's tattoo
1991
Vintage: London
1993
Proust
Marcel
In Search of Lost Time: Sodom and Gomorrah
A la recherche du temps perdu: Sodome et Gomorrhe
1921-2
Kilmartin, T, Moncrieff, C K Scott
Chatto
1992
hb
639
16.99
Proust
Marcel
In Search of Lost Time: Swann's Way
A la recherche du temps perdu: du côté de chez Swann
1913
Kilmartin, T, Moncrieff, C K Scott
Chatto
1992

hb
522
16.99
Proust
Marcel
In Search of Lost Time: The Captive
A la recherche du temps perdu: la prisonnière
1923
Kilmartin, T, Moncrieff, C K Scott
Chatto
1992
hb
639
16.99
Proust
Marcel
In Search of Lost Time: The Guermante's Way
A la recherche du temps perdu: le côté de Guermantes
1920-21
Kilmartin, T, Moncrieff, C K Scott
Chatto
1992
hb
706
16.99
Rabinowitz
Shalom
Rabon
Israel
Street: a novel, The
Gas
1928
Wolf, L
Four Walls Eight Windows
1985
192
Rabon
Israel
Street: a novel, The
Wolf, L
Schocken
1985
192
Raboy
Isaac
Jewish cowboy
Shapiro, N
Tradition Books
1989
297
Ramraz-Ra'ukh, G; Michman, J
Facing the Holocaust: selected Israeli fiction
Jewish Publication Society: Philadelphia
1985
292
Rappoport
Solomon
Dybbuk, The
Alsberg, H & Katzin, W
Liveright
1971

145
Rappoport
Solomon
Dybbuk, The : between two worlds
Der dibek
Engel, S M
Nash Pub
1974
157
Rappoport
Solomon
Dybbuk, The : between two worlds
Der dibek
Engel, M von
Winnipeg Prov. print (Canada)
1953
68
Reisen
Abraham
Heart-stirring Sermon, The, and
other stories
Leviant, C
Overlook Press
1992
204
Renglich
Szloma
In the heart of Warsaw: an
autobiographical novel
Vehicule Press (Canada)
1993
326
Renglich
Szloma
When paupers dance
Jampel, Z
Vehicule Press (Canada)
1988
227
Richler
Mordecai
Apprenticeship Of Duddy Kravitz,
The
Penguin
1964
pb
Richler
Mordecai
Solomon Gursky Was Here
Viking
1989
pb
Ronch
Isaac E
Awakening of Motek, The
Bunting Books
1953
336
Ron-Feder-mit
Galilah
To myself
Zisquit, L
Adama Books
1987
133
Rosenfarb

Chawa
Tree of life, The : a novel about life
in the Lodz Ghetto
Der boym fun lebn
Rosenfarb, C; Morgentaler, G
Scribe: Melbourne, Australia
1985
1080
Rosten
Leo
Education of Hyman Kaplan
Penguin
1988
pb
Roth
Joseph
Job. The story of a simple man
Hiob, Roman eines einfachen
Mannes
1930
Thompson, D
Chatto & Windus
1983
hb
238
ROTH
Philip
Anatomy Lesson, The
1983
Vintage
1995
304
6.99
ROTH
Philip
Ghost Writer, The
1979
ROTH
Philip
Portnoy's Complaint
1969
Vintage: London
1995
5.99
pb
ROTH
Philip
Prague Orgy, The
1985
Vintage: London
pb
4.99
Roth
Philip
Zuckerman Bound
Penguin UK
pb
8.99
Roth
Philip
Zuckerman Unbound
1981
Cape: London
hb
10.95
Rothgiesser

Ruben
Well of Gerar, The: a novel
Schneiderman, H
Jewish Publication Society of
America
1953
287
Rubens
Bernice
Elected Member, The
Abacus: London
1987
pb
240
6.99
Sadeh
Pinhas
Life is a parable
Ha-hayyim kemashal
Flantz, R
Carta (Israel)
1989
380
Sadeh
Pinhas
Life is a parable
Ha-hayyim ke-mashal
Flantz, R
Jerusalem, Carta
1989
380
Samuel
Maurice
Prince of the Getto. A revelation of
the life and work of Polish Jewry
through a retelling of the tales of the
Yiddish master, I.L.Peretz
Jewish Publication Society of
America: Philadelphia
1959
294
Meridian Books
1959
249
Schectman
Elya
Erev
Erev
Singer, J
Crown
1967
268
Schneour
Zalman
Restless spirit: selected writings
Spiegel, M
Yoseloff
1964
312
Schuchinski
Osher Jaime
Broken Roots: a collection of stories
Vantage Press
1993
232
Schulz

Picador: London
1988
304
6.99
Schwartz
Israel Jacob
Kentucky
Dubrovsky, G
University of Alabama Press
1990
238
Schwartz
Miriam
Lonely search, The
Korot Havah Gotlib
Ben-Yosef, R
Sabra Books: NY
1970
377
Scliar
Moacyr
Strange Nation of Rafael Mendes
Sefer
Aleksandrus Mukdon
Tales of Alexander the Macedonian,
with a literary and historical
commentary (Heb, Engl)
Ktav Pub. House: NY
1972
143
Sforim
Mendele Mocher
Adventures of Mendele the Book-
Peddler
Kuperard (dist.)
16.99
Sforim
Mendele Mocher
Fishke the lame
Fishke der krumer
1869
Stillman, G
Yoseloff
1962
221
Yoseloff: London
1960
221
Sforim
Mendele Mocher
Travels and adventures of Benjamin
the third, The
Spiegel, M
Schocken Books
1949
124
Schocken Books
6.99
Sforim
Mendele Mokher
Parasite, The
Stillman, G
Yoseloff
1958
174
Sforim

Mendele Mokher
Nag, The
Spiegel, M
Beechhurst P: NY
1957
223
Semel
Nava
Becoming Gershona
Gershonah shonah
Simckes, S
Viking-Penguin: NY
1990
153
Semel
Nava
Flying Lessons
Simon & Schuster: NY
1995
Sendak
Philip
In grandpa's house
Barofsky, S
Harper and Row
1985
42
Sendak
Philip
In grandpa's house
Barofsky, S
Bodley Head
1986
423
Sened, Yonat & Alexander
Another attempt
Ha-nissayon ha-nosaf
Conin, N
Institute for the Translation of
Hebrew Literature, Tel Aviv, Israel
1981
190
Shaanan
Avraham
Writers in war and resistance
Editions Naaman (Canada)
1986
2v
Shabtai
Yaacov
Past continuous
Zichron devarim
1977
Bilu, D
Schocken Books
1985
389
Shabtai
Yaacov
Past continuous
Bilu, D
Jewish Publication Society of
America
1985
389
Shabtai
Yaacov

Past perfect
Zichron devarim
1984
Bilu, D
Viking
1987
291
Shabtai
Yaacov
Uncle Peretz takes off & other
stories
Mosaic Press: Oakville (Canada)
1993
119
Shaham
Nathan
Bone to the bone
Etsem el atsmo
Bilu, D
Grove Press
1993
345
Shaham
Nathan
Rosendorf quartet, The : a novel
Reviiyat Rosendorf
Bilu, D
Grove Weidenfeld
1987
357
Shaham
Nathan
Other side of the wall, The: three
novellas
Gold, L
Jewish Publication Society of
America
1983
281
Shahar
David
His Majesty's agent
Sokhen hod malhuto
Bilu, D
Harcourt Brace Jovanovich
1980
392
Shahar
David
News from Jerusalem; stories
Bilu, D et al
Houghton Mifflin
1974
310
Elek
1976
310
Shahar
David
Palace of shattered vessels, The
Hekhal ha-kelim ha-shevurim
Houghton Mifflin
1975
212
Shahar
David

Bellow, S et al
Farrar Straus Giroux
1981
610
Cape
1982
h
610
Singer
Isaac Bashevis
Collected stories of Isaac Bashevis
Singer, The
Bellow, S et al
Penguin
1984
p
610
Singer
Isaac Bashevis
Crown of feathers and other stories,
A
Farrar, Strauss & Giroux
1973
342
Cape
1974
h
342
Singer
Isaac Bashevis
Crown of feathers and other stories,
A
Penguin
1979(1977)
303
Singer
Isaac Bashevis
Day of pleasure, A; stories of a boy
growing up in Warsaw
Farrar, Straus & Giroux
1969
227
Singer
Isaac Bashevis
Death of Methuselah, The and other
stories.
New American Library
1988
p
244
Singer
Isaac Bashevis
Death of Methuselah, The and other
stories.
Franklin Library
1988
244
Singer
Isaac Bashevis
Death of Methuselah, The and other
stories.
Farrar Straus Giroux
1988
244
Singer
Isaac Bashevis

Death of Methuselah, The and other
stories.
Jonathan Cape
1988
256
Singer
Isaac Bashevis
Isaac Bashevis
Death of Methuselah, The and other
stories.
Penguin
1990
p
244
6.99
Singer
Isaac Bashevis
Death of Methuselah, The and other
stories.
Penguin
1993
p
336
Singer
Isaac Bashevis
Elijah the slave
Shub, E
Farrar, Straus & Giroux
1970
1v
Singer
Isaac Bashevis
Enemies, a love story
Sonim, di Geshichte fun a Liebe
Shub, E & Shevrin, A
Farrar
1972
hb
280
Cape
1972
hb
280
Singer
Isaac Bashevis
Enemies: a love story
Sonim, di gesichte fun a liebe
Shub, E & Shevrin, A
Penguin
1979(1977)
p
220
6.99
Singer
Isaac Bashevis
Estate, The
Singer, J & Gottlieb, E & Shub, E
Penguin
1979(1975)
335
Singer
Isaac Bashevis
Estate, The
Singer, J & Gottlieb, E & Shub, E
Farrar, Straus & Giroux
1969
374

Cape
1970
h
374
Singer
Isaac Bashevis
Family Moskat, The
Gross, A H
Penguin
1980
636
Singer
Isaac Bashevis
Family Moskat, the
Gross, A. H.
Knopf
1950
611
Singer
Isaac Bashevis
Family Moskat, The
Gross, A. H.
Bantam
1967
626
Secker
1966
h
611
Singer
Isaac Bashevis
Family Moskat, The
Gross, A. H.
Panther
1969
p
604
Singer
Isaac Bashevis
Family Moskat, The
Gross, A. H.
Cape
1979
p
611
Singer
Isaac Bashevis
Fearsome inn, The
Singer, I B & Shub, E
Scribners
1967
1v
Singer
Isaac Bashevis
Fools of Chelm and their history,
The
Farrar, Strauss & Giroux
1973
57
Singer
Isaac Bashevis
Friend of Kafka, A, and other stories
Penguin
1979(1975)
282
Singer

h
519
Magna Print (Large Print)
1979
h
519
Singer
Isaac Bashevis
Passions and other stories
Penguin
1979
271
Singer
Isaac B
Passions, and other stories
Farrar, Straus and Giroux
1975
312
Cape
1976
312
Singer
Isaac Bashevis
Penitent, The
Farrar Straus Giroux
1983
169
Cape
1984
h
169
Singer
Isaac Bashevis
Satan in Goray
ha-Satan be-Gore
Sloan, J
Penguin
1981
158
Singer
Isaac B
Satan in Goray
Sloan, J
Avon
1963
p
173
Transworld
1967
p
173
Singer
Isaac Bashevis
Satan in Goray
Sloan, J
Noonday P.
1955
250
Owen
1958
h
239
Singer
Isaac Bashevis
Scum
Shoym

Schwartz, R D
Plume Book
1991
217
Cape
1991
h
217
Singer
Isaac Bashevis
Scum
Shoym
Schwartz, R D
Farrar Straus Giroux
1991
217
Penguin
1991
p
217
5.99
Singer
Isaac Bashevis
Seance, The and other stories
Ginsburg, M et al
Penguin
1979(1974)
p
240
Singer
Isaac Bashevis
Seance, The and other stories
Klein, R H et al
Farrar, Straus & Giroux
1968
276
Cape
1970
h
276
Singer
Isaac Bashevis
Short Friday and other stories
Singer, J & Klein, R
Farrar Straus Giroux
1964
h
243
Secker
1967
h
243
Singer
Isaac Bashevis
Short Friday and other stories
Singer, J & Klein, R
Penguin
1983
p
201
Singer
Isaac Bashevis
Shosha
Singer, J
Penguin
1979(1993)

p
255
Singer
Isaac Bashevis
Shosha
Singer, J
Prior (Large Print)
1979
509
Singer
Isaac Bashevis
Shosha
Singer, J
Cape
1979
277
Singer
Isaac Bashevis
Slave, The
Hemley, C & Singer, I B
Farrar
1962
h
235
Secker
1963
h
235
Singer
Isaac Bashevis
Slave, The
Hemley, C & Singer, I B
Penguin
1974
p
235
5.99
Singer
Isaac Bashevis
Slave, The
Hemley, C & Singer, I B
Cape
1973
h
311
Singer
Isaac Bashevis
Spinoza of Market Street
Farrar Straus Giroux
1961
h
214
Secker
1962
Singer
Isaac Bashevis
Spinoza of Market Street
Cape
1973
h
214
Singer
Isaac Bashevis
Spinoza of Market Street
Penguin
1981

1973
Gollancz
1974
311
Tammuz
Benjamin
Minotaur
Parfitt, K & Budny, M
Enigma
1983
210
Tammuz
Benjamin
Minotaur
Parfitt, K & Budny, M
New American Library
1981
210
Tammuz
Benjamin
Orchard, The: a novella
ha-Pardes
Flantz, R
Copper Beech Press: Providence,
Rhode Island
1984
88
Tammuz
Benjamin
Rare cure, A
Angiokhsil, terufa nedira
Schachter, J
Institute for the Translation of
Hebrew Literature, Tel Aviv, Israel
1981
216
Tammuz
Benjamin
Requiem for Na'aman
Budny, M & Safran, Y
New American Library
1982
228
Tamuz
Benjamin
Castle in Spain
Bobbs-Merrill:NY
1973
311
Taube
Herman
Empty pews
Lesser, S
N.A. Grossman Pub. Co.
1961
216
Taube, H & S
Remember
Di umfargeslekhe, etc.(1948)
Frank, H
N.A. Grossman Pub. Co.
1951
182
Tavory
Doron
Stories for Sharon

Sippurim le-sharon
Arzouni, O
Haifa Pub. Co.: Haifa (Israel)
1964
103
Tene
Benjamin
In the shade of the chestnut tree
Be-tsilo shel ets ha-armon
Ben-Joseph, R
Jewish Publication Society
1981
136
Tomer
Ben-Zion
Children of the shadows
Yalde hazel
Halkin, H
Institute for the Translation of
Hebrew Literature, Tel Aviv, Israel
1992
90
tr Sabar, Yona
Folk literature of the Kurdistani
Jews, The : an anthology
Yale University Press
1982
250
Tsanin
Mordechai
Artapanos comes home
Artapanos kumt tsurik aheym
Lask, I M
A. S. Barnes
1980
332
Yoseloff
1980
332
Tsernowitz
Jacob
Artzi: The Palestine Almanac
WIZO: Tel Aviv
1948
95
Vogel
David
Married life
Chai nissuim
Bilu, D
Grove Press
1989
486
Vogel
David
Married life
Chai nissuim
Bilu, D
Halban
1988
486
Weinstein
Rachel
Way back, The
Woman's League of Yeshiva Beer-
Sheva: NY

1977
282
Weinstock
Moshe D
Light in the darkness: selected
stories
Sz sz, K
Bezalel Art
1982
84
Weinstock
Moshe D
Scandal in Brooklyn
Tabori, P
Horizon Pub.
1972
217
Weissbrem
Israel
Israel Weissbrem and his work:
novels and poems
Crown, A
Tcherikover (Israel)
1983
414
Weissbrem
Israel
World of Israel Weissbrem, The :
novels
Westview Press: Boulder, Colorado
1992
1v
Westview Press: Oxford
1993
Weissenberg
I.M. et al
Shtetl, A and other Yiddish novellas
Wisse, R
Behrman House
1973
364
WEST
Nathanael
Day Of The Locust, The & The
Dream Life of Balso Snell
1939 & 1931
Penguin UK
pb
7.99
WILSON
Jonathan
Schoom
LIME TREE
pb
217
9.99
Wisler
Israel Menachem
Methusaleh's Gang
Ha-Havurat Metushelah
Segal, N
Dodd:NY
1980
Yehoshua
Abraham B
Continuing silence of a poet, The

Halban
1988
480
Halban
1988
480
Yehoshua
Abraham B
Continuing silence of a poet, The:
the collected stories of A. B.
Yehoshua
Penguin
1991
328
Yehoshua
Abraham B
Continuing silence of a poet, The:
the collected stories of A. B.
Yehoshua
Flamingo
1990
359
Yehoshua
Abraham B
Early in the summer of 1970
Heinemann
1980
165
Yehoshua
Abraham B
Early in the summer of 1970
Doubleday: Garden City, NY
1977
165
Yehoshua
Abraham B
Five seasons
Molkho
Halkin, H
Doubleday
1989
359
Yehoshua
Abraham B
Five seasons
Molkho
Halkin, H
Collins
1989
359
Yehoshua
Abraham B
Late divorce, A
Halkin, H
Harcourt Brace
1993
354
Yehoshua
Abraham B
Late divorce, A
Halkin, H
Doubleday
1984
354
Yehoshua
Abraham B

Late divorce, A
Gerushim me'uharim
Halkin, H
Abacus / Steinmatzky
1985
352
Yehoshua
Abraham B
Late divorce, A
Gerushim me'uharim
Halkin, H
Harvill
1984
352
Yehoshua
Abraham B
Lover, The
Simpson, P
Harcourt Brace
1993
352
Yehoshua
Abraham B
Lover, The
Simpson, P
NY, Doubleday
1978
Heinemann
1979
352
Yehoshua
Abraham B
Mr Mani
Mar Mani
Halkin, H
Doubleday
1992
368
Yehoshua
Abraham B
Mr Mani
Mar Mani
Halkin, H
Halban
1993
368
15.99
Yehoshua
Abraham B
Mr Mani
Mar Mani
Halkin, H
Phoenix
1993
pb
368
6.99
Yehoshua
Abraham B
Open Heart
Bilu, D
Halban
1996
498
16.99
Yehoshua

Abraham B
Three days and a child
Arad, M
Doubleday
1970
260
Owen
1971
260
Yehuda
Amichai
Battle for the hill
Grumet, E et al
Jewish Publication Society of
America
1984
199
Yizhar
S
Midnight convoy & other stories
Sheyyara shel hazot
Louvish, M
IHT:Jerusalem
1969
273
ZANGWILL
Israel
Children of the Ghetto
1895
Wayne Stae University Press:
London
1998
pb
22.50
ZANGWILL
Israel
King of Schnorrers
1897
H.Pordes: London
1972
hb
156

·K·U·P·E·R·A·R·D·

**The Best of Jewish Reading from Around the World
and Throughout the Years**

KUPERARD provide a unique service in supplying a wide range of books of Jewish interest from publishers around the world to both the general and the specialist markets. We provide a wide selection of books for communal literary events, author appearances as well as organising book fairs.

Our Mail Order department prides itself on offering an efficient service to members of the public wishing to acquire the best of Jewish publications.

Specialist subjects;

Childrens' Books • Israel & Zionism • Anti-Semitism & The Holocaust
Classical Texts & Commentary • Customs & Practices
Fiction & Folklore • Mysticism & Kabbalah • Cookery
Hebrew Courses & Dictionaries • History & Current Affairs
Bar & Bat Mitzvah • Gift Selection • Jewish Life

Should you wish to order any book from our extensive catalogue please contact us using either our FREEPOST service
or tel. 0171 424 0554
fax: 0171 424 0556
email kuperard@bravo.clara.net.

Kuperard
FREEPOST LON 12097
LONDON
NW5 1YR